The Cheapskate's Guide to
VACATIONS

The Cheapskate's Guide to
VACATIONS

How to Save Thousands of Dollars
No Matter Where You're Going

Stephen Tanenbaum

A Citadel Press Book
Published by Carol Publishing Group

Dedicated to Patty,
for inspiring and sharing
our many dream vacations

A Citadel Press Book
Published by Carol Publishing Group
Citadel Press is a registered trademark of Carol Communications, Inc.

Editorial, sales and distribution, and rights and permissions inquiries should be addressed to Carol Publishing Group, 120 Enterprise Avenue, Secaucus, N.J. 07094

In Canada: Canadian Manda Group, One Atlantic Avenue, Suite 105, Toronto, Ontario M6K 3E7

Carol Publishing Group books may be purchased in bulk at special discounts for sales promotion, fund-raising, or educational purposes. Special editions can be created to specifications. For details, contact Special Sales Department, 120 Enterprise Avenue, Secaucus, N.J. 07094.

Manufactured in the United States of America

10 9 8 7 6 5 4 3 2 1

Library of Congress Cataloging-in-Publication Data

Tanenbaum, Stephen.
    The cheapskate's guide to vacations : how to save thousands of dollars no matter where you're going / Stephen Tanenbaum.
        p.   cm.
    "A Citadel Press book."
    Includes index.
    ISBN 0-8065-1832-4
    1. Travel.   2. Travel costs.   I. Title.
    G151.T36   1996
    910'.2'02—dc20
                                                    96-9771
                                                    CIP

Contents

Preface

There I was, a baby-boomer, growing up in Brooklyn in the sixties and ready to go where none of my peers had gone before—out of the neighborhood, out of New York state, and beyond the very shores of our great nation. I was ready for adventure...to cross the Atlantic Ocean...to travel!

I am a bit ahead of myself. During my early teen years, in the late fifties, I first experienced the joy of low-cost travel. My buddies and I met early in the morning. We rode the Church Avenue bus for fifteen cents, used a free transfer to the Rogers Avenue bus, and thirty minutes later arrived at Sheepshead Bay. A ten-minute walk from the bus stop took us to our final destination: the Atlantic Ocean seashore at world-famous Brighton Beach.

To the chagrin of many I have met on the West Coast, I was not a "deprived child" growing up on the harsh pavements of Brooklyn. A funny thing about being poor...often you are the last to know. My friends and I were from first- or second-generation Jewish families. Our fathers worked in one old-world trade or another. My Dad, Sam Tanenbaum, was a buttonhole maker who enjoyed his fifteen minutes of fame in the fifties, becoming a neighborhood hero when he appeared on *What's My Line?* answering the questions of Bennett Cerf and Dorothy Kilgallen.

Now, where was I? Oh yes, Brighton Beach. There we were, a group of "poor suffering" teenagers with names like Hoc, Jake, and Big Irv, coping with the oppressive heat of Brooklyn summers, basking in the sunshine on one of the world's most beautiful beaches. In Brooklyn, you say? You bet! Miles of beautiful, wide, white-sand beach, with hundreds of thousands of bodies lying blanket to blanket. After all, with four million souls living in Brooklyn alone, this was one crowded piece of real estate. The water matched the beach and, unlike in northern California where I now reside, the water was glorious, warm, and swimmable. It was, to be blunt, a teenage delight. Lying on my towel, with closed eyes pointed toward the sun, my mind took flight. I traveled to the farthest corners of the globe. When a breeze swept across my face, I was in the South Pacific awaiting the arrival of Polynesian nymphettes. It was about then that someone inevitably would kick sand into my face, returning me to a pleasant if not exotic reality.

Boardwalks are special, perhaps magical, especially when they lead to magical places. Brighton Beach's boardwalk led to such a place. When we had our fill of sand, sun, and surf, we hiked a mile or so down the boardwalk to the world's capital of seashore entertainment, Coney Island. Although its heyday was in the forties, Coney Island remained vibrant and alive in the fifties. Visitors enjoyed the original Cyclone roller coaster, the Steeplechase Park, and the famed Parachute Jump—a genuine army paratrooper training machine hundreds of feet high and a forerunner of today's high-tech rides. There was also the world's largest Ferris wheel, the Wonder Wheel, with its tilting cars that seemed to shoot its passengers into the void. On top of that there was the world's ultimate eatery, the original Nathan's hot dog stand. To us it was heaven. I was a teenager enjoying the best summers of my life.

Although money was scarce, my family was a warm and happy one. My mother, Ruth, was and continues to be the ultimate caring, loving parent. Amazingly, my older sister, Phyllis, and I never fought, which greatly perplexed my friends. At this time, real travel to exotic destinations such as Rome, Paris, and Africa occurred only in our dreams. With that said, my parents did their best. The lack of a family car, though a major hindrance, did not stop them. We forged ahead on mini-adventures, such as our trip via the New York Central Railroad to Niagara Falls, one of the world's greatest natural wonders. On that trip "it" happened. I crossed our national boundary and entered a foreign land. No matter that it was Canada, it *was* a foreign country! At that moment I felt a slight sting. The proverbial travel bug had bitten me.

Some summers my family spent two weeks at one of the

smaller borscht-belt hotels in the Catskill Mountains. Here young comics like Jerry Lewis and Red Skelton were honing their craft. On these occasions, Phyllis and I communed with our second mother—Mother Nature. Other summers we stayed at Catskill Mountain bungalow colonies. (Bungalows are family cottages rented for the summer, where fathers enjoyed weekend "visitation" privileges.) First, I experienced endless varieties of insects. Next came the fishing, and finally I encountered a snake that sent me screaming for a SWAT team.

By the time I was twenty my body, mind, soul, and spirit were ready to merge with the real world of travel; I simply needed a plan and the money to fund it. It must have been divine intervention, in light of my average high school grades, that I won a coveted New York State Regents college scholarship. This changed my life. Upon acceptance to New York's City College, a nontuition school, I received the minimum Regents College Scholarship award of $1,200. They had funded me! By the end of my sophomore year I had the means and opportunity to forge ahead. The die was cast and nothing, not even a cataclysm, would stop me.

In January 1965 I finally broached the subject with my parents. Their reaction went something like this: "Who puts these crazy ideas in your head?," "Ridiculous!," "You will throw $1,200 away?," "Go to the movies if you want to see France!," "If you want Italian, go to Vinnie's Pizzeria!" Then they played the "compelling argument" trump card. "Use the money for your own car, something you can see, touch, and feel." Now *that* hit close to home! At age twenty I knew I was facing the rarest of opportunities, a chance to spend three months traveling throughout Europe and Scandinavia. I knew this opportunity occurred rarely in people's lives and might not present itself again. In my heart of hearts I knew that it was now or never.

In 1965 the words *discount travel* were not yet part of my consciousness. I knew one thing and one thing only: I had only $1,200 to fund my travel adventure. At that defining moment I commenced my first effort at "cheapskate" travel. My first plan envisioned the use of Icelandic Airway's bargain fare to London. The trade-off for the low fare was a circuitous route to London via Iceland. In the end I booked a low "group" fare on an Air India's New York to London flight. I drafted a fraternity brother, and we set out to meet the world. My second companion was Arthur Frommer's hallmark book, *Europe on Five Dollars a Day*, the bible of travel in the sixties. My budget was a frivolous $7 per day to cover both lodging and food.

Our rule of travel was simple: We stayed in low-cost hotels, spending $2.50 to $3 per day, per person, for lodging. We traveled in our "luxurious" leased Citroen 2CV, a vehicle as famous and common in Europe as the VW Beetle was in America. Puttering along at its maximum speed of 55 miles per hour, our 2CV was the workhorse of our trip. By trip's end we had visited thirteen countries and thirty-two cities, traveling more than seven thousand miles. We explored London, East Berlin, Rome, Copenhagen, and everything in between.

As early as our initial arrival in London, I was already looking for bargains. Instead of taking a torturous boat-crossing from England to France, I followed a suggestion in Arthur Frommer's book. For the $26 cost of a boat ticket we took a flight from England to France using fledgling Skyways Airlines. It worked like a charm. The airline bused us from London to Dover, where we boarded a "questionably" small plane that hopped the channel and deposited us in rural France. There, another bus awaited our arrival and took us to Paris. I still recall sheep lining the short, narrow runway at Dover and the beautiful Dover cliffs. I was in awe as I viewed the beaches of Normandy from the excellent vantage point of our low-level 3,000-foot flight.

Over the decades I have traveled, not as extensively as some but more than many others, and I freely admit the travel bug has been one constant in my life. Since 1983 my best friend, lover, and companion, Patty, and I have enjoyed traveling the world and living one adventure after another. I mention Patty often in this book because she deserves credit for being there when I needed her. (After all, most packages are double occupancy!) Patty has made it all worthwhile. Sharing life and our adventures together gives them all meaning. From photo safari-ing in Africa to shark diving in Moorea, we have done it together and loved every minute of it, and each other. The *Cheapskate's Guide to Vacations* tells of our travels while pointing the way to your own exotic cheapskate adventures.

In recent years Patty has retired from the labor market to

embark on a law school education, putting a big squeeze on our travel budget. The pressure was on to travel at cheapskate prices to world-class destinations, not the easiest of tasks. The results speak for themselves.

In 1990 and again in 1992 we embarked on photo safaris to Kenya and Tanzania, also visiting Mombasa, the tropical Kenyan coast. *Our airfare was free on both trips.* We have traveled to Tahiti's crown jewel, the island of Moorea, four times since 1993. In 1994 our total cost to visit Moorea was just $499 each! The price included nonstop airfare from Los Angeles, transfers, eight-days' and seven-nights' hotel lodging on Cooks Bay, and all service charges.

In 1992 we took in a scuba-diving adventure at Club Med on Turquoise Island in the British West Indies. This Club Med is a dedicated dive center, rated one of the best diving destinations in the Caribbean. Our airfare to Turquoise Island was free.

In 1994 we visited London for eight days of theater, sightseeing, and day trips in the countryside. The vacation package from California, including airfare, hotel, and breakfasts cost only $517 each. Three months later, in April 1995, we vacationed in Paris for eight days. The entire vacation, including airfare, hotel, and daily breakfasts, cost $565 each. In October 1995 we visited Israel, with side trips to Jordan and Egypt. Again, the round-trip air travel to the Middle East was free for both of us.

Let me emphasize that I am not wealthy. I am a salaried worker's compensation attorney who earns and wisely uses one month of vacation per year. The reason for this book is that I am tired of repeating travel advice to friends and acquaintances so often that it becomes a mantra of sorts. On a weekly basis I was grilled for information on my cheapskate travel escapades. In recent years I found myself giving advice even to travel professionals and airline personnel. Eventually I began carrying a mini–travel file in my briefcase, and I was soon replying to requests with instant informational handouts.

The Cheapskate's Guide to Vacations is a key to dream vacations at dirt-cheap prices. It is about doing it your way and going on the vacations of your choice. The guide refers to legitimate tour operators from well-known Pleasant Hawaiian Holidays to little-known France Vacations, which uses even lesser known AOM

Airlines. It is about hundreds or even thousands of free travel dollars. It is not about standby or courier travel that helps only those who are able to pick up and leave on a moment's notice.

This guide is user-friendly and points the way to dream vacations at low prices. It also provides down-to-earth information needed to make the crucial decision to do it! It is one thing to realize you can afford a world-class vacation to Tahiti and quite another to know exactly what you will find, from hotels to restaurants to night snorkeling and shark diving. I realize that foreign travel, including travel to Africa, Europe, and the South Pacific, may be intimidating to some. After all, we are dealing with foreign languages, currencies, and customs. My discussions of favorite exotic places will put you at ease so that you may comfortably make the best travel decisions of your vacation life.

Do not be held back by artificial barriers. My recommendations, strategies, and advice help topple them one by one. Soon you will be lying on a sun-drenched beach in French Polynesia or some equally exotic destination of your choice. To this noble end, this book is your ticket to world-class vacations at unheard-of rock-bottom prices. *Dare to live your dreams*!

PART I

The Principles of Free Cash and Dirt-Cheap Vacations

1

Hundreds, Even Thousands, of Free Travel Dollars!

No One Gives Away Free Money, Do They?

I know the cliches: "Nothing is for nothing!," "Do not take money from strangers!," and "You get what you pay for!" Forget them. They no long apply to you. During the past twelve years I have received thousands of dollars of free travel cash from corporate vacation cash giveaways. During the past two years alone, I requested and received $3,700 of free travel cash from such American icon companies as Kraft and Nabisco. Free travel dollars may be used like cash to help pay for virtually any vacations.

Over the past three years Patty and I used $400 of Kraft's free travel cash on each of four vacations. The trips were exciting and varied. We took eight-day vacations that included airfare, hotels, and most breakfasts, to Tahiti ($499 each), London ($517 each), and Paris ($565 each). We enjoyed a full-week Carnival cruise to the Mexican Riviera for the cheapskate price of $449 each. Scores of family, friends, and acquaintances were, at first, amazed and skeptical, but later they happily followed in my footsteps. I found myself constantly explaining all this to more and more people. This book will save my vocal chords while empowering readers to pursue their own dream vacations at cheapskate prices.

Since 1984, major corporations have used vacation cash giveaways to promote their product lines. Time and again my friends and associates are shocked to learn that such free travel cash promotions exist.

It seems the very people who would benefit most from free travel cash know the least about this windfall. Year after year new companies jump onto the vacation savings promotion bandwagon. During the past twelve years, new and sometimes more valuable promotions have replaced expiring ones. Often multiple travel-cash giveaways run simultaneously. This happened with the Country Time Lemonade, Jell-O/Cool Whip, Kodak, Carlton cigarettes, and Nabisco promotions.

Longevity is another wonderful feature of these programs. For example, the recent Kraft Jell-O/Cool Whip promotion ran for two years, until April 1995. Just as the Kraft program expired, Nabisco issued its spanking-new travel-cash giveaway promotion, scheduled to run for a whopping twenty-one months.

You lucky readers are about to be given the chance to get on an inside track to International Travel House (ITH), the company responsible for creating the vast majority of these marvelous giveaways. ITH has run free travel cash giveaways since their 1984 Castrol Oil promotion. In April 1995, ITH released the Nabisco promotion. Soon you, too, will discover such programs and use them to reduce your vacation costs to cheapskate proportions.

Free travel cash giveaways customarily require that you purchase the company's products. In return for proofs of purchase—UPC codes—participants receive "travel cash," or script. The script is applicable against the cost of vacation trips of your choosing. Keep in mind that the promoting companies have no say regarding where or when you travel, or the price you pay. Simply shop for the best vacation at the lowest price, and let a corporate benefactor pay hundreds of dollars toward the bill.

I recently spent just $38 to purchase sufficient Nabisco products to receive $1,700 in free travel cash. If this sounds unbelievable, do not forget that I am talking about Nabisco, a company as rock solid as Oreo cookies. I am not talking about offers made by people bearing a striking familiarity to con artists seen on the television show *America's Most Wanted*. These offers are as American as Oreos, Triscuits, and Jell-O!

Let me say, right up front, that I am an avid consumer advocate with no respect whatsoever for misleading offers, deals, or promotions. That said, consider the following:

U.S. Currency: Legal tender, coins of the realm, cash.
Free Travel Dollars: "Travel cash" or "script" certificates in $50 and $100 denominations issued by sponsoring companies. The script is usually picturesque, fun to look at, and even more fun to use! It is redeemable as a cash credit toward vacations booked through the travel agency chosen by the sponsoring company. My own experiences will convince you that free travel dollars are equivalent to real dollars when used toward your dream vacation.

Are Free Travel Dollars Available Now?

The honest answer is: yes, no, and maybe. Not perfectly clear? Let me explain. Free travel dollars have been continuously available during the past twelve years! ITH has launched one promotion after another using this time-proven, successful advertising technique. Depending on when you are reading this guide, free travel cash is either available or we are awaiting the release of the next travel cash giveaway promotion. This chapter teaches readers to discover new programs that ITH should be releasing in 1997 and beyond. There is no better time to learn of these promotions than now.

As this guide goes to press, I must report both good and not-so-good news. First the not-so-good. Sadly, the twenty-one-month Nabisco giveaway recently entered its wind-down phase. This means that Nabisco has ceased issuance of free travel cash. Those who have surplus Nabisco dollars may continue to use the script until January 1, 1997. (More details about the Nabisco program later in this chapter.) Following is the good news.

ITH does it again! Its newest promotion, another free travel cash giveaway was released on July 1, 1996. The promotion is for Zostrix, a major name-brand pharmaceutical product used as a surface treatment for relief of arthritis discomfort. The selling price of the product, depending on its size, ranges from $10 to $15. Participants will receive $50 in free travel dollars for each proof of purchase. This promotion's rules are similar to Nabisco's promotion, but there are some differences. Nabisco allows $300 to $500 of free script for a two-person, seven- to fourteen-night vacation; however, the Zostrix giveaway permits less, that is, $200 to $400 of free cash for a two-person, seven- or fourteen-night air and land package. Note: the initial phase of the promotion runs through January 31, 1997. Zostrix travel cash must be requested by March 31, 1997. Vacations must be booked by November 15, 1997, and travel must be completed by January 1, 1998. Another big plus: the minimum vacation package for two is just $800 (seven nights) and $1,200 (fourteen nights). This means the offer is valid for most cheapskate-priced vacation bargains. On the negative side, cruises alone do not qualify and must include air to the departure point. You may call Zostrix (Genderm Company) cutsomer service at 201-605-8979 and ask for a Vacation Cash mail-in rebate form.

Though I previously obtained $3,700 of free travel from the combined Kraft and Nabisco giveaways, I will be conservative with this promotion, since the price of Zostrix is far greater than that of a box of Oreos or Jell-O. I will shop for the best bargain prices on Zostrix and then order $600 of free travel cash, sufficient to use on three future vacations. What I will do with twelve tubes of Zostrix is another matter. Certain arthritis-related ideas spring to mind. There is my mother, Patty's parents, and an assortment of baby-boomer friends. It is possible that associates may find a tube sitting on their desks, a gift from an anonymous good samaritan. (Okay, I admit it, I will keep a couple for myself.)

➡ **Steve's Instant Free Cash Tip:** *Don't feel left out during the transition periods between promotions. Readers who book cheapskate vacations directly with Pearson Travel Company may obtain $100 in free American Express traveler's checks. See my special section on Pearson's "cash in your pocket" promotions at the conclusion of chapter 4.*

Look for displays on pharmacy counters with peel-off, mail-in program certificates. Read the rules carefully. Review my description of past promotions so you know exactly what to look for. As always, good luck in becoming involved in this newest ITH free cash giveaway program. Can't find a Zostrix display? ITH promises to answer written requests and provide the Zostrix promotion flyer. Read on for ITH's address.

1997 Promotions and Beyond

ITH anticipates that 1997 will be a banner year, with a larger-than-ever number of new free travel-cash promotions. However, should the worst scenario occur and there is no current program available, do not despair. You will be prepared to plug into the next program just as soon as it hits the advertising marketplace.

Oftentimes multiple promotions begin and overlap one another. When this occurs, select the best program, considering the amount of free travel dollars usable per vacation, the nature of the product being promoted, and the cost of the product. Your aim is to amass a sizable reserve of free travel cash as quickly as possible. This permits your immediate, spur-of-the-moment use of free travel dollars. Those who lack such a ready reserve may not make vacation reservations during the four to six weeks it takes to request and obtain free dollars.

Keep a constant vigil for new programs. Rhondee, my company's assistant office manager, followed my advice and vacationed in Moorea with her husband and friends. Their group paid the ultimate cheapskate price of $499 per person for the entire eight-day vacation package. A few months later, Rhondee, exercising the highest level of promotion "awareness," came upon the incredible 1995 Nabisco giveaway. She handed me the promotion advertisement that appeared in a local Pak 'N' Save supermarket flyer. I immediately began my participation in the program and, six weeks later, I received $1,700 in free Nabisco travel dollars from ITH.

Check your Sunday newspaper's travel section and also the glossy coupon section. Kraft placed advertisements for its 1994–1995 Jell-O giveaway in both of these sections on different occasions. Check with friends and family who live in distant areas—occasionally programs are released in limited geographical areas. Finally, contact the good people at ITH. I am assured they will respond to written inquiries about programs and "doubling" offers that may be currently available in your area. I suggest that you check with ITH every three months to be kept abreast of the most current travel-cash giveaways and other free travel-cash–type programs. Also keep a sharp vigil on printed advertising media. In the past, free travel-cash promotions have been advertised in weekend newspaper coupon and travel sections and supermarket flyers.

Direct inquiries about current ITH programs to:

International Travel House
24 Columbia Road, Suite 210
Somerville, New Jersey 08876
Fax: (908) 429-1022

Are There Restrictions on Vacation Choices?

Virtually none! Although promotions differ slightly, they usually apply to eight-day, seven-night vacation packages that include airfare and hotel. The Nabisco promotion applied to four-, seven-, and fourteen-night packages. A mind-boggling giveaway of $500 of free travel cash was available for vacations of fourteen nights or longer. One immediate caveat: Most promotions exclude charter flights. For those who have used larger charter companies, such as Sun Trips, I point the way to little-known alternatives that offer an opportunity to save big bucks. Still not convinced?

My favorite use of free travel cash was on our eight-day vacation to the island of Moorea (Tahiti) for the outrageous cheapskate price of $499 per person. On other occasions I have paid $665 for the same package. Even at $665, without using free travel dollars, this package is a cheapskate bargain extraordinaire. It is the dream vacation of a lifetime, paradise on earth. Quickly I became a pied piper, enticing scores of family and friends to follow in my footsteps.

First, I discovered the cheapskate-priced program called Tahiti Escapes, run by the tour operator Islands in the Sun. This special program uses a French airline, Corsair, for nonstop 747 wide-body service from LAX to Papeete. Corsair is a French-certified airline owned by Nouvelles Frontières. It offers scheduled charter service that includes weekly flights from Paris to Los Angeles and then on to Papeete. Island in the Sun's major competitor is Tahiti Vacations, another Los Angeles tour operator that offers nearly the identical eight-day Moorea vacation at the same cheapskate price of $699. Only Tahiti Vacations offers transportation on a regularly scheduled airline, AOM French Airlines, at this bargain-basement price.

➡ **Steve's Tip:** *Unhappily, I recommend against using Corsair's new nonstop service from Oakland International Airport. My top recommendation is Tahiti Vacations' scheduled AOM flights from Los Angeles as the best bargain choice. See chapter 11 for full details on package choices to Moorea. Remember, free travel dollars are not necessary to enjoy a dream Tahitian vacation at a cheapskate price.*

In 1994 the cost of a Tahiti Escapes vacation package was only $699. In 1996 Pat and I made our fourth visit to Tahiti at the same 1994 price of $699, less a 5 percent cash rebate. We received the 5 percent cash rebate on the total cost of our vacation packages using Travelers Advantage. but more on that later.

The complete air-and-land Tahiti Escapes package includes lodging at Cooks Bay Resort on the island of Moorea. Depending on the time of year and flight schedules, the package includes either six or seven nights at Cooks Bay Resort. In the former instance the seventh night is spent on the island of Tahiti in order to catch an early-morning flight home. The price also includes transfers from Tahiti's main airport on Papeete to Moorea via the high-speed ferry *Aremiti II*, and from the ferry dock to Cooks Bay Resort. In September 1994 we used $400 of Kraft's free travel cash to further reduce the $699 price to an all-time low of $499. On the other hand, Tahiti Vacations offers seven full nights on Moorea and throws in a free interisland flight on Air Tahiti from Papeete to the island of Moorea. All this at the same cheapskate price of $699 (plus $50 for weekend departures).

Are the Free Travel Dollars Truly Free?

Smart program participants spend only nominal dollars to purchase the products needed to obtain large amounts of free travel cash. For example, in 1995 I spent $38 to purchase Nabisco cookies at a local flea market. In return for the UPC proofs of purchase, Nabisco sent me almost $2,000 in free travel cash. Our collective goal is to spend as little as possible to obtain free travel dollars. One big plus is that sponsors' products are often staples we use every day, and many of the products can be stored or frozen for later use. When I purchased the fifty boxes of Nabisco cookies at a local flea market, I quickly became a cookie Santa, giving cookies to family and friends. (I admit it: we kept every single box of Oreo cookies for ourselves!)

Some promotions are cheaper than others. The Nabisco program was a snap. It required the purchase of three boxes or packages of cookies or crackers, of five ounces or larger, to obtain $50 in free travel cash. Occasionally, there are "doubling" offers that cut the cost of purchases by 50 percent (see page 15).

What if a promotion involves an expensive product such as Zostrix, which costs more than cookies or Jell-O? I am philosophical about this type of situation. If the product is usable and not obnoxious, I can deal with the cost by using creative strategies. Let's say the product is priced at $10 and each purchase qualifies for $50 in travel cash. This amounts to an expenditure of $40 to obtain $200 in travel cash. Is anyone else offering you $200 in travel cash in addition to $40 of usable product you may purchase? Probably not. Should a doubling offer be available with this program, it would cut the purchase price by 50 percent.

You must be creative to cut your purchase costs to the bare minimum. Often, when a new promotion commences the product will be offered on special sale, so look for sale ads and discount coupons. Shop to find the lowest price. A local store may have an advertising bulletin board, or perhaps there is a flea market newspaper offering cheap or free advertising. How about advertising your interest in obtaining UPC proofs of purchase? Friends or family members who use the product may donate UPC proofs of purchase or may allow you to purchase it for them. Use any of these strategies and come up with new and better ones. Where there is a will, there is usually a money-saving way.

Some promotions require the submission of store receipts while others require only the submission of UPC proofs of purchase. Always review the few rules governing each program.

Finally, if a product does not work for you, skip it and wait for the release of the next program. Fortunately for me, the far better Kraft and Nabisco programs ran simultaneously with a Carlton cigarette promotion, so I purchased cookies instead of cigarettes.

What Makes This Author an Expert?

Since 1984, Patty and I have participated in vacation travel cash giveaways. One of the earliest 1984 promotions was sponsored by Castrol Oil. We used our free travel dollars to pay for several memorable scuba-diving vacations to Mexico's largest island, Cozumel. As I recall, the Castrol giveaway allowed us to use $200 of free travel cash per vacation. In a word, we were hooked on these corporate deals.

In late 1993, while reading my Sunday newspaper, I rummaged through the coupon inserts—the infamous coupon magazine section that many immediately dispatch to the trash bin or use as kitty-box liner. Suffice to say my curiosity paid off big-time when I spotted a full two-page spread announcing Kraft's "Jell-O/Cool Whip Vacation Cash Giveaway." Okay, I admit I am a peruser of the coupon section, but then again, the fruits of my efforts have altered the course of our travel lives. As far as I can determine, the Kraft advertisement appeared only once in its original full-two-page format in the Bay Area, though I did notice smaller, one-eighth-page ads that were run on two subsequent occasions over the next two years. With the original two-page advertisement in hand, I immediately set up a Kraft promotion file. In a flash we were planning several dream vacations.

At around the same time as the release of the Kraft Jell-O/Cool Whip program, I spotted promotions by Kodak, Carlton cigarettes, and Northern toilet tissue. Prior to the Kraft Jell-O promotion, I participated in another Kraft promotion involving Country Time Lemonade. I gathered the newest promotion advertisements and studied the brief rules governing each program. Though the programs are all similar, there are usually threshold differences, the major one being the amount of free travel cash that couples (and more recently singles) may use on typical seven-night vacations. I am always determined to locate and participate in the best promotion available, giving due consideration to the amount of travel cash usable per vacation and the nature of the product involved. My quick study concluded the easy winner to be the Kraft Jell-O/Cool Whip promotion.

Another decision was what to do with the $800 in free travel cash I had already amassed from Kraft's earlier Country Time Lemonade program. I compared the Country Time limit of $250 in free travel cash per vacation to the $400 limit in the Jell-O/Cool Whip program. Without hesitation, I donated the $800 of Country Time script to family and friends.

Why give the script away? This was an easy mathematical calculation. I spent $40 to obtain the $800 in Country Time script. Our first vacation using Kraft's Jell-O script, at $400 per trip, would save an additional $150 over the Country Time program. On top of that, I spent only $40 on sufficient Jell-O products to obtain $2,000 of Kraft's travel cash. No doubt about it, we were off and running with the incredible, newer Kraft Jell-O/Cool Whip promotion. For the next two years, this travel cash helped fund our world-class dream vacations, from Paris to Tahiti and beyond.

It is one thing to learn about travel-cash programs and quite another to be savvy enough to use them. I have talked to people who customarily trash such offers as "too good to be true." They are the same people who routinely spend hundreds of dollars per year on losing lottery tickets. When I tell such people I received and used $2,000 from Kraft Foods just by participating in the very program they ignored, I am met with looks of disbelief. I firmly believe that knowledge is power, and with this book, you become empowered to obtain and enjoy hundreds to thousands of free travel dollars that are virtually yours for the asking.

The Great Kraft Giveaway

During 1994 and 1995, I obtained and used $2,000 from the Kraft's Jell-O/Cool Whip Giveaway, and also gained an intimate working knowledge of the promotion. The Kraft program is an excellent example of how most giveaways work, from day one until the participant is departing on a dream vacation. Here are the nuts-and-bolts details of the Kraft program:

1. I shopped at a local discount market where Cool Whip sold for $1 per large tub. Each $1 purchase represented $50 in Kraft

Travel cash. My net product cost, to qualify for $400 in travel cash, was an astounding $8.

2. I mailed proofs of purchase (UPC codes) to ITH, along with the Kraft mail-in form. Eight weeks later I received Jell-O script in $50 and $100 denominations.

3. The promotion applied to vacations of at least seven nights' duration that included airfare on a regularly scheduled airline. As always, the free travel cash could be used toward the vacations of my choice at the best prices I could find.

4. Finally, I inserted the specifics of my chosen vacation on the travel certificates (script) and mailed them, with a $100 deposit, to ITH. Later, I was contacted by Kraft's travel agency, Liberty Travel of New York City. Liberty promptly booked the vacation, provided written confirmation, and a week or so prior to departure sent us all the necessary travel documents.

➡ **Steve's Tip:** *Charter flights are excluded from most vacation cash giveaways. However, there are occasional exceptions, a major one being the wonderful Tahiti Escapes package that uses Corsair Airlines, a scheduled French charter airline. For reasons unknown to me, Liberty Travel permitted the use of Kraft travel dollars in the amount of $400 per couple on Tahiti Escapes' packages. This resulted in a net price of $499 per person for the entire Moorea vacation. When in doubt, always check with ITH or its selected travel agency.*

Not certain if a package uses charter air? Just ask the tour operator. If still in doubt, ask whether you are required to complete a charter agreement as a condition for participating in the vacation. That is a surefire indication the tour operator is using a charter company.

The Great Nabisco Promotion!

ITH's recent travel cash giveaway, the twenty-one-month Nabisco promotion, commenced in April 1995. It has been one of the finest and longest running programs offered during the past twelve years, which portends well for upcoming new promotions. Sadly,

Nabisco recently concluded its two-year giveaway of free travel cash. Nevertheless, it is another excellent example of just how these ongoing programs work. Your familiarity with and understanding of the program will enable you to promptly participate, to your maximum advantage, in the Zostrix and other soon-to-be-issued new promotions.

Nabisco provided $100 to $500 of free travel cash per couple for vacations of four to fourteen nights' duration. Within hours of learning of the Nabisco program, I contacted ITH in New Jersey, inquiring about all aspects of the promotion.

Once again, the twelve-year pattern of these wonderful cash giveaways continued. Another American food icon, Nabisco, had replaced Kraft's Jell-O/Cool Whip program. The Nabisco giveaways' few rules are summarized as follows:

1. Nabisco paid $50 in travel cash for three proofs of purchase submitted from packages of their cookies or crackers (of five ounces or larger). There was *no limit* on the amount of free travel dollars participants could request—hundreds or even thousands. This is true of most prior promotions as well.

2. Participants could use their free travel cash in the following manner:

- $100 per couple toward a vacation of at least four nights that includes the purchase of round-trip noncharter airfare.
- $300 per couple toward a vacation of at least seven nights that includes the purchase of round-trip noncharter airfare.
- $500 per couple toward a vacation of at least fourteen nights that includes the purchase of round-trip, noncharter airfare.
- All of the above applied to cruises with one exception: cruises did not require the purchase of airfare.
- Vacationers had to use regularly scheduled airlines. Charter airlines did not qualify since if the plane was not full, the flight might have been canceled.

3. Nabisco proofs of purchase were mailed to ITH with a $2 check and the official mail-in certificate, or a facsimile.

4. In four to six weeks the participant received free travel cash in $50 denominations.

5. Next was the fun part. Participants shopped for the vacation

of their choice at the best price available. Weekend newspaper travel sections often contain the best money-saving deals. The *New York Times* and *Los Angeles Times* offer the most comprehensive newspaper travel sections. Their advertisers routinely announce super money-saving bargains on international vacations departing from East and West Coast gateway cities. Participants would choose a vacation and send ITH the travel cash script along with a vacation request form. ITH's selected travel agency, Zenith Travel, booked the vacation.

➡ **Steve's Tip:** *On one occasion my submission to ITH for $1,700 was temporarily lost in the mail. Based on my photocopy of the UPC proofs of purchase, ITH sent me the full $1,700 I had requested. Without doubt ITH proved to me they are a first-class operation. The lesson: Be smart and keep a copy of all submitted UPC proofs of purchase.*

Doubling Free Dollars?

The Nabisco giveaway promotion announced a new friendly feature not found in prior programs. It is important to keep the Nabisco doubling feature in mind, since this may appear in newly released promotions. Here is how it worked. If a participant obtained $200 in store receipts from a participating local supermarket, Nabisco doubled the amount of free travel cash. For example, I submitted to Nabisco $200 in local store receipts together with fifty-one proofs of product purchases. Normally this would qualify for $850 in script ($50 for each of three UPC codes). Instead, I received double the amount—$1,700—of free travel cash. During 1995 and 1996 Nabisco repeated the offer intermittently in different areas of the country. A friend followed my advice and participated in the Nabisco giveaway. First, she found a local market running a doubling promotion. Though she could have spent the $200 on any grocery items, she chose to purchase $200 worth of Nabisco cookies. Then she donated them to Glide Memorial Church in San Francisco and received a record-breaking $3,700 in travel cash from Nabisco. She wins my admiration for being an ultimate promotion participant.

➡ **Steve's Tip:** *Recently my mother, Ruth, sent me a Nabisco advertisement that asked readers to join the "Nabisco Family," and it included a mail-in coupon. Nabisco promised to inform all those returning the coupon of future offers and promotions. I suggest you write to Nabisco and request to be placed on its mailing list for announcements of future offers or promotions. Write to:*
Nabisco Special Offers
P.O. Box 7147,
Easton, Maryland 21606

Travel cash giveaway promotions are not limited to couples. For example, Nabisco's free travel cash was equally usable on the basis that "single travelers receive half the savings, four travelers receive double the savings." The four-traveler rule is understandable, since each pair of travelers may use $400 on an eight-day vacation. The best news was that singles could also use free travel cash. Single travelers received $150 to use on seven-night vacations and $250 on fourteen-night packages.

Using Your Free Travel Dollars

Some tour operators run bargain advertisements in major newspapers' travel sections before their brochures are available. Regardless, it is always prudent to request major airlines' bargain-tour brochures. Keep an ongoing watch of your local newspapers' weekly travel section. If possible, periodically pick up the Sunday *Los Angeles Times* and *New York Times*. These newspapers contain the two finest travel sections in the country.

➡ **Steve's Tip:** *Cruise lines often advertise seven-day cruises, which usually refer to full days on the ship, with seven nights, so that passengers qualify for free-travel-cash promotions. But just to be safe, call your cruise company to confirm the trip length.*

Here is a small selection of my best use of free travel dollars during the past two years:

1. In April 1995 we vacationed in Paris. The eight-day, seven-nights vacation included lodging and daily breakfast at the Hotel Amsterdam. This two-star hotel was cozy and comfortable, offered a super breakfast, and was well located in central Paris. The regular package price of the vacation, through France Vacations (AOM), was a cheapskate bargain at $765 from the West Coast. After deducting $400 of free travel cash we paid the incredible net price of $565 per person.

2. During 1994 we took a full-week Carnival cruise to the Mexican Riviera, which included stops at Puerto Vallarta, Mazatlán, and Cabo San Lucas. The full-week cruise was a bargain at $645 per person. After deducting $400 with our Kraft travel cash, the net price was an incredible $445 each for the entire cruise. These cruises have recently dropped their prices to just $549 per person (or a net price of $399 using free dollars).

3. We also took a third trip to Tahiti using the Kraft promotion. Again we used Islands in the Sun's Tahiti Escapes package. The regular cheapskate price is $699; we used Kraft free dollars to reduce this to $499.

4. In 1994 we traveled to London with American Airlines' "London on Your Own" package. In the bargain, I picked up 11,000 American AAdvantage miles. The regular cheapskate price for this eight-day, seven-night London vacation, including airfare, hotel, daily breakfast, and a three-day London Underground pass, was $718 each. After deducting our free Kraft travel cash, the net cost was an incredible $518 per person.

5. In June 1996 we traveled to mainland China with tour operator China Focus Travel, which offered a twelve-day, all-inclusive, historical tour of China. The twelve-day tour included round-trip airfare to China, hotels, meals, sightseeing, and intra-country transportation with buses, trains, and one plane flight. The regular cheapskate price for this high-season tour is $1,399. Our net price, less $300 with Nabisco free cash, was just $1,249 each. Truly a world-class cheapskate vacation.

I will end this section by noting that several of my associates and friends give hundreds of dollars of colorful free travel script to their family members as gifts. Chris, a fellow employee, gave $300 of free travel cash to her son, who promptly applied the money toward his Hawaiian vacation. Do you recall my friend who obtained $3,700 in free travel cash? Her excess travel cash turned into numerous free travel gifts to family members. I gave Patty's son $800 in free travel cash that he wisely used to help pay for his Paris and Tahiti vacations. This is a wonderful way to be a benefactor while using "free" corporate funds.

Recent Deals Using Free Travel Cash

Weekend newspaper travel sections usually reveal new money-saving tidbits of travel information. I am primarily interested in seven-night or even fourteen-night vacation packages so that available free travel cash may be used. The following examples are just that—examples. Prices of these packages are constantly changing, depending on the season of travel, airlines prices, and other factors. All these deals were advertised in 1996, and each easily qualifies for the cheapskate rating whether or not free travel dollars are used. The Hawaii packages reflect West Coast departures. Cruises are "cruise only." Caribbean cruises usually depart from Miami, Puerto Rico, or New Orleans, while Mexican Riviera cruises depart from Los Angeles. See chapter 14 for a variety of global bargains, and the appendix for details on tour operators.

Let me begin with an astounding example of how your diligence can pay big vacation dividends whether or not free travel dollars are used. In July 1996 Carnival placed a large advertisement for its seven-day southern Caribbean cruises in the weekend travel sections of major newspapers from coast to coast. The price per person with four passengers sharing a stateroom, *including round-trip airfare to Puerto Rico*, was just $649 from New York and $749 from California. Readers had just five days to book the cruise, although travel was good on sailings from late August to early October. Those using free travel cash paid just $499 from New York and $599 from California. This deal was beyond cheapskate!

• Eight days, seven nights in Waikiki, including air and hotel through Pleasant Hawaiian Holidays for only $399. This means a net price of just $249 for those using free travel dollars.

- Eight days, seven nights on Maui, Hawaii, which includes airfare, hotel, and car rental for the week, through Pleasant Hawaiian. This package was advertised in July 1996. It was priced at only $519, or just $369 using free travel dollars.
- A seven-night eastern or western Caribbean cruise with Celebrity or Carnival priced at only $549, or net price of $399 with free dollars. Many other cruise lines offer the same prices on selected sailings.
- A seven-night Carnival cruise to the Mexican Riviera, priced at $549, or a net price of $399 using free dollars.
- A seven-night London package from United Airlines at only $692. This included round-trip airfare from the West Coast and daily breakfasts. The price using free travel dollars dropped to $542. This same package was priced at $625 from New York City and $674 from Chicago, less $150 using free travel dollars.
- A seven-night Paris package from United Airlines at $775 from New York on the West Coast ($674 from Chicago) included round-trip airfare and daily breakfasts. Free travel dollars reduced the price by $150.

Okay, I could go on and on, but I do think you get the idea. Look for bargain packages offered by legitimate tour operators. It is one thing when American Airlines offers its London on Your Own package and quite another when you see some unknown company announcing below wholesale prices. When I learned of the super-bargain-priced China tour offered by San Francisco–based China Focus Travel, I learned from my colleague Ann that this tour operator had a solid reputation in the travel industry. Also, Ann herself had traveled to China on a China Focus tour, and she offered wonderful firsthand testimony regarding the tour and the services provided by China Focus Travel.

If a tour operator is not known to you, be sure to obtain their brochure, ask them for references, and check with travel agents and better business bureaus in the area where their home office is located. Remember, always be a good travel consumer!

Purchasing Air-Only or Land-Only Packages

I know there are times when air-and-land packages do not meet our travel needs. When Patty and I used free AAdvantage miles to fly to Kenya, I still had to purchase a land package. Other times, when we visit Maui or are staying with friends, we require only air transportation. Chapter 4 offers savings on such air-only and land-only packages.

As you read on and delve into the fascinating world of cheapskate travel, think in terms of free travel dollars. When I discuss packages, I note whether they involve charter flights or regularly scheduled airlines. I always emphasize the exact number of nights in a given air-and-land package. Occasionally, packages are offered exclusively through a single tour operator so that free travel cash cannot be used.

Above all else, never forget that your dream vacations are as close as your spirit of adventure and willingness to pack your bags, feed the pets, and head to the nearest departure gate at the airport!

2

Better Than Cheap: Free Travel

Patty and I have enjoyed the ultimate vacation adventure of an East African safari not once but twice. Our first trip was a two-week photo safari to Kenya in 1990. Our second trip, in 1992, included a one-week photo safari in Tanzania and a one-week stay in Mombasa on Kenya's tropical eastern coast. From Mombasa we explored Wassini and Medina, two of the country's finest Indian Ocean marine preserves. Our airfare, from California to Nairobi, the capital city of Kenya, was free for both of us on *both* trips. Let me repeat: Our travel was 100 percent *free* on *both* trips! Soon after our return from Kenya, we vacationed at Club Med on Turquoise Island in the Turks and Caicos chain of the British West Indies. This is widely considered one of the best Club Med scuba-diving destinations in the world, and it was superb. While diving we found ourselves swimming side-by-side with the island's resident dolphin, an unforgettable experience. Our travel to this expensive destination was 100 percent free for both of us. In October 1995 we traveled to Israel, with side trips to Jordan and Egypt. Again, travel on this trip was free for *both* of us.

Frequent Flying on Terra Firma

This chapter emphasizes an overlooked fact of travel life. Major U.S. corporations are ready and willing to give away free travel to

21

most worldwide destinations. The sad truth is that most people don't take advantage of it.

The best source of free travel is frequent flyer miles, known today as program miles. Okay, you do not enjoy reading this because you rarely fly. You know all too well that such programs are meant for corporate types but definitely not for you. However, here is the rest of the story:

At least 90 percent of our program miles are not from flying. How do we do it? How do landlubbers like Patty and me obtain free travel to Africa, the Middle East, and the Caribbean? Better yet, how can you bank these miles and obtain free travel awards? My recommended answer is the partnership between American Airlines and Citibank.

➡ **Steve's Tip:** *Call American Airlines' AAdvantage program at (800) 882-8880, or call any American Airlines phone number and ask for their AAdvantage department. You will be signed up on the spot and given a program number. That's it. You have completed phase one on the road to free global travel. If you prefer, you may check a box on the Citibank Visa/MasterCard application (lower-left corner), and an American Airlines AAdvantage number will automatically be assigned to you.*

Let's start at square one: American Airlines. I recommend that all readers immediately join the American Airlines AAdvantage program. But let me put your mind at ease: There is no obligation and no fee to join.

A bit of history would be helpful. Originally, the American Airlines program was a frequent flyer program awarding miles for flights completed by passengers. The frequent flyer miles were later turned into free-travel awards. Recently, free-travel programs have cropped up everywhere, and fierce competition forced American to vastly expand its frequent flyer program. Since many people earn free travel without setting foot on a plane, American Airlines no longer uses the term *frequent flyer*. In its place came the American AAdvantage program. The most successful aspect of this program is its association with Citibank Visa/MasterCard.

The special Citibank AAdvantage card allows card holders to bank one mile for each dollar charged through purchases. American Airlines issues free-travel awards based on banked program miles. As in the past, program miles are also earned for each mile flown on American Airlines' flights.

➡ **Steve's Tip:** *Do not get confused. There are different types of Citibank credit cards. You need the Citibank AAdvantage card tied in to the American Airlines AAdvantage program. As this book goes to press, Citibank is offering a super 3,000-mile bonus for new card holders. This is a long-running offer that will hopefully be available when you sign on.*

While phase two is not free, it is inexpensive and will eventually pay for itself: You must sign up for either the Citibank American AAdvantage Visa or MasterCard. Anyone can apply for this card, and most applicants qualify. The minimum income requirement to apply is a reasonable $15,000 "from all sources." Okay, I do not believe in paying annual fees on credit cards. In fact, I carry numerous cards and all are free of annual fees with one exception. But because the payback on this one is so great I am willing to pay the annual fee for my Citibank AAdvantage card. The regular card has a $50 yearly fee; the Gold Card has an $85 fee. Let's start with the regular card. To obtain an application, contact Citibank at (800) 950-5114 or (800) FLY-4444, and ask for a Citibank AAdvantage Visa or MasterCard application.

The Citibank AAdvantage card has some fine features, one being great customer service; a "humanoid" (real-live operator) is available seven days a week and twenty-four hours per day, which comes in handy when there is an occasional problem with a merchant. Also, Citibank will, upon request, issue an additional card to a second authorized user at no charge.

Plastic Rules!

Your winning strategy should incorporate two major goals: First, you want to amass megamiles by using the Citibank card for all your purchases. Second, you want to enjoy thousands of free-mile perks along with other valuable freebies.

➡ **Steve's Cardinal Rule:** *Stop using your checkbook. Charge everything you would normally purchase with cash or by check with your Citibank AAdvantage card. (Since I do not wish to carry debts on a credit card, I pay off each monthly bill in full to avoid paying finance charges. Hence, I am not concerned with interest rates. However, you should know that Citibank's interest rate is 18.15 percent.)*

What follows are my time-proven, day-to-day strategies for garnishing the miles needed to achieve free travel to the exotic destinations of your dreams. Today, more than ever, businesses are allowing customers to charge most purchases and services. A great place to start is your local supermarket, where you can now charge everything from soup to nuts and much more. In my neck of the woods we have supermarkets that sell Chinese food, pizza, every imaginable food product, and most household products. One may charge everything from beverages to pharmaceuticals, and more. I think you get the picture. The point is to use your Citibank card for everything. The average family spends approximately $150 per week on such purchases. This alone amounts to an impressive 7,800 miles that can be banked in one year, or 11,700 in just eighteen months.

Don't feel nauseous over missed opportunities! There is no looking back! Too many people are unaware of how to use this program if they do not fly. I use a cellular phone for business, with an average monthly bill of $150. I charge the payments with my Citibank Visa card. The net result is an additional 1,800 miles per year. (By the way, my cellular bill offered no provision for paying by credit card. By contacting customer service, I learned they permit payment by charge card only when the customer makes a special request. Always think credit card!)

Let's return to my strategy for banking miles. Do you go to the barber or beauty salon periodically? Do you purchase refrigerators, washers and dryers, stereos, television sets, computers, cameras, video gear, or clothes? Every "yes" answer means more megamiles in your program account when you charge the purchases on your Citibank card. Take your pen and add a conservative minimum of $10,000 to $20,000 per year as the amount spent in all of these categories, hence, 10,000 to 20,000 additional program miles. Did I mention home repairs and home-related purchases? At this point the total could easily exceed 25,000 miles in the first eighteen months.

Shall I continue? Unfortunately, automobiles are expensive to purchase, maintain, and operate. On the other hand, we should charge everything, from repairs to gasoline. Often major expenses, such as tuition costs for private schools, colleges, and vocational classes can be charged. Patty charged thousands of dollars of her law school tuition on our Citibank card. Today it is common for charities to solicit by mail, and more often than not they allow credit card charges. The same applies to magazine subscriptions.

When we travel, the first thing I do is charge all related expenses, including the cost of the vacation package, on my trusty Citibank card. As I am paying for a vacation, I know full well that my payments are already helping to pay for future vacations.

As an electronic and video junkie, I receive all sorts of mail-order catalogues. Each year I purchase cameras and other electronic products from established, out-of-state discount firms such as Damark International (800-827-6767). These purchases amount to hundreds and sometimes thousands of dollars—and thus miles—per year.

One example still hurts—figuratively speaking. Recently when I visited Norm, my dentist, the bill was $390. In the past Norm took only cash payments, but six months ago I noticed a Visa sign on the reception desk. Norm was finally catching up with modern times. As the nitrous took effect, I began to dream of the tropical islands I will one day visit thanks in small part to such dreaded dental visits.

By now your total miles has likely hit the first plateau—the 25,000-mile mark. Perhaps you have reached the second or even third free-travel plateau. Currently American Airlines will award a free ticket to any destination in the continental United States for

25,000 miles. At 30,000 miles you qualify for free travel to Hawaii or any destination in Canada, Mexico, the Caribbean, the Bahamas, Bermuda, or Central or South America. The 40,000-mile plateau qualifies you for a free round-trip ticket to any destination in Europe. It is amazing, but true, that this plateau—40,000 miles—qualifies you for a free round-trip ticket to Tel Aviv. Other examples of major free round-trip travel awards include Tokyo (50,000 miles), Australia, New Zealand, or Fiji on American's sister airline Quantas (80,000 miles), or Nairobi, Kenya, using sister airline British Airways (75,000 miles). The Nairobi flight represents the most expensive major air destination in the world. A round-trip economy ticket usually sells for $2,500 to $4,000.

Any doubts remaining? Consider that Citibank will, at no extra cost, issue additional cards to a spouse, siblings, or anyone you authorize. For years Patty has been charging her bills to my account using just such a Citibank card issued in her name.

Recently, Citibank requested I upgrade to a Gold Card account. This required an increase in the yearly fee from $50 to $85. For that nominal increase, Citibank gave me a free companion domestic airline ticket that was valid for free round-trip travel anywhere in the continental United States. Later, I used the companion ticket when booking my annual four-day trip to New York City. I paid a reasonable economy coach fare of $353, but Patty's ticket was free. Such a companion ticket may be worth up to $600, depending on the U.S. destination. I think you will agree this was one sweet deal for my extra $35 payment. Citibank also offers another companion ticket each year thereafter for those taking an American Airlines flight during the year.

Want to bank even more miles? When Patty and I were getting ready to spend a week in London using the Kraft/Jell-O promotion, my goal was to locate a cheapskate package using American Airlines. My strategy worked. The American Airlines package to London, called London on Your Own, provided the lowest price. I was able to earn 11,000 frequent flyer miles by flying American. The total cost of the London trip for two was $1,034. Of course, I then charged this on my Citibank card, adding another 1,034 miles to my account. When traveling in foreign countries, we charge everything on our Citibank Visa card. And we get an extra bonus when using a Visa card in foreign countries—all purchases at the highest exchange rate available that day!

A few major recurrent bills, such as rent and mortgage payments are exceptions and may not be paid by credit card. But then, who knows when this will change?

➡ **Steve's Tip:** *If you are one of many readers who own a large or small business and are not already using a Citibank AAdvantage card, then a free travel "pot of gold" awaits at the end of your business rainbow. Consider all of the commercial purchases made each year on such items as furniture and equipment. All of these thousands of dollars will translate into banked program miles when the purchases are made with a Citibank card. By year's end these miles alone may qualify you for a free round-trip ticket to any number of global destinations.*

Be innovative and assertive! There is no shame in failure. When making our recent car purchase, Patty and I asked if we could charge the deposit on Visa. Reluctantly, but because of our insistence, the salesman checked with his manager. Unfortunately, the dealer did not allow it. However, we tried. Use initiative! Our mantra is: "I will not use my checkbook, I will not use my checkbook." Repeat this chant daily until your checkbook gathers dust. A warning, however: Never charge frivolously! Charge only those items you would otherwise be purchasing. After all, the fun and enjoyment of free travel is worthless if you are headed for bankruptcy court! Keep track of charges and be aware of your monthly charge-card balance, and be sure to earmark sufficient funds to cover all purchases. If possible, pay the entire charge card bill each month to avoid high interest rates or finance charges.

Free Miles and Other "Freebie" Perks

Welcome to the American Airlines AAdvantage program, a new and unique universe. Be ready to receive valuable perks that will no doubt be coming your way. American Airlines sends members periodic statements and newsletters. Read them meticulously. During the past year the American AAdvantage newsletter contained the following free miles and related offers:

- Each newsletter lists chains of hotels, such as Sheraton and Forte, that offer hundreds of free miles for each stay. It also lists car rental companies that offer up to 1,000 free miles per rental. Often, there are doubling offers on hotels and car rentals.
- A 1,000-mile bonus, plus a flight upgrade for a stay of one night or more at a Holiday Inn.
- Periodically, the newsletter announces "sales" on travel. For example, a 25 percent sale on the miles normally required for a travel award to Australia. The usual "charge" of 80,000 miles for a free round-trip ticket to Australia was reduced to 60,000 miles.
- The special dining club offer of 5,000 free miles for those joining Citibank's free-dining club and buying ten meals over a two-month period. The club includes such low-priced eateries as Numero Uno.

In early 1996 my associate, Nancy, dutifully reported the valuable "junk mail" she had received. But this time she had received a "selected" mailing and a numbered promotion certificate from Citibank that offered up to 15,000 free program miles. If she deposited $6,000 in Citibank accounts and agreed to use Citibank's "free" electronic banking service, similar to the Quicken service that charges $9.95 per month, she would receive 12,500 free program miles. If she agreed to the direct deposit of her paycheck, Citibank would have given her an additional 2,500 free miles.

Here is the "magic" of my strategy: by finding and participating in the above mini-promotions over a matter of eight weeks, I instantly obtained 20,000 free miles. This is the equivalent of one-half of a round-trip ticket to the Middle East or any European city. This shows just how easy and fast one may bank program miles.

The key is getting into the game. Become a member of Citibank AAdvantage and become a player, not an unknowing observer. If I had a dollar for each person who plays the lottery and ignores corporate handouts of free airline tickets and travel cash, I would become a wealthy man.

➡ **Steve's Tip:** *Often such special offers are randomly mailed by Citibank to some members and not others. In this case I did not receive the promotion certificate. When Citibank would not mail me a certificate in response to my phone request I did not give up. I called a local Citibank office and learned they had a limited number of in-office certificates, so I could participate in this particular "freebie" deal. Three days prior to the expiration of the offer I appeared at the Citibank office, and moments later left with 12,500 free program miles. Last year I received a free companion ticket, randomly mailed by American Airlines, just for being an AAdvantage member!*

Here is what happened when a friend followed my advice. Ann, an associate attorney in my office, booked a free flight from California to North Carolina to visit her mother through the American AAdvantage program only eight months after she obtained her Citibank card. She also switched to MCI and received their 5,000-mile new member bonus. Recently Ann used another free ticket to North Carolina. She is a perfect example of a savvy program member. During the past year MCI has been offering a more modest bonus of at least 2,000 free miles for new subscribers. For some of the latest and best deals, check American Airlines' newsletter, which regularly lists current MCI specials.

What About Competing Programs?

During the past year, several new types of programs have hit the marketplace. One was issued by a local bank and another by the California Automobile Association of America (CAAA). The bank promotion awarded 5,000 miles to new customers. Thereafter, miles were accumulated through use of a noncredit bank card known as a debit card. In both instances these programs have no relation to the American AAdvantage program. When the bank mentioned that their miles could be used on any airline, I checked further and learned that the program was exclusive to this bank. These programs may or may not be to your advantage, but one thing is certain: They will *not* allow their miles to be added to your existing American program account, even though both programs offer free travel on American Airlines.

The 1996 CAAA program is another good example. The program uses CAAA's Bank One Visa card. They presently issue the card without a yearly fee, a definite plus. Members using their CAAA Visa card accumulate one Diamond Dollar for each dollar charged, similar to the AAdvantage program. For you, all that remains is to compare awards and expiration dates. The CAAA program miles expire at the end of the year following the purchase, bad news that means that miles earned in December 1996 will expire just thirteen months later, at the end of 1997.

CAAA's colorful award brochure is enticing. It describes the various awards, including luggage, domestic and international flights on United Airlines, and a $400 cash discount on vacations booked through the CAAA travel office. Comparing free air travel is the easy part. American awards a free domestic ticket for only 25,000 program miles, while the CAAA program requires 35,000 Diamond Dollars for the same ticket. More interesting is the CAAA offer of a $400 cash award against any travel booked through its travel agency.

In comparing cash equivalents, I assume that a 25,000-mile American award equals, at the very minimum, a low-priced $400 seat to New York City from the West Coast. That translates to 1.6 cents per program mile. Applying that standard, the CAAA program requirement of 35,000 Diamond Dollars for the $400 travel award is the equivalent of $640 in AAdvantage miles. Another way to phrase it is that at 35,000 miles, CAAA awards a $400 travel credit. American, for an additional 5,000 miles and a total of 40,000 miles, awards a round-trip ticket to most European cities or Tel Aviv. This is worth far more than $400.

Compare all these programs and do your own calculations. I am sticking with American AAdvantage. Their program continues to be the easiest to use and offers the greatest value. You may recall that I received a free companion ticket for any U.S. destination just for being a program member. That same free companion ticket is listed as an award in the CAAA brochure, costing a hefty 20,000 Diamond Dollars.

➡ **Steve's Tip:** *Over the years I have joined several airline frequent flyer programs. In the spring of 1996 I received a piece of valuable "junk" mail from the United Airlines Mileage Plus program offering a free companion round-trip airline ticket, good for any U.S. destination, if I signed up for a United Mileage Plus First Visa card. I opted for the regular (non-Gold) card, paid a $60 fee, and received a companion ticket that will provide Patty with a free $400 flight when we next visit the Big Apple. Card holders are not required to renew the card after the first year. I urge you to take advantage of these bargains. To learn whether United's program is currently ongoing, call United Airlines at (800) 767-9839 or (800) 421-4655. Also check with Delta at (800) 323-2323 and Continental at (800) 525-0280 for any promotions they may be offering.*

Wisdom! Do *Not* Leave Home Without It!

I do not have Solomon's wisdom, but my New York street smarts have sharpened over the years. After returning from Africa, Pan American Airlines awarded us 30,000 frequent flyer miles for the flights, which qualified us for free travel anywhere in the United States or the Caribbean. I knew Pan American was financially in trouble, so we used the miles quickly. Occasionally, I delve into *Skin Diver* magazine, a publication for scuba-diving enthusiasts. I found an exotic destination, Turquoise Island in the Turks and Caicos chain of the British West Indies.

Before you grab your atlas, the island is a short but expensive twenty-minute flight from Florida. The article described the Club Med village on Turquoise Island, which is touted as one of the best Club Med scuba destinations in the world. It is a diving-oriented facility with its own boats that offer participants at least two dives per day. A resident dolphin habitually follows the dive boats and allows divers to swim nearby. My eye turned to another page that contained a telltale photo of the island's airport runway.

And there it was. Sitting on the runway was a small commuter plane with very large letters reading Pan Am! I instantly realized the photo's significance. Exotic tropical islands are costly destinations. Few people visit such an island, often only serviced by a single airline. Here that airline was Pan Am, and we had two free tickets good for any destination in the Caribbean!

I contacted Pan Am to ask about the airfare from San Francisco to Turquoise Island. The price quoted was approximately $700 per person for the trip, routed through Miami. In a flash we booked the free flights. The land package was to be our first Club Med vacation. In my experience most Club Med villages, including Turquoise Island, charge about $1,000 per week, with no airfare included. This covered all of the usual Club Med amenities, such as food, wine at meals, and all activities. Our Turquoise Island Club Med vacation was superb in all respects. And yes, we did dive and swim in tandem with the island's resident dolphin!

➡ **Steve's Rule:** *Always push your travel dollar to the limit when using free airline ticket awards. Focus on the "now or never" scenario. Read the award schedule from top to bottom, including footnotes, asterisks, and all the small print. Free tickets in hand today may not be available tomorrow.*

Generally, some fares are consistently low. This applies to heavy traffic routes, like flights between New York and the West Coast, and flights to Hawaii or Mexico from the West Coast. So avoid using a free ticket for such high-volume, low-fare destinations. East Coast residents receive good value when using a free travel award on a memorable Hawaiian vacation; however, most of us on the West Coast will eventually vacation in Hawaii using bargain airfares. While a domestic ticket award (25,000 miles) also permits travel to "any" Caribbean destination, a mere 5,000 more miles qualifies for a free ticket to any South American destination, while another 10,000 miles qualifies for any European destination or Tel Aviv. Always spend your program miles wisely.

Congratulations! You are now a graduate of Program Miles 101.

A Bed at 40,000 Feet!

Another truism known by savvy air travelers is that during a flight it is not mandatory that you remain in your assigned or reserved seat. Once a plane is airborne and reaches cruising altitude, it is okay to move around the cabin or to any empty seat or even an entire row of seats. If you are willing to abandon your seat for a more comfortable one, then read on.

Night, or "red-eye," flights are my specialty. For twenty years I have annually flown to New York City on such flights. On the West Coast these leave at 10:00 P.M. and arrive in New York at about 6:30 A.M. The length of the flight is five hours, with four hours of sleep opportunity. My strategy has been honed to so fine a craft that Patty and I have a 90 percent chance of sleeping in a "bed" of three to four seats. Add blankets and pillows, and *voilà!*—we are in airline heaven, enjoying solid sleep during most of the flight.

First, an old legal adage: Possession is nine-tenths of the law. Use simple strategy. My goal is to take possession of an entire center row of four or five seats. If at all possible, I try to prebook our seats, each of us occupying a middle seat within a five-seat center row. As much as Patty and I care for one another, we agree, before we board the plane, that we also care to get a good night's sleep. I have seen numerous couples attempting to sleep in uncomfortable positions when they could have had their row, or "bed," of five seats.

During check-in, I determine whether the plane is full. Once onboard I store my carry-on luggage in the overhead compartment, settle in, and immediately consider what I will need to take with me should I need to change my seat. If I am already in the middle of an empty row, this is an excellent starting position. Otherwise, I keep tabs on open rows as other passengers continue to board, checking the aisle to determine whether the stream of passengers is thinning. When seven to ten empty rows remain, I make my move. Often, a knowing attendant gives me a friendly nod.

Occasionally I am holding a solid empty row, sitting comfortably in the center of five seats when another passenger invades "my" row by taking an end seat. The passenger has only two seats, which makes it difficult to sleep. But with three seats I will do fine. If last-minute passengers with assigned seats show up, I take my belongings and head for a new empty row. When moving from my assigned seat I make certain to take a jacket or sweater with me. On one flight I did not think of this. I left the seat to visit the rest room and returned to find a stranger lying in "my" row. As I said, "possession *is* nine-tenths of the law." Now I simply place my jacket or other belongings on the seats if and when I must leave the row.

One exception: On Corsair airlines, the flight attendant nearly decapitated me in French style when I moved, before takeoff, to an empty row. The French rule permits passengers to make a run for empty seats only at cruising altitudes, which reminded me of the old-fashioned land rush of the 1850s. As the seat belt light went off, many savvy passengers made the dash for a night of precious sleep.

Do you like to sleep in the dark? I am not big on silly-looking sleeping devices, however, I dearly love to use my super Mindfold sleep mask. This product features a lightweight plastic outer "lens" that is totally impervious to light. The body of the mask is soft foam, with large cutouts that allow the user to blink in total darkness. And it includes foam earplugs to silence conversation and screaming children. The mask works like a charm, and I highly recommend it. It is currently available through Brookstone's mail catalog as item number 183731, priced at $15. You may contact Brookstone at (800) 926-7000. I guarantee that you will enjoy using this mask. Do you want to keep the flight attendant away while you sleep? Buckle your seat belt on the *outside* of your blanket when heading off to dreamland, but be certain to tell the attendant whether or not you wish to be awakened for meals.

The bottom line is the importance of a good night's sleep. For me it means optimum enjoyment of my first day of vacation.

3

Entertainment Publications and the World of Freebies

For some years I have been a minor member of the Entertainment Publications distribution team. I regularly deal with Entertainment's Concord California office and enjoy using the various Entertainment editions. These publications are an important asset, providing discounts on travel, recreation, food, and sightseeing. For those who are not familiar with these money-saving publications, read on.

Entertainment Dining Discounts: U.S. Editions

Entertainment books average about two hundred pages each, two thirds of the contents being two-for-one dining discounts. These are subdivided into dining categories. The fine-dining section consists of upscale restaurants that offer a $15 to $25 discount per entrée. The books provide sample menus and photographs of the participating establishments. The fine-dining section of the San Francisco edition includes the Tonga Room at the Fairmont Hotel and the Carnelian restaurant at the top of the Bank of America building, two of San Francisco's premiere restaurants. The New York edition includes fine restaurants such as Cecil's Grill in the Tudor hotel and Giovanni's Atrium on Washington Street.

The book is further divided into categories of "informal dining" and "fast-food dining." Also listed is the amount of discount offered by each establishment. Selecting a restaurant according to the size of one's pocketbook is easy. Every imaginable type of fast-food eatery is also listed, and surfing the fast-food section is always money-saving fun.

The U.S. editions are too numerous to list, currently totaling 137. Five editions cover the San Francisco Bay area and six editions cover the New York City area. Editions are presently available in eighteen states, from California to Florida to New York.

Entertainment Publications functions as fund-raising tools for charities, schools, and other qualifying organizations. The selling organization retains a percentage of the money raised by book sales. Most U.S. Entertainment editions cost $40 each, though users will find that after two or three uses their book pays for itself. Because of the fund-raising connection, these books are not sold in retail book stores. However, they are not difficult to find. I have seen them at flea markets, Sam's Club, and at PriceCostco. The U.S. editions, released annually in September, are printed in limited editions because this ensures that participating businesses will not be "swamped" with more participants than they can financially handle. Popular editions are usually sold out by midyear. If you have trouble finding a local distributor, call Entertainment Publications at (800) 374-4464. Also see the appendix for further information. I guarantee that your Entertainment book will pay for itself many times over. In return, I want you to promise one thing and one thing only: Use it!

Entertainment books are easy to use. Fine-dining restaurants require use of a membership card that is punched after each use. Tear-out coupons are provided for the remaining restaurants and fast-food eateries. Participating restaurants deduct the lower-priced entrée from the bill, the customer only paying for the higher-priced meal. The cheaper restaurants and fast-food emporiums allow you one menu item free when another of equal or greater value is purchased. Sometimes the maximum discount available is printed on the coupon. Coupons generally apply only to the price of one entrée or one à la carte item. Drinks, appetizers, and desserts are excluded. Family-style restaurants may include soup and/or salad with each dinner. Chinese restaurants offer family dinners that include five to seven courses. These restaurants offer the best savings on meals, so be a wise coupon and card user.

➡️ **Steve's Tip:** *Always call a restaurant to confirm that they still honor their Entertainment discount coupon. I find this necessary because of the great turnover in restaurant ownerships, and new owners may or may not honor the discount. Also, when six of us are celebrating a family event we use three cards, the maximum allowed at one meal, and enjoy three free dinners.*

Entertainment Dining: International Editions

Twenty-five foreign cities are available in separate international editions. These include London, Paris, and major cities in South America, Australia, Mexico, and Canada.

The international editions are slightly different from the domestic editions. European editions offer a straight 25 percent deduction off the total cost of the meal. The result is better than it first appears, for the meal may include appetizers, desserts, and alcoholic drinks. Ordering is a carefree exercise, since everything qualifies for the 25 percent discount. These editions sell for only $25.

The Paris edition is written in French, making discount life a bit more interesting. During our recent eight-day vacation to Paris, we quickly overcame the language barrier. With only a few uses, during our brief visit, the book paid for itself. Make no mistake about it, the costs in Paris are high—very high. A can of Coca Cola or bottle of Perrier runs about $3. Meals at middle-range bistros can cost $40 to $100 per person. We discovered L' Accordion, a lively cafe in the Latin Quarter. Our full three-course dinner, including aperitifs, cost only $12 per person after the Entertainment discount.

We used the London/U.K. edition during a recent vacation to Great Britain. A single coupon, for a half-day Frames tour of Windsor Castle, saved us $35 when Patty received her free ticket. We enjoyed free pub meals and various London discounts.

Currently international Entertainment editions are available for:

Anvers and Brussels, Belgium
Amsterdam and Rotterdam, Holland
Canada, with eight different geographic editions

France
Great Britain
Gothenburg, Germany
Malmo, Sweden
Mexico
Stockholm, Sweden
U.S. Virgin Islands

Hotel Discounts

Entertainment editions encompass more than just meals. Entertainment books contain extensive hotel directories with listings for most states and a good selection of foreign countries. These listings promise a discount of up to 50 percent off published hotel "rack rates."

The subject of rack rates requires some brief discussion. A rack rate is "supposedly" the highest rate a hotel will charge a guest when no other form or type of discount applies. Based on my own experience, I believe that many hotels use a "phantom" rack rate.

Last year my buddy, Stuart, and I visited Washington, D.C., for a four-day tour. My assigned task was to set up our hotel accommodations. Using my Entertainment hotel directory, I found an all-suite hotel in Georgetown, one of Washington's classiest suburbs. This hotel listed the rack rate for a suite as $240 per night. My cost, they told me, would be 50 percent of the rack rate, or $120 per night.

I requested a brochure. When it arrived in the mail, I saw that the hotel listed the price of our suite as $180, not $240. I called the hotel and spoke with an honest-sounding registration employee. He indicated that during his years of employment with the hotel, it had never charged a guest the $240 rack rate. The published $180 rate was the highest price ever charged for our suite. I contacted my local Entertainment people and informed them of the phantom rack rate. In turn, they contacted their Washington counterparts. In short order, I received a new reservation confirmation with an adjusted price of $90, 50 percent of the real published rate.

Is there a moral here? Yes. Do not be bashful! Ask about rack rates. Ask for a brochure and a copy of published prices. Perhaps the hotel is offering a special deal, a very low rate, far below the rack rate. For example, a hotel may state that it has a rack rate of $150 but there is an ongoing "special price" of only $99. The hotel may then state that the Entertainment rate is $75. Get it? I doubt the $150 rate exists and $99 is the likely regular price for the room. However, the $75 Entertainment rate is still a solid 25 percent discount.

Always ask if the hotel accepts other discounts, such as AAA, a corporate rate, or others. These discounts may be greater than the Entertainment rate. Hotels will typically state that the Entertainment rate is their lowest available price. The Georgetown Hotel discount price for AAA was $125, whereas our Entertainment rate was only $90. I always compare rates using my AAA guide. For example, I found that in the Georgetown area prices ranged from $125 to $170 for comparable hotels. In the end I was still far ahead in using the Entertainment discount.

My goal is to use the Entertainment hotel directory to obtain a reasonable discount. Usually the Entertainment rate is best, with real savings of 20 to 50 percent. When I recently traveled to San Diego, most hotels were charging $80 to $100 per night. By using the Entertainment rate of $60, I saved $20 to $40. The savings for my five-night trip was substantial, a total savings of at least $100. We may not always save the promised 50 percent but then again a savings of 20 percent or more off a hotel's lowest rate is still a solid savings.

While planning our recent trip to Israel, I found that the U.S. Entertainment books do not list Israeli hotels in their hotel directory. However, the London and Paris editions list some fifteen Israeli hotels, with a wide range of prices. In response to my inquiries, a Tel Aviv hotel informed me that it reduces its rate from $86 to $43 for Entertainment members.

➡ **Steve's Tip:** *Need a list of international hotels but lack a foreign Entertainment edition? I am told you do not need to purchase a foreign edition only because you need a list of some international hotels. Call Entertainment at (800) 374-4464 or contact your local Entertainment office and request a list of participating hotels in the area you will be visiting. I am told that your local Entertainment card is also valid for foreign hotel use.*

Other Entertainment Travel Discounts

Entertainment editions have many pages devoted to other travel discounts, including cruise and airline tickets. During our 1994 trip to Maui we visited the island of Hawaii, home of Hawaii Volcanoes National Park and Hawaii's only active volcano. The one-day trip required an inter-island flight on Aloha Airlines from Maui to the "Big Island" of Hawaii. The round-trip fare was $130 per person. My Hawaii Entertainment edition contained a free companion ticket coupon for Aloha Airlines. That single coupon saved the cost of one $130 fare, a dramatic example of the powerful savings available when using an Entertainment book. At $25, the cost of the Hawaiian Entertainment edition is itself a bargain.

There are some negatives. For example, I take the advertised cruise discounts with a grain of salt. Cruise companies' ads often state, "One person cruises free!" Such offers require that the second person must pay the full cruise fare. Be warned: This is generally not the best available deal, no matter how good it sounds. Currently, the lowest advertised price for a Mexican Riviera cruise is $549. However, a major commercial brochure lists the lowest published fare as $1,269. I know you can do the math on this one. We all do better paying two full discounted fares totalling $1,098 than paying for one full fare at $1,269.

As for discount cruise coupons, my best advice is to check the weekend travel section in a Sunday newspaper. Check the travel sections of the *Los Angeles Times* and the *New York Times*. Look for the best advertised discount price for the cruise of your choice. A great price for a one-week Alaska cruise would be $700, without airfare. Current Caribbean bargains are $549 for seven-night cruises. Mexican Riviera cruises are also currently $549. All these sale prices are for the cruise and exclude air travel. Aim to match or beat these prices.

Entertainment's Dirt-Cheap Recreation

Entertainment books are a great recreational resource. Following are examples of ways we have saved using our Entertainment books:

- One free $45 parasailing ride off Maui's historic whaling town of Lahaina. A magnificent three-hundred- to four-hundred-foot-high ride along the west Maui coast.
- During our last visit to Maui we took a half-day, Zodiac rafting trip. The Zodiac raft is a large, hard-shelled, motor-powered raft. It quickly traveled to the nearby island of Lanai and circled the island, stopping often for sightseeing and great snorkeling. This was a three-quarter-day adventure with a price tag of $240 for the two of us. The Entertainment coupon saved us $120.
- One free $50 luau at the Royal Lahaina Hotel. It is rare that any full-fledged luau offers a significant discount. This hotel luau does it all, from a full dinner and open bar to a live show with fire dancers.
- We saved $65 on a snorkeling cruise to the famed Molokini Crater Marine Preserve. Molokini is a picturesque, crescent-shaped, volcanic rim that sits about ten miles off the west Maui coast. The boat, the Frogman, is fabulous. It has a friendly, knowledgeable crew and offers an excellent lunch buffet and two hours of super snorkeling at the crater. The beautiful catamaran returned to Maui under full sail.
- One free $130 Aloha Airline flight from Maui to the island of Hawaii
- Our London book had a coupon for a visit to Windsor Castle on a Frames half-day tour, saving us $35.
- In Paris, we used a coupon for a boat tour on the Seine with Les Vedettes de Paris and saved the cost of one ticket. There also were coupons for many restaurants, movie theaters, shows, and jazz clubs. The edition included coupons for the Museum of Wine and Paris Historique, a unique sound and light show, that took us through two thousand years of French history.

Entertainment editions contain literally hundreds of discount coupons for movie theaters, bowling alleys, museums, parks, sporting events, theater, comedy clubs, and more. Movie prices too high? We pay the bargain matinee rate at all evening performances using Entertainment's discount movie tickets.

Entertainment Publications remains a powerful tool in our

efforts to be fun-loving world-class "cheapskate" travelers, whether this involves travel, dining, or recreation.

Loving Your Junk Mail

Not a thrilling concept, is it? I will try to change your perspective on this one. My name exists on every junk mail list known to man. One reason for this is my mail order shopping. One day I opened a piece of solicitation "junk" mail—an offer to join an auto club. The offer was linked to my Citibank Visa card—Citibank was promoting its own Citibank Autovantage Club. Since I was a twenty-year member of the California Automobile Association, I had zero interest in switching my allegiance. With that in mind, I should have deep-sixed this piece of junk mail, right? Wrong?

➡ **Steve's Rule:** *Always assume a gift is offered with the sincere hope it will be appreciated and accepted. When junk mail demands that I spend time reading the sender's pitch, I go more than halfway; I do exactly what is asked of me. When I see an offer for a valuable gift, such as a free night of lodging, I don't hesitate to accept such a generous gift.*

Do not judge junk mail by its cover! Fully half of my junk mail deserves and receives immediate tossing into the "circular file." However, I am never certain that the remaining mail is equally useless. The above auto club's outer envelope stated, "Free Gift for You." That mildly piqued my interest. I needed to know what favor the auto club was bestowing on me. Also, a bank's involvement with a promotion is always a good sign. I opened the envelope to find a sales pitch touting the auto club. The letter said "Simply return the enclosed envelope and card, pay only $1 for a ninety-day trial membership and receive, as our gift, a voucher good for a free night of lodging at several participating motel chains." At the end of the ninety days they would automatically charge my credit card a one-year membership fee of $50. This was good and bad news. The free night of lodging was great, but what if I forgot to cancel in time? The letter went on to give an iron-clad guarantee that I could cancel anytime and still receive a full 100 percent refund of my membership fee. The free hotel voucher was still mine to keep. I am *sold* on such offers. My interest doubled when Patty received the same offer the next day.

In the above case, Autovantage wished to give me the hotel voucher and I was happy to accept it. Autovantage anticipates that many recipients of the promotion are CAAA members and asks only the opportunity to pitch their service. Many people sign up for these clubs, fully intending to cancel, and then forget to follow up. After ninety days Autovantage automatically charges the membership fee to the new member's credit card. Both Patty and I joined the Citibank Autovantage Club and received our free one-night lodging certificates, good at several middle-level national chains.

Several months later we headed out on a long weekend. We traveled to an American city listed in *Time* magazine as one of the ten most romantic cities in the world. Need a clue? It is a small southwestern city and was number ten on the list. (Dwell on this one for a moment.) I checked the Autovantage free hotel brochure and found two hotels in our destination city. One confirmed that we could use our two certificates on two consecutive nights. We had free hotel lodging for the weekend, compliments of Autovantage! We booked airline flights with Southwest Airlines using its long-running Friends Fly Free program that allowed Patty to fly free.

Give up? *Time* magazine's tenth most romantic city in the world is none other than Tucson, Arizona. *Time* wrote about the desert night sky with its myriad of stars and also mentioned the unforgettable saguaro cactus. This unique combination makes Tucson one of the most romantic spots on the globe.

Fifteen years had passed since my earlier visit to Tucson, and I could only hope my memories were true. I happily report that we experienced an unforgettable weekend. There they were, the thousands of giant saguaro cactus dotting the mountainsides and standing tall alongside the back roads. The world-class Tucson Desert Museum contains examples of most varieties of desert plant and animal life. Exhibits include bighorn sheep, tortoises, eagles, wildcats, and other indigenous animals, fish, and birds.

Because of the intense heat, many exhibits are underground and use state-of-the-art audio and video systems. Aboveground, animals roam in natural, man-made enclosures. The famed movie set known as Old Tucson remains a memorable local attraction and was, for many years, the location for hundreds of Westerns. This artificial town is fun, with its daily gunfights and stunt gunfighters falling off second-story balconies—hokey but fun!

In Tucson, dining at Pinnacle Peaks is essential. A stagecoach sits precariously atop a man-made mountain in front of the restaurant. Neckties are not allowed. Violators are summarily "punished," when the famous bell rings. At that moment the "criminal" customer's tie is cut from his body by a pair of large, sharp scissors, and the tie is hung from the ceiling, joining hundreds of others already on display. Forget coupons, the specialty is a thirty-two-ounce T-bone steak dinner that sells for $12.95!

The total cost of our three-day getaway was $224, including air, hotel for two nights, and rental car for three days.

Another piece of "junk" mail arrived from Best Western motels. Inside the envelope was an application to join Best Western's Gold Club. The application was a freebie, thus meeting my basic criteria for joining such hotel-related clubs. When the company's literature arrived, I learned that each stay entitled me to points. When sufficient points were accumulated they could be exchanged for cash or gifts.

Flash forward to our return flight from Paris. It brought us into Los Angeles at 10:30 P.M., too late to catch a flight home. I cashed in my Best Western points, accumulated over the past year, and obtained $50 in Best Western script. I applied it to our overnight stay at a Best Western Airport Plaza Inn near LAX, so the total room price was just $6. (I think it fair to consider this another free night of lodging.) This is a good example of a mini-corporate giveaway, a solid money-saving promotion of not-so-junky "junk" mail!

I have a seldom-used account with United Airlines, and one day I received a Mileage Plus account statement. Enclosed was a solicitation for a Mileage Plus First Visa card that charges an annual fee of $60. Since all of my credit cards, except for Citibank AAdvantage, are free of annual fees I was on the verge of "deep-sixing" the offer. Then I read a bit further and realized the value of this "junk" mail. Upon payment of the $60 annual fee United Airlines was sending new card holders a free companion ticket good for travel to any United Airlines U.S., Mexican, or Canadian destination, an incredible offer that could save new card holders $500 or more on a round-trip ticket. Call United Airlines at (800) 368-4535 for details on current offers.

In chapter 2 I mentioned the CAAA Diamond Dollars program, which mimics the great American AAdvantage program. How exactly did I learn of the CAAA program? Yes, it was a piece of "junk" mail stuffed in with my yearly CAAA bill.

Catching on? If in doubt, check it out! In no time at all you too will be reaping valuable "junk" mail rewards.

Winning Contests

I admit it, our first trip to Africa only came about because we won two free airline tickets in a Pan Am contest. Impressed? Probably not. When I hear of other people winning contests, an inner voice says, "They are not run-of-the-mill Earthlings. They belong to that species that receives visitations from the Publishers Clearing House." On the other hand, many of you "shoot for the gold" by purchasing lottery tickets with the hope of winning "the big one."

For my part, I do not like contests and, generally speaking, I do not enter them. All and all I consider them a waste of time. So how did Patty and I head to Africa with $4,000 to $5,000 in free plane tickets?

In 1989 Pan American Airlines published a full-page advertisement in the *San Francisco Chronicle* announcing its fiftieth anniversary contest. All customers flying across the Atlantic Ocean would receive a game card with three "scratch" boxes similar to California's "scratch-and-match" lottery tickets. Any customer finding the words ECONOMY TICKET in three boxes was the winner of a round-trip ticket to any worldwide Pan Am destination. Amazingly, Pan American was giving away 2,400 sets of such tickets. I am not a gambler and do not routinely purchase lottery tickets. I do know that the odds of winning the big lottery prizes are slim, very slim, which translates into astronomical odds, thousands upon thousands to one. But Pan American's odds were fixed because a limited number of cards were available. The exact odds were 440 to 1. Even I recognized this was very unusual, considering the value of the prizes. Entering the contest was another matter, since game cards were distributed to those flying the Atlantic route. However, following local "no purchase necessary" rules, the fine print stated that game cards could be requested by mail.

I decided to act on this contest. I prepared and mailed eight entries, and in a matter of four weeks or so we began receiving game cards. I arrived home to a wonderful greeting as a stunned Patty displayed two of the cards. I stared at the three scratched-off boxes on each card. All six of the squares read "Economy Ticket." Both of them were winners! We were stunned, dumbfounded, and incredulous.

When I studied Pan American's routes, I noticed an intriguing line that ran from Frankfurt, Germany, to Nairobi, Kenya. I studied the line with great interest, turned to Patty, and innocently asked, "Is this where people go on safaris?" I freely admit it, at that time I had not been watching my quotient of Discovery Channel programs on African safaris; otherwise I would have known that Kenya is the number-one destination in the world for photo safaris. Without further hesitation I looked at Patty and said, "We are going on a safari." Patty smiled broadly—very broadly. A few weeks later we were standing at the Pan American counter at San Francisco Airport picking up our tickets, holding $5,000 worth of the most valuable airline tickets one can buy. The greatest adventure of our travel lives was to come. Without a doubt, we used the winning tickets wisely. The safari was nothing less than an incredible odyssey.

Since our Pan Am fortune of 1989, I have found similar quality contests. A United Airlines contest involved a giveaway of free round-trip tickets to fifty of the airline's worldwide destinations. We tried, but were not among the fifty winners.

Another time, I spied a full-page advertisement in *Time* magazine for a contest that caught my eye for two reasons. First, it involved prizes that included a Carnival cruise, one year of free Alamo car rentals, and, perhaps best of all, Continental Airline tickets. Second, the contest was similar to the old Pan Am contest. Days Inn motels offered this contest, which used a lottery scratch-off game card. Once again, we gave it the good contest try!

I ask you to keep an open mind. When you see a contest, check it out. Consider the prizes. Do they interest you? If so, are they valuable? Consider the odds. How many prizes are being given away? Forget single grand-prize contests. Seek the occasional contest offering scores of top-notch prizes. If you find a rare contest, give it your best shot. Read all the small print and go for it. After all, it *is* free—unlike those lottery tickets.

Wonderful "Short-Lived" Offers

Special company offers and contests, unlike free-travel-cash promotions, are usually short-lived. What follows are good examples of such opportunities. All too often we ignore or overlook them.

Post Cereals: Recently Post cereals placed a two-page advertisement in the weekend coupon section of our local newspaper. The advertisement pictured three small boxes of Post cereals in the palm trees above happy-go-lucky vacationers playing in the surf on a Hawaiian beach. The text, in large bold letters, read POST OFFERS YOU 50% IN HOTEL SAVINGS and featured Marriott, Ramada Inn, and Best Western as participating hotel chains. The text continued: "Over 1,400 participating hotels! Savings good for one year!" An official mail-in certificate provided the details in small print and confirmed the offer was a true freebie. The requirement for participation was the purchase of any three cereals. I mailed three proofs of purchase and the original mail-in certificate and soon received the Post cereals "Hotel Savings Club" directory. It, in fact, turned out to be an Entertainment-related national directory, which included the necessary membership card. The membership, with discounts of up to 50 percent, is valid for one full year and honored at more than 1,400 participating hotels.

Budget Gourmet Foods: In late 1996 Budget Gourmet Foods also ran a full-page advertisement in the *San Francisco Chronicle*'s weekend coupon section. This was a variation of the above Post Cereals hotel directory. The Budget Gourmet advertisement exclaimed, "Delicious Escapes Compliments of Budget Gourmet." The one-year *VIP Delicious Escapes Travel Directory,* also packaged by Entertainment Publications, included airline discount coupons good for up to $100 off per ticket, a 50 percent–off hotel directory good at "over 2,000 leading properties nationwide," and savings at major attractions nationwide. Since these free travel directories are not 100 percent clones of Entertainment books' regular hotel sections, they offer different money-saving opportunities. Let's also not overlook the fact that they are mostly freebies. The Budget Groumet directory required only five proofs of purchase. I searched our freezer, found five budget dinners, and awaited delivery of my free Delicious Escapes Travel Directory. I love these money-saving options!

MCI: Several months ago I spotted a full-page MCI advertisement, obviously part of the current telephone wars. MCI was offering a free domestic round-trip airline ticket to "new" members. The nominal requirement was that the "new" member's monthly bill must be at least $25. I took immediate exception to the "new member" requirement. After all, why punish loyal MCI users? It turned out that MCI would allow current subscribers to sign up for the promotion. At year's end I will receive a free round-trip ticket worth up to $600 on domestic travel. Another great freebie!

Nancy's Free Country Inn Promotion: Once again, early purchasers of my guide may reap an instant reward. As press time approached I noticed another valuable promotion in my local newspaper's weekend coupon insert section. Nancy's Specialty Foods offers fine products that include Nancy's frozen quiche, appetizers, and petite desserts. The initial promotion runs until November 30, 1996. It offers participants one free second night of lodging at any of 1,700 bed and breakfast inns in the United States when the first night of lodging is purchased at the inn's regular rate. Nancy's representative assures me that readers may submit their UPC proofs of purchase with a typed or handwritten mail-in coupon facsimile. Simply purchase three Nancy's frozen products and mail three UPC bar codes along with a note that reads "Please send me Nancy's *B & B and Country Inn Guidebook* and free night lodging certificate." Include your full name and mailing address on the facsimile coupon. Mail your request to:

Nancy's Free Night Offer
P.O. Box 1290
Grand Rapids, Minnesota 55745–1290

Remember, this is a limited-duration offer that expires on November 30, 1996. On the plus side, the certificates may be used until December 31, 1997. But each certificate can save a participant $50 to $300 on the second free night of lodging. This is not a typo. Nancy's tells me that the best of their listed B&Bs charge $300 per night! I expect to request several certificates that Patty and I hope to use by January 1998. Are we surprised that not one of the dozen or so friends and associates I have spoken with noticed this colorful half-page free lodging advertisement in their weekend newspaper? Nancy's informs me that the promotion advertisement ran one time only in various national newspapers—a one-shot offer for free lodging certificates that are fully valid for *eighteen* months from the date of the advertisement. I just love those weekend newspaper coupon inserts!

No-Surcharge Bargain Phone Cards

Shortly before departing on my recent trip to Israel I heard about two super phone cards issued by independent companies. World Link is one, American Travel Network is the other. These cards are not tied into a home phone service such as AT&T, MCI, or Sprint. Simply request the cards and you will promptly receive them in the mail.

I used my World Link card while in Israel and it worked flawlessly. I simply called a toll-free number, and a prompt from World Link asked for phone and PIN numbers. No surcharge is billed for foreign calls, and the minute rate from Israel to California was only $2. Billing is easy, since World Link directly charges my Citibank AAdvantage card for the call. The minimum monthly charge is a nominal $1.

For domestic calls, the best deal in the United States is the American Travel Network Card. This phone card is also issued free of any charges. There is no monthly minimum and no connecting charge. The cost is only 17.5 cents per minute to any location in the United States, including Hawaii. The company does not take charge-card payments. Instead, it bills the cost of the calls directly to its customers. *Money* magazine rated American Travel Network among the ten best deals in the country, and to my knowledge no better or cheaper independent phone card exists.

Forget thirty-cents-per-minute cards. Forget cards that have you running out of time mid-sentence. Treat yourself to the best and lowest priced phone cards. Here are contact numbers:

American Travel Network
10211 North 32nd Street,
Suite A5
Phoenix, Arizona
85028-9826
(800) 477-9692

World Link
3399 Peachtree Road, N.E.
Lenox Building, Suite 400
Atlanta, Georgia 30326
(800) 432-6169

4

When All Else Fails, Take a 5 to 20 Percent Discount!

What happens if your best deal involves a charter package? Or you require only land or air reservations? Our Tahiti trip was a package tour through Islands in the Sun, but the flight was on Corsair Airlines, a charter company. While our round-trip flight to Kenya was free, I still needed to purchase the two-week land package (the safari). What to do? When all else fails we can still enjoy discounts ranging from 5 to 20 percent or more!

Travelers Advantage

This service has existed for years. Its major advantage for members is a 5 percent rebate on all travel arrangements. Members must book through a special toll-free number. Travelers Advantage is a subsidiary of CUC, which runs Shoppers Advantage and Autovantage. The company sells reasonably priced memberships on the information superhighway using America Online, Prodigy, and CompuServe.

Travelers offers a three-month trial membership for only $1. Better yet, it offers great incentives to new members. It often gives new members a one-night free hotel voucher good at popular national hotel chains such as the Ramada Inn, Days Inn, Howard Johnson, Park Inn, and Choice Hotels. Let me emphasize, this is *not* a two-for-one voucher that requires the purchase of a one-night stay to receive the second night free. This voucher is worth one absolutely free night of lodging with no strings attached.

For example, if Patty and I sign up for separate memberships, both vouchers can be used on consecutive nights, so we could travel to Las Vegas for a three-day weekend getaway with two free nights of lodging. Yes, I am always reading big, bold Las Vegas ads offering $29 per night for rooms at the best main-strip hotels. Funny though, when I strap on my reading glasses, I see the small-print restrictions limiting these great offers to Sunday through Thursday reservations. Enter the Travelers hotel voucher, valid *seven* days of the week—a definite winner!

As the evening infomercial people say, "Don't go away! There is more!" Travelers also gives new members a $50 voucher good toward any travel arrangements of $50 or more. When the voucher is used, the member receives 5 percent or $50, whichever is greater. If a member were to fly one-way to Los Angeles, pay $65 for the ticket, and use the voucher, the member would receive a $50 cash rebate. Want more?

Travelers Advantage also sends new members four American Airlines vouchers for discounts of $40 to $80 off their lowest excursion fares. If a family of four travels from New York to the West Coast and pays $379 for each American Airline ticket, the member will receive a cash discount of $240.

Okay, another incentive: Travelers Advantage also sends new members a national hotel directory at 50 percent off list price. Since parent company CUC owns Entertainment Publications, the hotel directory is a clone of the one found in Entertainment editions. There is one important distinction: The national hotel directory lists 2,500 hotels, while Entertainment editions list only 1,700 hotels. All of us are big winners with this program freebie.

Additionally, Travelers Advantage offers an iron-clad guarantee. Cancel your membership for any reason during the year and receive a full refund, whether or not the hotel and $50 vouchers were used. Also, keep in mind that unless you cancel your membership, the $49 annual fee will be automatically charged to your Citibank card.

Not married but residing in the same household with your significant other? Travelers Advantage allows the 5 percent rebate against an entire trip for *all* household members. If the Travelers representative insists the 5 percent applies only to blood relatives and married couples, simply call their customer service department at (800) 648-4037. Have someone there make sure that the discount is applied to the entire booking. Join Travelers Advantage by phone or by writing:

Travelers Advantage
Box C32123
Richmond, Virginia 23261
(800) 843-7777

➡ **Steve's Tip:** *If you have are any problems with Travelers Advantage's service, request cancellation of your membership. The company will offer you new incentives and discounts if you relent on your cancellation request.*

Sears Discount Travel Club

When I received confirmation of our Tahiti reservation, the return address on the Travelers envelope read "Sears Travel Club." This piqued my curiosity. I called Sears and learned that CUC runs both the Travelers Advantage and Sears programs. These are pretty much identical, but the incentives may differ. Also, the Sears club requires a Sears charge card. Own a Sears charge card? Feel more comfortable joining a club associated with the Sears name? Then go with Sears. Call this customer service number to join either the Sears Discount Travel Club or Travelers Advantage: (800) 835-8747.

PriceCostco Travel

PriceCostco Travel started doing business in 1994. Presently the often-changing program offers a 5 percent discount only on cruises and selected vacation packages. Remember: only members may use this discount service.

How does the program work? First, a member makes a reservation directly with the cruise company. At the same time, the member tells the company that PriceCostco will be issuing the tickets. The member then calls PriceCostco's toll-free phone number and, at the computer prompts, gives the details of the cruise. Tickets are picked up at the nearest PriceCostco outlet. Talk this over with PriceCostco's customer service rep if you have any questions. One cannot tell when the scope of the discounts will change. Consequently, members should ask about the program periodically or when visiting a local PriceCostco warehouse.

Pearson's "Cash-in-Your Pocket" Promotions

Pearson Travel Company of Providence, Rhode Island, an American Express–related, full-service travel agency, offers exciting money-in-your-pocket promotions, and they will give special attention to clients identifying themselves as *Cheapskate's Guide* readers. While I have yet to use Pearson's services, the company's vice-president has provided me with impressive references and notes Pearson's history dating back to 1929. I do encourage readers to check out these great "cash-in-hand" deals. Unlike other savings options, there are no fees to pay or clubs to join.

American Tourister Promotion: I learned of Pearson when visiting a local American Tourister factory outlet and I was handed a flyer advertising Pearson's American Tourister–related promotion. This very same deal is available until January 1, 1997, to readers calling Pearson and identifying themselves as being part of the American Tourister promotion. This entitles you to:

- $100 in American Express travel checks per couple on any one-week Royal Caribbean cruise
- A two-category upgrade on the cruise
- A Royal Caribbean travel clock

Book a similar one-week cruise on another cruise line and identify yourself as a *Cheapskate Guide* reader and receive $100 in travel checks and a one-category upgrade. Bargain-priced Caribbean and Mexican Riviera cruises selling for $549 to $599 will be net priced at $499 to $549 per person, and include a guaranteed upgrade.

Vacation Package Savings: Pearson will guarantee $100 per couple in American Express travel checks for any one-week, air-and-land vacation package booked with them. (This reduces my favorite one-week Moorea package to just $649.)

Miscellaneous Savings: Call Pearson for their latest deals. Vacationers booking cruises are winners. Pearson often offers other discounts, such as $200 ship credits or 50 percent off for third and fourth passengers. There is also Pearson's Last Minute Club, specializing in last-minute travel discounts.

As another convenience to West Coast readers, Pearson's offices are open until 7:30 P.M. on weekdays. Be sure to call Pearson for information on their 1997–98 offers.

Pearson Travel
93 Dyer Street
Providence, Rhode Island 02903
(800) 336-1066 or (401) 274-2900
Fax: (401) 831-5328

National Rebate Travel Agencies

I love savings options. Another option for you to consider are national discount, or rebate, travel agencies. These agencies rebate their commission (usually 10 percent to customers) and charge a booking fee based on the total cost of the trip. Simply compare the services and discounts each provides and decide which offer the greatest savings. These agencies also offer discounts on air-only or land-only bookings.

Pennsylvania Travel: This independent discount travel retailer has fine credentials. It rebates its commission, usually 10 percent, to its customers, and charges a booking fee scaled to the total cost of the booking. I called Pennsylvania Travel, and they immediately faxed a brochure that provided all necessary details. Call Pennsylvania Travel at: (800) 331-0947, (610) 251-9444, or fax (610) 644-2150.

Travel Avenue (Chicago): This discount retail travel agency offers a 7 percent rebate on vacation packages and cruises. Unlike other similar agencies, it charges a flat booking fee of $25 if a single payment is made and $35 if a deposit is made and final payment comes later. Travel Avenue also faxed me their brochure. Call them at: (800) 333-3335 or fax (312) 876-1254.

➡ **Steve's Tip:** *Pearson's offer of $100 in traveler's checks for cruises and air-and-land vacation packages promises the greatest savings on bargain-priced vacations. On higher-priced bargain sojourns, Pennsylvania Travel offers greater savings. For example, on a low-end cruise costing $1,098 per couple, Pearson offers $100, versus Pennsylvania's net savings of $60. However, on a bargain China tour costing $2,799 per couple, Pennsylvania Travel offers net savings of $180 that exceeds both Travelers Advantage's and Pearson's discounts and rebates. Compare, shop, and make the best choice.*

5

Peace of Mind and Security of Pocketbook

A bit of philosophy is in order. Vacations are sacred to me. They are synonymous with serenity of spirit and peace of mind. I wish to enjoy every moment of my stay in a tropical paradise. I want to lie on a beach, savor beautiful sunsets, and chase rainbow-colored tropical fish. The last thing I want to do is worry about thousands of dollars of camera equipment, scuba gear, and other valuable personal belongings.

Insuring Personal Property

Before leaving on vacations I customarily purchase personal belongings coverage, technically called travel baggage insurance. What does this cover, you ask? This wonderful policy covers not only luggage but virtually everything you bring with you on your vacation, including items such as cameras that you may have borrowed from another for the trip.

For vacations that are six to ten days' duration, the "cheapskate" price for this peace of mind is $20, which buys the required minimum $500 of coverage for baggage and personal belongings. The cost for $1,000 worth of coverage is $30 and a hefty $50 buys the maximum coverage of $2,000.

In deciding how much coverage to buy, I consider several factors. What equipment do I need to cover? Am I traveling with my lower-priced 35mm camera or expensive camcorder? Is the vacation a high-risk one, involving constant exposure to sand and water? My rule of thumb is: Insure the cost of the most expensive camera or camcorder plus $250 to cover the replacement value of miscellaneous clothing, belongings, and luggage. I purchase additional coverage for Patty, usually the minimum of $500, since she rarely travels with electronic or photo gear. Remember, *never* over-insure.

Travel Pak (short for Travelers Travel Insurance Pak) coverage is very broad and consumer-friendly. It excludes autos, boats, commercial equipment, and bicycles, except during transit. More important, it covers cameras, photo equipment, jewelry, and watches up to $1,000 per loss. It also covers sporting equipment such as scuba gear, tennis racquets, and golfing equipment. The only limit on losses is the limit of the overall policy.

Occasionally, I buy trip cancellation coverage as well. Here are examples of the value of Travel Pak from my personal experience.

Theft of Personal Belongings

Upon arriving at San Diego Airport, I learned that one of our bags was missing. Hours earlier I had used the convenient curbside check-in service at San Francisco Airport. (I strongly discourage curbside check-in.) The missing bag contained $1,400 of mostly new scuba gear. The maximum legal liability of a domestic airline for lost or damaged luggage and contents is $1,250 per passenger. Approximately two weeks after the loss, the airline offered to settle my claim for only $700. The offer, based on improper depreciation of my almost-new scuba gear, was too low. I informed the airline and Travelers that I expected to be fully reimbursed and suggested they pay me and share the loss. My trusty Travel Pak policy provided $1,000 per person coverage for our luggage and possessions. A couple of weeks later I received a check from Travelers for $1,350—virtually full reimbursement.

Passengers may purchase additional airline coverage at check-in. This coverage costs $1 per $100 of coverage but is effective only during transit. On the other hand, Travel Pak coverage is in effect during the entire length of one's vacation.

Carelessness

Before our trip to Moorea in late 1994, I inspected my Nikonos V 35mm underwater camera and was shocked to find its shutter was frozen. Mortifying news followed when I received a repair estimate—for $500! I should mention that the Nikonos V is one of the best 35mm underwater cameras made and sells for $750. An accidental buildup of salt near the shutter mechanism caused the problem. It seems that I carelessly neglected to have the camera professionally cleaned after our previous vacation to Tahiti three months earlier.

There I was, the victim of my own human frailty. I was careless and had to pay the price big time, right? Not so! The result of this incident is dramatic proof of the value of Travel Pak coverage. I quickly retrieved my previous Travel Pak policy and reviewed it. Just as I recalled, the policy is truly "no fault." It does *not* exclude damage resulting from accidents even when the policy holder is negligent. This is the best type of *all risk* coverage one can buy. In fact, the only listed exclusions are such as wear and tear, insects, vermin, and war. Within a week or two I received Travelers' $500 check.

Lost Items

While scuba-diving, my camera's $75 optical viewfinder was "lost at sea." It was accidentally detached from my camera and never seen again. On a later dive, my video housing lens was scratched when a strong current slammed the camera into a large piece of coral. Travelers Insurance dutifully paid $75 to replace the viewfinder and $100 to repair the lens.

Damaged Items

Patty and I use underwater transceivers to talk to each other while scuba-diving. When I inspected them, between vacations, they were not working. The manufacturer, Ocean Technology, inspected the units and declared both were "dead," a result of saltwater corrosion. Salt water had entered the two units from small pinholes in the wires. The president of Ocean Technology confirmed in writing that both units were accidentally damaged when last used. The damage likely occurred when someone on the deck of the dive boat stepped on the wires. Travelers lived up to its policy and fully reimbursed me $800, the full cost of replacing both units.

Camera Coverage

So you don't scuba-dive or travel with expensive electronic gadgets or sports equipment? Do you travel with a $1,000 camcorder or valuable 35mm camera? Consider the following scenarios:

- While lying on a beach in the sunny tropics, do you wish to go swimming or snorkeling? What do you do with your camera? Bury it in your beach bag and jump in for a quick dip, constantly straining to view your blanket and beach bag? Even if the camera is still there, you have spent most of your time worrying.
- While sunbathing on the beach, a teenager runs by and kicks sand on your blanket, covering your camcorder with the deadly particles.
- You are enjoying a fine lunch when your camera topples off a table or chair onto a concrete floor.
- While resting in a beach chair and staring at the distant island of Lanai, high tide sneaks in. A large wave rolls over your feet and your very expensive camcorder. The next "wave" is one of nausea.
- Do you recall an ominous sign over the hotel or condo registration desk that reads "We are not responsible for valuables left in the rooms"?

Believe it or not, such losses often spoil the best of vacations, but Travel Pak covers all the above scenarios. When I suffer a loss I experience a feeling of horror only for a fleeting moment until I remind myself that Travelers will come to my rescue.

Why Choose Travel Pak Over Other Policies?

Because the features most desired in a travel policy are found in Travel Pak:

Primary Policy: This means that *no* claim is filed on your homeowner policy. This is a great feature because claims against a homeowner policy may increase the premiums or cause cancellation of the policy. Once Travel Pak or a good policy is purchased, do not be bashful. Go ahead and make a small claim as long as it is valid.

Broad Coverage: Coverage for baggage and personal belongings should be extensive, with few exclusions. I have listed Travel Pak's broad coverage and a very few but reasonable exclusions. Also, limits on expensive items such as cameras should be reasonable. Travel Pak covers cameras and jewelry up to $1,000, with $2,000 worth of coverage available for sports equipment. Many other policies severely limit photo equipment and camera coverage, from none at all to a nominal amount. Some policies limit a claim to 25 percent of the value of a camera or camcorder or to a strict $250 per item.

I am always on the lookout for better or cheaper policies, despite my deep appreciation of Travel Pak's extensive protection. Some travel insurance brochures are plainly misleading. One claims $2,000 worth of coverage for baggage and personal belongings, but its microscopic print warns customers that the brochure merely summarizes the benefits. Customers must carefully read actual policy provisions. I called the company previously mentioned and learned it had a $250 coverage limit on cameras. The same is often true for jewelry. Whenever checking a policy, look for the company's toll-free number, then call and have them disclose any and all policy exclusions, the items not covered, and the claim limits for cameras, jewelry, sporting gear, and other items.

Some policies require customers to purchase a total package that includes medical and accident coverage. These add-ons are often unnecessary. Buy only what you need. Travel Pak's "à la carte menu" permits customized coverage for each vacation.

Over the years I have found that only a select few travel agencies sell the superior Travel Pak policy. If you cannot locate one, help is at hand. At my request, my friends at Downtown Travel in Walnut Creek, California, became agents for Travelers' Travel Pak, offering and issuing the policy on the spot. Send them a written request and they will mail you a brochure and application. Complete the application and return it to Downtown Travel together with your check for the premium. Your policy will be issued and returned to you by mail. Personal belongings coverage begins on the date of departure on your vacation. Cancellation coverage begins on the date of the application, which is the date you sign and mail it. Keep a copy of the application for your records.

➡ **Steve's Tip:** *If you are mailing in the application, do so at least one week early so that you may call Downtown Travel to confirm its receipt. If you wish, they will fax you the issued policy page. If you must mail the policy late, up to the day of departure, try to obtain either proof of mailing from the post office or send the application via certified mail. The latter should be done only if you worry about lost mail.*

Obtain your Travel Pak policy application by contacting:

Downtown Travel
1609 Locust Street
Walnut Creek, California 94596
(510) 945-9004; fax: (510) 945-8081

Trip Cancellation Coverage

You have paid thousands of dollars for your dream vacation and the trip is only days away, when you, a family member, or travel companion falls ill or has an accident causing you to cancel the trip. The tour operator sadly explains that your insurance does not entitle you to a refund. One dramatic example occurred during our Tanzania safari when an elderly traveler suddenly had chest pains. He and his wife were quickly flown to Nairobi where they paid thousands of dollars for an immediate flight home. Trip cancellation insurance is intended to pay for nonrefundable vacation expenses as well as emergency medical transportation back home, whether the illness or injury happens before departure or during the vacation.

This is a favorite consumer topic given the misleading advertising of many insurance companies that fall back on technical policy language to avoid paying when a vacation gets canceled. While this coverage is far less frequently used than is personal belonging insurance, the financial stakes are potentially higher.

Trip cancellation coverage should *not* be limited to cancellations resulting from the illness or injury of family members. It should include mishaps involving travel companions as well, which would allow reimbursement if your travel companion becomes ill, injured, or called to jury duty. The policy should also cover "unforeseen emergencies" that occur en route to a departure point. Travel Pak includes this coverage if a delay is at least one hour and prevents a party from taking a vacation.

This is my best example of an unforeseen emergency. You are driving to the airport to catch a flight to take a cruise. You are stalled by an accident up the road and consequently miss your flight. Believe it or not many policies provide no coverage since you were not actually involved in the accident. Travel Pak will pay whether or not you were directly involved as long as the accident was an unforseen emergency.

Travel Pak covers any illness or injury that occurs after a policy is purchased. It also covers any preexisting illness or injury *if* the condition was "under control" for sixty days before the purchase date. ("Under control" means that no treatment has been received or required for the last sixty days.) Purchase the Travel Pak trip cancellation coverage quickly. Once you are committed to a vacation and if you are in good health, waste no time in buying a Travel Pak policy—and there is no extra charge for buying insurance early. The illness, injury, or flare-up that occurs tomorrow will be covered *only* if the policy is purchased today.

➡ **Steve's Exception Tip:** *When should the purchase of a trip cancellation policy be delayed? Suppose your back flares periodically. Your vacation is in eight weeks. Forty-five days ago, your back flared up. Because of the sixty-day rule, no coverage is available for preexisting conditions, like your back, until sixty days have passed with no treatment from the last flare-up. In this case wait another fifteen days before purchasing the policy. Then, if a flare-up occurs at any time before departure, you are fully covered.*

Turning in an Insurance Claim

The Travel Pak claim form is simple to complete, since Travelers does not require submission of original receipts. Simply list the place and date of purchase and an estimate of the repair or replacement cost. If the loss is less than $500, the claim need not be notarized. During the past ten years, my many meticulously prepared claims have always been promptly processed and paid.

What does *meticulous* mean? Let's revisit my salt-damaged Nikonos V 35mm camera. The $500 repair estimate listed twenty damaged parts that needed to be replaced. Had I submitted that estimate it is likely my claim would have been delayed or denied out of hand. The problem is that most retailers, including camera shop salespeople, do not think in terms of insurance *language*. Upon reviewing the estimate, I made a visit to the repair shop and had the owner prepare a new one. The new estimate honestly stated that the damage was the result of saltwater buildup. And it continued, "According to the owner, the unit was last exposed to salt water during eight days in Tahiti three months ago." He added, "The damage is consistent with such exposure." Such a solid claim form offers no "out" for an insurance company. I proved that the damage must have occurred during my prior vacation, the place where the camera was last exposed to salt water.

My travel motto is "Don't worry...be happy!" In this way Travel Pak has helped keep Patty and me smiling through occasionally nasty and unpredictable events that occurred on our many and extended travels.

"Safety" Insurance

Peace of mind, safety, and comfort come together in the exceptional *Magellan's Travel Catalogue*. Magellan's has been selling high-quality travel items since 1989. The company offers its products by mail order and provides a 100 percent unconditional "no time limit" guarantee on every item sold.

Two years ago I purchased two of its Magellan's unique smoke hoods. Those of you who often fly or wish to have the same type of hood airline personnel carry should consider buying this item. In the event of a takeoff or landing mishap, the lightweight hood (five ounces) provides precious extra minutes of protection from poisonous fumes, permitting you to safely exit the craft. Presently, Magellan's is selling the British-made Provita hood, priced at $69 (item no. SP626). The sixty-page catalogue contains two full pages on electrical adapters and converters, and lists most countries along with a diagram of corresponding adapters that are necessary to use with their proper converters. You will marvel at the variety of safety, comfort, and convenience of the items available. Contact Magellan's to request a free catalogue.

Magellan's Travel Catalogue
P.O. Box 5485
Santa Barbara, California 93150-5485
(800) 962-4943

Don't Be Shocked by Foreign Electricity

For a moment I must talk about Benjamin Franklin's favorite pastime—electricity. It goes like this: In the United States and North America electrical appliances run on 110 volts. Tahiti and most of the rest of the world operate on 220 volts. This is the stuff that drives American travelers nuts. On our first trip to Moorea I dutifully went to a local travel shop, told them we were going to Tahiti, and purchased their recommended 50-watt transformer. So, why did it turn out to be useless? It seems the "expert" who sold me the transformer failed to include the $2 adapter that allows the transformer to be plugged into recessed wall sockets, the very kind I found in my room at Cooks Bay Resort. Enter Hybrinetics Company and Magellan's catalogue to the rescue.

➡ **Steve's Tip:** *Call Hybrinetics, Inc. at (800) 247-6900 or fax (707) 585-7313 and request their "Foreign Electricity Guide." Also call Magellan's at (800) 962-4943 and request their current catalogue. Hybrinetics distributes an entire line of converters and adapters and sells many of its products to Magellan's. The Hybrinetics brochure is heaven-sent for consumers, for it lists almost every country in the world, from Australia to Zaire, and the adapter(s) used in each. Magellan's catalogue devotes two full pages to a similar listing.*

Just so you understand the problem, consider that there are low wattage, 50-watt converter/transformers that allow you to use battery chargers, oral hygiene gizmos, radios, and personal tape and CD players. But this transformer will not handle high-wattage hair dryers. There are high-wattage converters, usually handling appliances up to 1,500 watts, which will handle hair dryers, irons, and coffee makers. A third type of transformer is specially designed to handle "continuous use" appliances such as notebook computers and other business machines. Want to go for broke? There are "combination" transformers that handle 50-watt appliances and switch to also handle 1600-watt items. In addition to the transformer, an *adapter* may be necessary to allow the transformer to be plugged into some foreign sockets. At Cooks Bay Resort the sockets are *recessed*, so an adapter plug must be used. The transformer, which must be flush with the wall or socket, then plugs into the adapter. Transformers without an adapter simply do not fit flush with the wall socket—which means that they do not work!

A word on prices. Magellan's sells its 50-watt transformer (EA234) for $14.85; its 1600-watt transformer (EA232) for $18.85; and the combination 50- and 1600-watt transformer for $27.85. A set of five worldwide adapters (EA239F) is only $9.85.

➡ **Steve's Hair Dryer Tip:** *How do you use the least expensive 50-watt transformer for battery-charging a Sony Walkman, for instance, and still use a hair dryer? Many "international" hair dryers, even low-priced models, incorporate a 110/220 switch that allows the dryer to be used worldwide. No need to buy a higher-priced 1600 transformer here. Magellan's deluxe "smallest, lightest hair dryer we've ever offered" is a full 1500-watt dryer that switches from 110 to 220 volts and includes a European adapter plug. The dryer is listed as item EP201R0 and sells for $24.85, but want a less costly model? I just purchased a made-in-America Hartman Protech 1250-watt dual speed and voltage dryer (model 1250MP) for just $8.95 at a local discount shop. For information, call Hartman Products at (310) 676-7700.*

Emergency Passport Service

Passport expired? Need a last-minute "new" passport or entry visa? Unfortunately, such emergencies occur. Help is at hand with Washington, D.C.–based Travisa Visa and Passport Service. I used this service when the Tanzanian embassy in Washington *lost* our passports, which had been mailed to the embassy for the required predeparture visa stamp. Although the company charges high fees, it offers essential last-minute rescue service. Call Travisa at (800) 222-2589 for a brochure that explains its services and fees.

PART II

Dirt-Cheap Global Vacations

6

Cruising: The New American Pastime

For many years Patty and I swore an oath. Taking a cruise was for senior citizens only, the over-the-hill crowd, bingo addicts, gambling addicts, but not—definitely not—for us. We refused to "cruise" until our proverbial rocking chairs started squeaking. Then a few things happened that changed our travel lives. Patty and I hit our forties. We desperately tried to avoid it, but alas, aging caught up to us. By this time I was aware of the cruising boom that was spreading to younger and younger crowds.

During one of my typical treks through the Sunday *San Francisco Chronicle*'s travel section, my eye was drawn to a particular advertisement that announced a really low price for early bookings. This was a Princess cruise to Alaska! The advertisement described two early June sailings from Whittier, Alaska, to Vancouver, British Columbia, via the inland passage. The ship was an older one, the *Fair Princess*. Suddenly my mind was filled with possibilities. Though I knew little or nothing about cruising, I did know my airfares. I also knew about hotel and four-star restaurant prices. This amazing cruise deal was all-inclusive for an astounding $849 per person. Incredibly, these two sailings included free round-trip airfare from San Francisco. The cost of round-trip airfare to Alaska was between $400 and $500 by itself. This deal was heaven-sent. It was time to head off to Alaska, a place I had always longed to visit. The allure was wildlife, incredible untouched wilderness, remarkable snow-capped mountains, scenery, and glaciers to boot. Patty was excited, although she had already seen most of this, having lived in Anchorage.

Today cruising is America's fastest-growing travel industry. The number of newly commissioned ships has soared in recent years. In fact, twenty-three new cruise ships will be launched between 1996 and 1999, adding approximately 35,000 new berths to the high seas. Moreover, the "seniors only" crowds have given way to younger passengers. Why did this happen? Fierce competition among the cruise lines has generated lower fares. Also, there is greater public awareness and appreciation of these all-inclusive vacations. Cruises offer fantastic amenities vis-à-vis food...fun...and service!

The Nuts and Bolts of Doing It!

Our Princess Alaska cruise represents the typical cruise offered by competing cruise lines. Amenities such as food, staterooms, service, and recreational activities are similar on most major cruise lines. After a whirlwind self-education on cruises, I was convinced that the Princess Line's Alaska offer was a remarkable bargain.

Think of the ship as a 747 "wide-body." Seats by the windows on either side of the plane are called outside cabins and the aisle seats are inside cabins. That's it. All cabins, excluding the suites, are mostly the same size with similar amenities. Outside cabins have windows and the same interiors and size as the inside cabins. All of them, inside or outside, usually have the same beds, closet space, and bathrooms. Very few ships will have inside cabins that are smaller than the outside ones. To be sure, the larger, deluxe cabins and suites with balconies are available at a cost of hundreds to thousands of dollars more per week. Patty and I were definitely not going to pay such high prices.

Following are examples of recently published prices for outside and inside cabins on a Princess one-week Alaska cruise. These were the lowest annual fares for selected May and September sailings. Do not be concerned that these are dated fares, since you will not be paying anything close to brochure rates. Also, these rates do not reflect upgrades.

Upper-deck cabin with a window	$2,499
Upper-deck cabin with no window	$1,799
Lower-deck cabin with a window	$2,149
Lower-deck cabin with no window	$1,549

➡ **Steve's Tip:** *Advertised cruise prices do not include the substantial add-on, "port charges." These range from $50 to $100 per person, depending on port of call, and are similar to airport taxes.*

What about cabin location? With her fifteen years of medical background, Patty is my resident "science officer." She assures me that all cabins on the dead center of the ship at the pivot point will hardly feel the movement of the ship in rough seas. All ships are designed with large underwater wings that prevent the ship from rolling sideways. Besides, during your dream cruise the various decks will be your home away from home. On tropical cruises, lounging, swimming, sleeping, eating lunch, and savoring tropical drinks deck-side are major activities. Even in Alaska you are on deck for four to six hours in Glacier Bay. On other days, sixty- to seventy-degree weather is perfect for lounging in the sun.

You may often wish to visit your cabin to retrieve something, change clothes, or get more film. Do you want your cabin to be ten decks down and half a football field away, at the far end of the ship? There are elevators, but they are not fast. Having your cabin in the middle of the ship is convenient, and the same is true of the ship's restaurants. Being close to your designated restaurant is a major convenience. Generally, a good cabin location is obtainable when you book early and know which cabin to choose. Once again, knowledge is travel power.

Our initial bargain-priced Alaska sailing was difficult to book. However, my perseverance paid off and I snagged a reservation. In fact, I booked through a specialty cruise travel agency that included $50 in stateroom credit per couple, which further reduced the price to $825.

Another interesting fact of booking is that occasionally the best cabins are booked on a first-come, first-served basis. Our booking was sufficiently early to secure an upper-deck, midships cabin where we were also conveniently one flight of stairs away from our restaurant.

Older ships, such as the *Fair Princess*, are quaint and retain old-world charm. The *Fair Princess* is 608 feet long and holds 890 passengers. On the negative side, older ships have less open decking than newer ships. Consequently, older ships are better suited for the Alaska cruises, where passengers spend less time on deck, than on tropical routes where greater deck space is desirable. On warm cruises, the more deck space the better.

Fair Princess's cabins have two twin beds that are immovable, which was a problem for us. In the end we decided to grin and bear it, just this once. After all, it was cold and chilly Alaska, right? Cruise ship brochures indicate whether beds can be converted to double or queen size. Some brochures contain maps of the ship's floor plans that show all cabin levels in different colors. Let's say you have picked a double cabin that is in the dark blue section. But the dark blue cabins are on different decks on the ship's map. When the time comes to book the cruise, try for a dark blue, double cabin closest to the center of the ship on the highest available deck.

Keep in mind that a few ships still offer low-end, unacceptable bunk-bed cabins. So check the micro-small print in the cruise advertisement! This usually shows the category included in the advertised price. I once assumed that the best bargain cruises were based on such bunk bed cabins, but I am happy to report this is not the case. Cruise lines usually apply their bargain fares to regular, inside double cabins. When the price is right, go for it. We booked inside cabins on each of our three cruises. The ships varied, from the older *Fair Princess* to the newer luxury *Star Princess*. Our inside cabins were entirely adequate, clean, and very comfortable. One quickly learns to move around in small quarters.

Sightseeing in Alaska

The major Alaska cruise activity is sightseeing, and I mean *sightseeing!* We flew to Anchorage and were bused to our cruise ship, docked at nearby Whittier. The excitement began as early as our bus ride. Suddenly, just outside Anchorage, we stopped for a major Alaskan photo opportunity. Just off to our left, in a picturesque meadow, were three moose! On the side of the mountain nearby, Dall sheep were clinging to the sheer rocks. We had arrived—this was Alaska!

Following is a brief overview of our itinerary. It was a typical one-week cruise on the Inland Passage:

Day One: Arrived in Anchorage and were bused to the cruise ship in Whittier.

Day Two: Cruised through the College Fjords in Prince William Sound. This is the site of sixteen glaciers, each named for Ivy League colleges sponsoring the expedition leading to their discovery.

Day Three: A full-day tour of Glacier Bay National Park. Muir Glacier, the major glacier in the bay, is almost two miles wide and twenty-five stories high. Passengers had about four hours to view and photograph the glaciers, birds, and sea mammals.

Day Four: Port of call: Skagway. Here passengers visited a picturesque gold rush town that is home to the famous White Horse Pass and Yukon Railroad. We took the railroad to the mountain summit.

Day Five: Port of call: Juneau. This is Alaska's landlocked capital city, accessible only by boat or plane. We enjoyed an excursion to the nearby Mendenhall Glacier and river rafting on Mendenhall River. Sport fishing is a major shore excursion activity.

Day Six: Port of call: Ketchikan, the "Salmon Capital of the World." Exciting shore excursions include seaplane trips to Misty Fjord National Monument. Passengers may visit a native village where natives expertly carve totem poles.

Day Seven: Cruised the inside passage past islands and forested coastline. There was plenty of time to view wildlife, mostly birds and sea mammals.

Day Eight: Arrived at Vancouver, B.C.

Make certain that your Inland Passage cruise includes a full-day tour of Glacier Bay National Park. Some Alaska cruises skip this park and instead visit the old Russian town of Sitka. The full-day tour of Glacier Bay is incredible. Our ship cruised the bay at a snail's pace, allowing passengers to view "calving," the natural ripping away of large chunks of glacier. We watched, in amazement, as mountains of ice split from the glacier and crashed into the bay, and we listened to the thunderous sounds of the ice hitting the water. Marine life is ever present, mostly seals and birds. Make sure you bring binoculars and warm clothes, especially good gloves. I remained on deck for about six hours, taking in the marvelous sights and sounds of the bay. Despite the great weather and temperatures in the fifties and sixties, I was nearly frozen after six hours on deck. I later offered eternal thanks to our steward for delivering a large pot of steaming hot chocolate.

Shore-Based Activities and Ports of Call

Shore-based activities are a bit costly, but they offer unparalleled experiences. In Ketchikan we took a seaplane tour over Misty Fjord National Monument. When the seaplane landed on a remote lake we got out, stood on its pontoons, and tried not to fall in. Our pilot was a Paul Bunyan lookalike with a long beard, someone right out of the Alaskan bush. On the return leg I sat next to him in the cockpit and gaped in awe as I looked out my *open* window. The cost was about $75 per person and well worth it. It was great!

In Juneau we took a half-day rafting trip on the Mendenhall River. This is a glacial river within eyesight of the edge of the Mendenhall Glacier. It was tame but fun, and cost $40.

In Skagway we rode the famous White Horse and Yukon Route Railroad. The train traveled from Skagway to the snow-capped White Horse Pass, and the scenery was spectacular. The cost was $20 per person.

Other adventures, such as remote, wild-river salmon fishing, sport fishing, kayaking, and more are available at the various ports. Before your departure, the cruise line provides a special brochure listing all of the diverse shore excursions, virtually something for everybody and every budget. Want to save money? Then walk, shop, and explore the picturesque and historic ports of call. There is excellent shopping for precious Eskimo soapstone carvings and beautiful wool sweaters. Or send family and friends packages of Alaskan smoked salmon purchased on Juneau's main street. The stops and excursions are exciting, memorable, and a wonderful part of the Alaska experience.

Meal Seatings

We are getting close to the heart of cruising—food. However, before the dinner plate arrives, you must make the important choice of an early- or late-dinner seating. This decision is *very* important; do not underrate it, for it may affect your overall enjoyment of the cruise!

➡ **Steve's Tip:** *When booking your cruise, select the late seating!*

First, here are the schedules for early and late seatings on most ships: The early seating is usually 7:00 A.M. for breakfast, and you must arrive on time or face the scorn of fellow passengers and the waiter. The second seating is usually 8:30 A.M. Lunch is served at noon for early diners and at 1:30 P.M. for the late seating. The all-important dinner seating is at 6:00 P.M. for early dining and 8:30 P.M. for the late seating.

Why do I strongly recommend the late seating? First, you will not need to be up at the crack of dawn, i.e., 7:00 A.M. for breakfast. Second, when the ship is in port for a full day, passengers can wait until 6:00 P.M. to return to the ship. See where I'm going? Those with the late seating may stay ashore until the 6:00 P.M. deadline. The trade-off for early diners is that they may go into a town at 9:00 A.M. instead of 10:00 A.M., but this is not much of a trade-off for my money. I am not interested in hitting the streets of Juneau or any other port of call at 9:00 A.M. I opt for a leisurely afternoon, remaining on shore until 6:00 P.M. or so. The early-seating negative comes into play in the afternoon. Not only must the passengers return for their 6:00 P.M. dinner, they must return sufficiently early to dress, perhaps in formal wear. Late diners may return to the ship at 6:00 P.M. and relax until their 8:30 P.M. meal.

There are two possible downsides to the late seating. First, some passengers prefer their dinners earlier, at the 6:00 P.M. time slot. Also, the late seating means those passengers must attend the late 10:00 P.M. nightclub show rather than the earlier 8:30 P.M. show. Pick the seating that is best for you.

Late seatings are by far the most popular. Therefore, choose your seating at the time of booking. Keep in mind that passengers are *not* usually permitted to change their seating once reservations are made.

Dinner on the High Seas: The Heart of Cruising

That is the truth! The food on cruises is sensational. Princess Cruises offered gourmet flaming desserts and a lobster dinner. On the other hand, to the chagrin of many passengers, Carnival did *not* serve a lobster dinner during our Mexican Riviera cruise. There are dinner ceremonies on cruise ships, such as the march of the flaming Baked Alaskas. As lights dim, the crew marches around the dining room, each member carrying a flaming platter. Really fun to watch *and* to eat!

Okay, this not only *sounds* decadent, it *was* decadent. People at our table initially frowned but later joined right in. The menu was superb, even too good. It listed mushroom-capped tournedos of beef (filet mignon) and roast royal pheasant flambé with cognac. For me the word was—dilemma. Recall my introduction, and my wonderful weeks in the borscht belt, staying at an early version of the "all-inclusive" hotel where food was unlimited and waiters would kill to please. Our eager-to-please, Italian dinner crew reminded me of those busboys and waiters of yesteryear. As déjà vu set in I asked our waiter if Patty and I could share another entrée besides the main dishes we had ordered. (Remember, this trip is *supposed* to be decadent.) The waiter eagerly complied. Some tablemates looked on with disdain. Then the metamorphosis took place. The next evening we watched these same tablemates trying to agree on the extra entrée they would order. Before long, most were joining in the decadent fray and sampled exotic entrées to their heart's content. This was not a nightly event, but something we did when the menu offered us impossible choices.

Here is a preview of a typical menu for the Captain's Gala formal dinner:

Russian Caviar
Shrimp Cocktail
Liver Paté
Soup
Salad
Entrée
   Broiled Rock Lobster
   Baked Salmon Hollandaise
   Roast Royal Pheasant Flambé with Cognac
   Tournedos of Beef
Vegetables
Chocolate Soufflé and Assorted Cakes
Seasonal Fruits and Cheeses
Coffee, Tea

Patty loves lobster. After her lobster dinner she asked the waiter if they would serve lobster again. The bad-news answer was no, it was a one-time culinary event. But there was also good news. The waiter told Patty the kitchen had leftovers. The next evening they served this delectable meal to her again, much to the envy of our tablemates.

I noticed another table enjoying a second evening of a flambé dessert. Our waiter explained that flambé desserts are served only once—unless a table makes a special request. I immediately polled my table and obtained the anticipated 100 percent vote in favor. Our waiter checked with the head waiter, and the next evening we enjoyed another flaming spectacle at our table. Everyone applauded the encore desserts.

Midnight buffet anyone? The infamous midnight buffets are served each evening in different forms on different ships. Princess offers some creative options. One evening, the waiters at the dessert stations created a variety of exotic delicacies right before our eyes. Another plus for me was that the late-seating dinner ended about 10:00 P.M., which pretty much killed my desire to dive into the midnight buffet! But we did marvel at it all, including the great swan ice sculpture.

Room Service

Now, we *are* talking decadence! The closest thing to legal slaves are floor stewards. These noble crew members are totally dedicated to passenger comfort, fully twenty-four hours per day. Room service is free on Carnival, Princess, and all major cruise lines. In fact, room service offers its own menu, albeit a limited one. A typical room service menu includes, coffee, tea, hot chocolate, continental breakfast, and sandwiches.

During several days of our cruise I was up and out early in the morning doing aerobics. Patty opted to sleep in and enjoy a late breakfast in bed, and she loved every morsel of it. This is set up the prior evening by leaving your order form hanging on the outer door knob. It includes the food order and delivery time. The next morning Patty's breakfast arrived on the button. What a life!

Perhaps you think I was high and dry, working my butt off doing aerobics during the breakfast hour? No way! A great breakfast buffet is usually served outside on an upper deck from 7:00 to 10:00 A.M. After aerobics my "reasonable" breakfast of juices, fruits, and cereals hit the spot in a big way. But you can imagine everything I passed up for my aerobically correct breakfast. Okay, maybe I snatched a small slice of bacon—but just one!

➡ **Steve's Tip on Tipping:** *You should tip the waiter, busboy, and floor steward according to the suggested schedule provided by the ship. So how do you also get program miles for the $100 to $125 in tips (for all meals and services for the week)? Not easily done, but this worked for me: Go to the casino and use your Citibank card to obtain $150 in cash. This is usually done as a credit transaction and not a cash advance. You may then use the money for tips.*

Entertainment

Generally fun, talented shows are on all cruise lines except for a couple of nights of amateur-type shows. But do not expect Las Vegas gala–quality shows every night. One comedy act came onboard for a single show and then returned to shore. On the

Alaska cruise, as expected, one-half of the shows were geared to the super-senior crowd and were reminiscent of the Tommy Dorsey–Benny Goodman era. However, a few nights were great. The best was a Broadway review with excerpts from five Broadway shows, including a fifteen-minute version of *Phantom of the Opera*. Some show people double in other shipboard capacities. In fact, one dancer doubled as the ship's aerobic instructor. But overall, I was disappointed. Perhaps I took Kathie Lee Gifford's commercials a bit too seriously, expecting super Broadway shows each night. That is definitely not the case. If you enjoy three or more very good to excellent shows during the week, you are doing well. I would say ours ranged from fair to good but were rarely excellent. However, the shows do provide variety, including singers, dancers, and comedians.

Onboard Activities

The activities offered depend on the cruise route. Without a doubt, the three most popular routes for Americans are Alaska, Mexico, and the Caribbean. Patty and I have cruised all three. I will discuss each route and show you life on the ship and, in particular, shipboard activities. I will also discuss some differences between the older ships, such as the *Fair Princess*, and newer ships such as the Carnival's *Jubilee* and the *Star Princess*.

This is where all-inclusive cruising and Club Med part company. Patty and I do not gamble and are not into Bingo. If this is your cup of tea, you are in grand shape. In colder weather, such as on the Alaska route, your choices are limited. The ship's pool is very empty, and there is only limited opportunity to enjoy lounging on an outside deck. We spent just one day—a sunny glorious day in the high sixties—sunbathing in shirt sleeves. I don't want to complain, but I do emphasize that while you're at sea activity options are slim. Try skeet shooting off the aft deck. Enjoy exercising? I found pedaling on a Lifecycle on the top deck incredible! As I pedaled, I viewed ice floes and snow-covered peaks.

The *Fair Princess* had a great option for me. At 5:00 P.M., when it was too cold for the outdoors and too early for dinner, I headed straight for the full-size movie theater that offered a regular schedule of feature films. The newer luxury ships have cable television so passengers may view a greater selection of movies in the comfort of their cabins.

The bottom line for Alaska cruising is that shipboard activities are limited. However, on the big plus side, there is little dead time at sea, since most days are spent visiting interesting ports of call, and one full day is spent at Glacier Bay. With some luck, during the dead time at sea one can enjoy warm, sunny weather.

Under the Caribbean Sun

We had to do it. We paid big dollars to sail on one of Princess Cruise's magnificent new ships, the *Star Princess*. The *Star* is 804 feet long, has twelve decks, holds 1,494 passengers, has a wine- -Russian caviar bar, and a spectacular, three-story atrium and staircase. Also, the *Star* has three swimming pools and four outdoor hot tubs, and all regular cabins have two beds that move side-by-side to form a queen-size bed. Cabins also have a television and refrigerator.

This is one of the luxury ships pictured in Princess brochure's two-page color spread, the one where you ask, "I wonder what ship that is?" Okay, it cost us $1,400 each for this extravaganza, but it included airfare from the West Coast to Miami and a second flight to Puerto Rico. A word or two about Caribbean cruise routes is in order. There are eastern, western and southern routes. The western route departs from Miami, Florida, and visits Cozumel and the Grand Cayman Islands. These islands are known for their world-class scuba diving. The eastern route also commences in Miami but wastes a day at sea while traveling to its first port. On the other hand, when a cruise ship departs from Puerto Rico on the southern route, it stops at a new island each day for five days. The southern route visits more islands than any other one-week cruise and offers the broadest sampling of Caribbean life.

We decided to take the southern route and our Caribbean adventure began as the *Star Princess* departed from San Juan, Puerto Rico, and cruised to Barbados, the most southern point of our trip. We joyfully island hopped during the next five days on our way back to Puerto Rico. Here is our route:

Day One: Leave Puerto Rico (U.S. territory)

Day Two: At sea (day on deck and in pool)
Day Three: Barbados (former British colony)
Day Four: Princess Bay (Mayreau is an island of pristine white sand beaches.)
Day Five: Martinique (former French colony)
Day Six: St. Maarten/St. Martin (former half-Dutch and half-French colony)
Day Seven: St. Thomas, Virgin Islands (U.S. territory)

Shore Activities in the Caribbean

Make no mistake about it, most passengers are biting at the bit to hit the stores at each port of call. Just before reaching port, our ship had a preport meeting in the nightclub that doubled as an auditorium. Being a mega-ship, *Star Princess* conveniently beamed the meeting to all cabins via closed-circuit television. They tell you which stores are "legitimate" and which to watch out for. Some will provide discounts for passengers—you may save at other stores but this decision is up to you. I recall *Princess* went so far as to guarantee any merchandise purchased from their recommended stores. Should a passenger have any problem with the merchandise en route to home the cruise line would take care of it—which could save a passenger big bucks.

On St. Thomas passengers hit the jewelry shops big time. Big dollars—thousands—were spent by many couples on glittering bangles of gold and diamonds. Instead, we were off snorkeling in the Caribbean at a great beach. Another wonderful day of sun, snorkeling, relaxing, and sipping BBC's (Baileys, bananas, and coconut in vanilla ice cream)—an incredible, refreshing drink aptly named for its ingredients.

The island of Martinique is truly a fun stop. The French capital is Port-de-France, a typical French town of quaint buildings with wrought iron balconies and cobblestone streets that resemble old Paris. Before landing I did some research and found out that Mercedes taxis offer a full-circle tour of the island. The ship offered the same package, using a crowded van or bus, for double the price—$40 per person. I hit the dock running and found several cab drivers hawking their tours. I negotiated with one, knocking the price from $30 to $20, a full 50 percent off the ship's price. The half-day tour was marvelous, including a walk through the ruins of St. Pierre, a Pompeii-like town destroyed by a volcanic eruption about seventy-five years ago. We completed the tour traveling through a lush green rain forest—all in the comfort of an oversize Mercedes!

St. Maarten, or St. Martin, Island is a unique stop because one-half the island is Dutch and the other is French, and it is split into Dutch and French towns on either side of Mullet Bay. Phillipsburg is on the Dutch side whereas Marigot is on the French side. Both are picturesque and offer many fine shops. We took a boat from Phillipsburg to Marigot for a one-hour shopping stop. Then, on the return trip, the boat stopped at a small beach in the middle of the channel. We had about an hour to have a picnic lunch, go swimming or, in my case, try a jet ski for the first time. For a fee of $20 a half-hour I was off and hitting the waves with a jet ski. It was great!

Scuba Diving

Who says you must "veg out" on a cruise? I have described the bush flight to the fjords in Alaska and jet skiing in the Caribbean. Patty and I are divers at heart and have taken more than our share of dive trips (about five to Cozumel alone). We knew this would be an R&R vacation with fun snorkeling at some island ports of call. Although diving was listed on the shore excursion list, I assumed it would not be up to our standards. It also seemed costly for a one-tank dive. My assumption changed when I happened upon the ship's scuba instructor at poolside. He gave beginner lessons at the pool and handled shore dives for certified divers. At $55 the cost was really not bad, about the same as in Tahiti.

While the southern Caribbean route offered us five different island ports, they are not, by any stretch, world-class dive destinations, unlike the western Caribbean cruise route, which includes Cozumel and Grand Cayman. So why did we not take that cruise? Fair question. In large part because we had been to Cozumel before and really wanted to see five new and different islands. A different island each day for five days was great fun.

While chatting with the instructor I asked the number-one question: Were any dive sites on this route very good or excellent?

Or were they simply average, as I expected? The answer surprised me. Three of the islands were average but two offered excellent dives. One was a shallow, forty-foot dive to a sunken ship that now teamed with marine life, while the second offered a beautiful coral bed. We opted to go for it and experienced two memorable dives, one at the "private" island of Mayreau and the other at Barbados. All aspects of the dives were handled professionally and the equipment was very good. The water was crystal clear and the dives were flawless. Diving to the sunken ship was best, with prolific marine life in all directions, while the coral gardens were majestic and colorful.

Cruising the Mexican Riviera

This was truly one of our best bargain vacations. Suffice to say, the Kraft free travel dollars allowed us to embark on this one-week Carnival cruise to the Mexican Riviera for the incredible price of $449 each.

Upon reaching Puerto Vallarta, a classy tropical resort, there was the usual preport meeting in the nightclub. What was interesting, the social director discussed shopping and sightseeing but not the best places to "veg out"—enjoy the beach, sun, and sand...the reason people pay big bucks to vacation there.

I finally cornered the social director and asked for some advice. After all, that was his job, right? It worked, though I felt I was privileged to be getting the scoop. "Just turn right and walk and you will head toward a few great hotels," I was told. This turned out to be terrific advice. We headed in the correct direction, and within a couple of blocks saw a young woman signing people up for a time-share presentation at a nearby property. The freebie included total use of the Crystal Hotel and a free buffet lunch. I signed up and received our written invitation. Up the street was the entrance to the Crystal Hotel. What a place it turned out to be!

You are cynical, I can tell. All I can say is that I trust my instincts and this one was 100 percent on the mark. The Crystal Hotel is part of a major chain of expensive, high-end properties. The Crystal Resort in Puerto Vallarta is part hotel, part time-share, and part condominium, and it sports its own bullfighting ring. As we walked through the ornate lobby, Patty and I were totally impressed. There, in the garden area, were little villas forming a crescent, with each grouping of four or five villas surrounding its own private pool.

We finally made it to the beach and main pool, where we found two lounge chairs and had an unforgettable day. Why unforgettable? The pool was elongated and kidney-shaped, with small bridges here and there. It was perhaps four feet deep—made for sun worshipers. In its center was a concrete "flower platform" upon which teenagers stretched out to enjoy quality sunbathing and misting from tiny fountains. Lounge chairs surrounded the pool, and soothing light rock music erupted from underground speakers spaced evenly around the area. The water spilled over the edge, giving the illusion of a waterfall emanating from the pool. Just beyond was the beach and ocean. Standing in the pool and looking toward the ocean, it seemed as if the pool was flowing into the ocean, merging with it—quite an extraordinary sight. As if that were not enough, all around the perimeter, in the water, were curved concrete lounges. We reclined horizontally, the water only reaching the mid-level of our bodies but keeping us cool and relaxed in the sun, the top of our bodies remaining dry as we lay in six inches of water.

We ordered giant cored pineapples filled with what tasted like nectar of the gods—a mixture of piña colada and other tropical flavors. We then feasted on our Carnival picnic lunch. At midday we walked to the beach and went parasailing.

➡ **Steve's Free Picnic Lunch Tip:** *The night before landing in each of our tropical ports, Patty and I placed a room service order for sandwiches and lots of fruit, delivered early the next morning. A great picnic lunch arrived at 7:30 A.M., and we happily headed off to the beach (or hotel pool), where we later devoured it. This seemed fair enough, since we were missing our regular shipboard lunch. Plan number two: Do you recall the famous midnight buffet? On one occasion I checked it out and returned to our cabin with all the necessary ingredients for the following day's picnic at our next island stop—Mazatlán.*

By 5:00 P.M. we were as rested and roasted as two people could be. We had passed on the buffet lunch, which meant we were not required to sit in on the ninety-minute time-share presentation. The day was a total success, truly what tropical vacations are made for.

On Mazatlán we shared a taxi to a recommended beachfront hotel. Although the hotel was more touristy, it was upscale and sported a giant man-made waterfall and pool. Full live orchestras played at poolside. There was no charge to use the facilities, as the hotel was happy to have us there, hoping, of course, we would buy lots of food and drinks. We certainly obliged in the exotic, fruity-drink department.

Bargains on the High Seas

Presently cheapskate cruises abound. One reason is a drop-off in bookings due to the aftermath of two 1995 hurricanes. These storms severely damaged the islands of St. Thomas, Antigua, and St. Martin. Despite this, the outlook for 1996 and beyond is total optimism. Of course, competition is more fierce than ever, despite the cessation of operation by two major cruise lines. The regular price for our Carnival Mexican Riviera cruise was $649. By using $400 of our Kraft free travel dollars, our net price was just $449. Today, cruise wars have dramatically reduced regular prices on most major cruises. In early 1996 Carnival advertised a seven-night Caribbean cruise departing from either Miami, Tampa, or New Orleans at the incredible price of only $549. Carnival is offering a Mexican Riviera cruise, departing from Los Angeles, for the same rock-bottom $549 price. Celebrity Cruises is advertising a Caribbean cruise at just $599, and Holland America cruise line has jumped on the bandwagon, offering a seven-night Caribbean cruise at $598.

You may take any of these first-rate cruises at low-end "cheapskate" prices and still feel like a first-class passenger. Gone are the days when such a low price guaranteed you a cabin just this side of the engine room, buried in the bowels of the ship. On the other hand, I thrive on discounts. Using free travel cash, Patty and I can book any of the above world-class cruises to either the Caribbean or the Mexican Riviera for only $399 each.

NOTE: In August 1996 Carnival advertised the mother of all cruise "sales." Its best southern Caribbean cruises during September and early October were sale-priced starting at $499!

➡ **Steve's Tip:** *No free travel cash? You can always save 5 percent by using Travelers Advantage or PriceCostco, reducing the low-end price to $521. Also, see chapter 4 for Pearson Travel's special cash-in-your-pocket promotions. Pearson offers its customers $100 in American Express travel checks and free upgrades on most one-week cruises. Chapter 4 also points the way to the best discount travel agencies. Whether you are using free travel dollars or any of the above discounts or promotions, you cannot go wrong on this one!*

A special word about the most common cruises, the one-week cruises to Alaska, Mexico, or the Caribbean. Many advertisements describe the length of these cruises as seven days. If you are using free travel cash, the cruise must be seven *nights* to obtain the current $300 discount. I did the necessary research on this one and was surprised. Most seven-day cruises are also seven-*night* cruises. For example, the Carnival line leaves Los Angeles at 4:30 P.M. on Sunday and sails for seven nights, returning to Los Angeles at about 9:00 A.M. the following Sunday. So the cruise lines are being honest by advertising seven full *days* on the ship. For us, the number of nights are the key to a dirt-cheap price. Whether the cruise of your choice says "one week" or "seven days," it will likely qualify. Pick up a brochure at any travel agency and check it out. Listed are the actual number of days and nights of each cruise. Just be certain you will be on the ship for seven *nights*.

When cruising the Caribbean, use Citibank AAdvantage miles for free travel to your departure city. As an alternative, look for a low-priced package that includes air from your home city to the departure point. In fact, many cruise lines offer special low airfares. I have seen Alaska airfares from West Coast cities as low as $250. On that basis, and using a low-end $650 fare, the net price will be as low as $900 per person.

Another interesting option is Southwest Airlines' super-liberal frequent flyer program. Customers receive a free round-trip ticket for completing any eight round-trip flights, regardless of the destination. I often commute between Oakland and Burbank and presently have two free Southwest tickets sitting in my file. For those of you who rarely fly, consider Southwest's latest promotion. Buy a full-fare ticket to the destination of your choice and take along one to three extra passengers for an additional $50 per round-trip ticket. This is how we plan to visit New Orleans.

Why New Orleans? There are two good reasons why I mention New Orleans. First, it is one of Southwest Airlines' easternmost destinations, and, second, many Caribbean cruises depart from New Orleans. Patty and I qualify to fly free to New Orleans, where we could use free travel dollars to catch another great Caribbean cruise. The total cost, including round-trip air, would be approximately $399 each.

If you already live near a port of departure, such as Los Angeles or Miami, you have it made. Airfare and port charges are the only "flies in the ointment" when it comes to cruising. The more distant you live from a departure port the more costly the airfare to get there. Fortunately, there are significant exceptions to this rule, the major ones involving high-volume air routes. Readers who live on the East Coast have an easy shot at cheap travel on the high-volume New York–Miami air corridor. The same is true of my home in the Bay Area. Presently, commuter-air wars have seen fares drop to as low as $19 one-way from San Francisco to Los Angeles. Any lower and the airlines will be paying *us* to fly.

➡ **Steve's Tip:** *For low air-only fares from New York area airports, call Cheap Tickets Inc. at 212-570-1179 or 800-377-1000. Since April 1996 they have offered round-trip New York–Miami area fares for as low as $178.*

Unlike most other vacations, a low-end cruise price is the bottom line, where a cheap airfare to Maui is just the beginning. Remember, you must still pay for food, recreation, and entertainment, while a cruise is truly all-inclusive. In fact, except for the variation in port charges, the actual cruise destination means little to cruise companies. They price cruises, like hotels do rooms, by the number of days of the booking, making any seven-night cruise at $549 or less a cheapskate bargain royale. Above all, I want to emphasize that paying a bargain cruise price does not in any way, shape, or form make you are a second-class passenger. Follow my advice, know your cabin location, book early, and be savvy. You will be rewarded with the cruise experience of a lifetime.

Oh yes, one more thing...Bon voyage!

7

Maui: Paradise in Hawaii

Maui is one of the world's special exotic places. It is known as the Valley Isle, owing to its formation by two volcanic peaks. A pristine, fertile valley connects its two extinct volcanos. One of the dormant volcanos, 10,000-foot-high Haleakala, House of the Gods, is the highest peak in the Hawaiian chain. A visit to its peak allows visitors to view a facsimile of the moon's cratered surface. Many visitors arrive at 5:00 A.M. to enjoy a spectacular sunrise. You feel otherworldly as the sun slowly emerges from the cloud-shrouded summit. Or you may take a four-hour drive to Hana, passing over forty small bridges.

Maui's beaches are some of the best in the world. In fact, Kapalua beach was voted best beach in the United States by *USA Today*. The nearby Kaanapali Resort complex is one of the finest in all of Hawaii, with its broad green belts, world-class golf courses, and, of course, broad white-sand beaches.

There are no real cities on Maui's western "gold coast." However, there is a jewel known as Lahaina Town. Historic Lahaina was a bustling, active whaling center more than one hundred years ago. Today, it is a bustling main street fronting the ocean, with quaint shops, many restaurants, art galleries, and two small museums.

Water sports abound. Maui offers great scuba diving, wind surfing, and snorkeling. Want more? How about jet skis, parasailing, surfing, boogie-boarding—and on and on. Land sports include hiking, tennis, golf, and bicycling—down Haleakala.

Remote marine preserves, such as Honoloa, offer another type of adventure. Honoloa is reached only in a four-wheel-drive vehicle or by hiking in a half mile or so. I think you get the idea.

Maui's new luxury hotels offer suites costing $400 to $700 per night with every conceivable amenity. Unlike on Moorea, seeing Maui requires that visitors rent a car to fully enjoy their vacations: There is simply too much to see and do away from your hotel or condo.

Our Home Away From Home

Let me be perfectly clear on this one: Patty and I have a special personal interest in Maui. We go there at least once a year, since we own two studio condominium apartments in a beachfront resort.

This is how it happened. In the late 1970s my employer indoctrinated me with the virtues of her favorite vacation escape, Maui. She traveled there annually and had been enjoying this ritual for ten years or more. Then, in 1982, I found myself rejoining the singles' ranks and badly needed an exotic getaway. I had just completed a scuba course and was eager to experience my first warm-water ocean dive. My trip to Maui, in 1982, was my first exposure to Hawaii, and more particularly, Maui. From the moment I stepped off the plane I was mesmerized by its beauty, from its pineapple fields to 10,000-foot-high Haleakala. I was totally in awe of this exotic and beautiful place. My first warm-water ocean dive was equally thrilling and unforgettable. My feelings for Maui have changed little over the years.

The following year I met Patty. We traveled to Maui and agreed it would be wonderful to own a piece of this paradise. We purchased two studio condominium apartments at the Royal Kahana, technically becoming licensed innkeepers and, of course, taxpayers. Our connection to Maui has enriched us in many ways. We visit the island at least once a year, so it is our home away from home.

Location, location, location, is the hallmark cry of real estate agents, and yes, this is also true in paradise. The best place to stay on Maui is the northern part of its west coast, the area near old historic Lahaina Town. Going north from Lahaina Town, you drive a mile or so to Kaanapali beach resort, then about two miles to the Kahana area and another mile or so to upscale Kapalua (the location of Kapalua beach—the best in the United States). The Royal Kahana is an oceanfront high-rise. Because it is V-shaped, all of its units face the ocean. It has its own beautiful golden stretch of sand and surf, and all of its units, including our studios, offer a vast array of amenities, including central air-conditioning, ceiling fans, microwave ovens, and full kitchens. All units also have their own washer/dryers, new TV's, recently installed VCR's, and a lanai (balcony).

I must add that the Royal Kahana is very moderately priced. You can easily select other properties that have more exotic, costly furnishings if you are prepared to pay more. By the same token, there are many lower-priced properties that are either located in the southern half of the island or do not qualify as ocean- or beachfront resorts. Other down-priced properties fail to offer various amenities. (Night tennis anyone?)

➡ **Steve's Tip:** *I have arranged a special $99-per-day rate for readers who require only lodging on Maui and wish to stay at our home away from home studios. This is a 37 percent to 44 percent discount off January 1997 published rates! For a colorful brochure and reservation form write to:*

Royal Kahana—Reservations
P.O. Box 1956
Lafayette, Calif., 94549

A word about resort condominium rentals. I will assume that some of you have no experience with this creature. You are *not* left adrift without the luxuries of a hotel. The Royal Kahana lobby has a guest check-in registration desk that appears no different from most hotel desks. Rooms have phones for in-house use and for outside calling. The units have daily maid service, the same as any hotel. The lobby has a tour desk so you may plan and purchase virtually any activity you wish, from tours of Haleakala to helicopter rides over volcanic peaks and hidden waterfalls. You have almost all of the benefits of a hotel, while enjoying either a studio, a one-bedroom, or a two-bedroom apartment. I should note that studios (both of ours) have king-size beds. You can also arrange a cot for a small child. One-bedroom units have a sofa sleeper in the living room so that four guests may share the unit. Guests with money to spare may check out the ultimate deluxe two-bedroom wraparound units that are dead center of the "V" of the building. Their wraparound lanais are approximately twenty feet long and offer astounding views up and down Maui's coast. But they are premium priced.

➡ **Steve's Tip:** *If you have a choice in selecting your arrival airport in Maui take an interisland flight from Honolulu to the new Kapalua West Maui Airport. This routing avoids Maui's heavily congested main airport at Kahului, and it also avoids the forty-five-minute drive from Kahului to the Lahaina area. The new west Maui airport is located in a pineapple field just across the road from the Royal Kahana. Do not worry, there are no large jets, only smaller interisland planes that all take off to the north, so you neither see nor hear them from the Royal Kahana. The bad news is that most bargain packages do not offer a choice of airports. If your package goes through Honolulu and provides an interisland flight to Maui, you may be able to fly into the Kapalua West Maui Airport at no extra charge.*

Some of Maui's newest megahotels, and many lower-priced older ones, are found on the southern part of Maui's west coast. The downside, for my money, is that you are in a more remote area of the island. There are no quaint towns, but simply off-the-road shopping centers, one after another. One must drive about forty-five minutes or longer to reach Lahaina Town, which precludes a spur-of-the-moment trip there. On the other hand, Lahaina is only a few miles away from all Kaanapali and Kahana area properties. I strongly feel that being near Lahaina, the Kaanapali Resort, Kapalua beach, and the Hanaloa marine preserve are compelling reasons to stay in this area and more than make up for the extra cost.

Maui Bargains

It's time to discuss free travel dollars and bargain vacations. Pleasant Hawaiian Holidays, a longtime leader in Hawaiian vacations, offers some of the very best available cheapskate deals to Maui. As recently as July 1996 packages from the West Coast were priced as low as $519 for eight days including air, rental car, and lodging at the Aston Maui Park resort. If free dollars are being used, the net cost is an astounding $369 per person. Of course, Pleasant Hawaiian package prices do change depending on travel economics and travel seasons. In addition, Pleasant Hawaiian offers packages to the Royal Kahana, one of their selected oceanfront properties.

My associate recently inspected the Aston Maui Park property and confirmed its excellent location near Lahaina. She inspected several units at the condominium property and was impressed. Although Aston Maui Park is not beachfront, it does have a lovely pool area. The interiors of the units are well furnished and very pleasant to view. What's best is its location, several miles from the Kaanapali Resort and Lahaina Town, and only a mile or so from the award-winning Kapalua beach. If you can get this package you should grab it! It is truly the best cheapskate bargain available to this island paradise.

I received mixed signals from two different Pleasant Hawaiian representatives. You may or may not find it difficult to book the low-end advertised special packages. But one source informs me there are a limited number of low-priced packages available for each flight. Be diligent and flexible in nailing down one of these packages. If you are using free travel cash, keep close tabs on ITH or its selected travel agency to ensure they get you the necessary booking. Good luck!

Pleasant Hawaiian Tours offers a Royal Kahana package for studio units. In May 1995 Pleasant Hawaiian offered an eight-day, seven-night package at a Royal Kahana studio priced at $730. The peak season price was $749. Of course, the price drops if you are using free travel cash or a 5 percent rebate. The lowest net price using free travel cash would be about $580 per person.

➡ **Steve's Tip:** *Upon arrival at the airport pick up a handful of money-saving local publications. The best are the rectangular weekly magazines* Maui Gold, This Week in Maui, *and* Today. *You not only learn what is going on during your week or two of vacation but will also find many money-saving discounts and coupons. These magazines also contain great free maps of Maui that are detailed and in sections, each covering a different part of the island.*

Check out any of the many advertised deals. Perhaps you can do better than the Royal Kahana (yes, there are many other top-notch condos in the area). There is certainly plenty of competition among properties these days. Just ask the right questions, stay near Lahaina, choose a condominium over a hotel room, and compare amenities that are important to you. The convenience of your own washer/dryer (such as our studios provide) may not, at first, be apparent. Consider that you can then take fewer clothes and will never find yourself sitting around some laundry room waiting for your wash. Remember, comfort and convenience are major goals when planning your tropical dream vacation. Select a condominium that is oceanfront and has its own beach. You want to be near the water's edge and enjoy spectacular views and golden sunsets. In whale season we sit on our lanai and watch humpback whales swimming by. Need I say more!

Following are some very special Maui recommendations. These are some nuts-and-bolts suggestions that may save big dollars and, perhaps even more important, turn a good vacation into a fantastic, memorable one.

Maui Restaurants

Kimo's: (in Lahaina at 845 Front Street, on the ocean side, at the north end of town) Kimo's is an absolute must! Arrive between 5:00 and 5:30 P.M. for a romantic sunset dinner. Dining is upstairs. Ask for a table along the rail for the best sunset view. The decor is rustic, featuring gas tiki lamps. The food is excellent. Prices are inexpensive to moderate, with entrées priced from $12 to $20. Kimo's special salad accompanies each entrée. My carnivorous recommendations include the teriyaki steak and the specialty, Kuola barbecued ribs in plum sauce. They also sell neat T-shirts! Kimo's comes through year after year with the best bargain sunset dinner in Maui.

Moanna Terrace: (in the Maui Marriott Hotel at the south end of Kaanapali Beach) This is absolutely our favorite hotel restaurant, another "must-do" on our bargain eatery list. The Marriott is an upscale hotel adjoining the top-rated Maui Hyatt Regency Hotel. It offers that scarce combination of elegant surroundings and incredibly low prices. For the past eight years it has offered the best cheapskate-priced prime rib buffet in the Hawaiian chain. The bargain bonanza continues in 1996 at the super-low price of just $13.95.

In addition to mouth-watering prime rib, the meal includes garlic mashed potatoes, fish and chicken dishes, and an incredible array of soups, salads, and exotic desserts. Prime rib too rare? Their chef will cook it to your specifications on the nearby open grill.

Some logistics: The prime rib buffet is offered only on Friday evenings. Immediately upon arrival, once you have settled in, call the Moanna Terrace and make a 5:00 P.M. or 5:30 P.M. reservation. This ensures that you will enjoy a super sunset dinner from the restaurant's open veranda seating. Also, you will dine to lively Hawaiian music at the hotel's luau as it swings into action a couple of hundred feet away.

Let me also reassure you that all is not lost if you are a vegetarian or simply desire a lighter meal. This year the restaurant is offering a soup, salad bar, and baked potato buffet. This midweek buffet is available Monday through Thursday at the bargain price of $10.95. Do not wait, call (808) 667-1200 and ask for the Moanna Terrace.

Swan Court: (in the Hyatt Regency Maui at the south end of Kaanapali Beach) Okay, you do not usually go out for breakfast. Suffer and go. This is not just any breakfast. It is another romantic "must-do" place. A gourmet buffet breakfast is served from about 7:00 A.M. to noon. It has a wonderful tropical setting with tables adjoining the hotel's lagoon and waterfall. You may even find the swans swimming up to your table. The cost is $16.25. Goodies include all the standards plus fresh local fruit and omlettes cooked to order. After breakfast be sure to tour the hotel lobby, with its $7,000 blue macaw parrot. Check out the South American penguin pool. (Yes, penguins!) Also be sure to tour the hotel's multimillion-dollar art collection. For reservations, call (808) 661-1234.

Longhis: (in Lahaina, at the north end of town, 888 Front Street) My sister and brother-in-law are longtime customers and swear this is the best continental restaurant in the area. It is an open-air restaurant and pleasantly decorated, but prices are on the high side. Their "thing" is a verbal menu and their scallops are "to die for." You also want to try their Prawns Amaretto. Call (808) 667-2288.

Hard Rock Cafe: (in Lahaina, on Front Street at the north end of town, across from Longhis) Great burgers and basics for moderate prices (under $10). Spacious and funky, decorated in the usual golden fifties motif with loud rock music. It sports the obligatory souvenir counter selling Maui Hard Rock shirts, hats, jackets, and so forth. For information, call (808) 667-7400.

The Grill and Bar at Kapalua: (on the eighteenth hole of the Kapalua Bay Golf Course) This is a nice splurge restaurant on the magnificent Kapalua golf course. Their special dinner entrées are priced from $17.95 (shrimp and scallop linguine) to $23.95 (Australian rack of lamb). Be sure to try their Hawaiian Hula Pie (easily enough for two). And be sure to check out Kapalua Condominium's lovely boutiques. Call (808) 669-5653.

Moose McGillycuddys: (in Lahaina on Front Street, on the mountain side of the street) A real hip, funky, fun place. Located on the second floor, it overlooks Front Street. This fun restaurant serves everything from burgers to prime rib and Mexican dishes. Prices are great, at $5 to $15 for most meals. Check *Maui Gold* for discount dinner coupons. Early-bird dinners, from 5:30 to 6:30 P.M., are even better deals, at $9.00 for prime rib. Call (808) 667-7758 for information.

➡ **Steve's "Dancing" Tip:** *Check out Moose McGillycuddys daily happy hour, at 3:00 P.M. to 6:00 P.M., and live music and dancing nightly, 9:00 P.M. to 2:00 A.M.*

Kobe Steak House: (136 Dickenson Street, Lahaina) This is a great choice for a delicious and fun dinner. Kobe provides authentic knife-wielding teppanyaki-hibachi artists who prepare steak, lobster, shrimp, scallops, and chicken at your table. Kobe is a super bargain pick if you are using your free dinner coupon from an Entertainment edition. Full dinners start at only $13.90 for chicken teriyaki and $19.90 for hibachi steak. And remember, these are full dinners that include an appetizer (teppan shrimp), soup (shabu-shabu), vegetables, rice, and tea. Call (808) 667-5555 for reservations.

After your meal hang a left out the door, stroll along Lahaina's Front Street, and enjoy the ocean view and many shops and galleries.

Planet Hollywood: Be sure to check out Lahaina's newest glitzy palace, Planet Hollywood. It opened recently and should be a "hoot." Head over to 744 Front Street in Lahaina Town to enjoy savory specialties such as St. Louis Ribs with a Maui onion barbecue sauce ($13.95), burger platters ($6.95), and spicy chicken and tomato pasta ($11.95). Or enjoy their simple Planet of the Apes concoction, made with Bacardi black rum, banana and blackberry liqueurs, fresh banana, and juices ($5.95). For information, call (808) 667-7877.

Fast-Food Hints: There is limited fast-food delivery available. Dominos Pizza has recently been servicing the Kaanapali and Kahana areas, and there are many fast-food restaurants in Lahaina. There is also a good food court in the Lahaina Mall. As you drive the road from Lahaina to Kahana you will see most of the well-known fast-food emporiums à la McDonalds, Jack in the Box, and others.

For good take-out food check out the new shopping center, Napili Plaza, located about a mile north of Kahana via the Honoapiilani Highway heading toward Napili. You will see it on the left. Its large supermarket has a good gourmet take-out counter with all sorts of goodies, including Chinese food.

➡ **Steve's Tip:** *Unless you're allergic to potato chips, they are a must in Maui. Buy the red bag, Kitch'in Cook'd brand. They are the original handmade Maui chips. Safeway may have them, or try any other small or large store. Eventually you'll find them. Forget fat for this one. They are incredible. Remember: Accept no substitutes!*

Northern Beaches
Black Rock

You will need a map of Kaanapali and the west coast of Maui. The easiest and best local snorkeling is at Black Rock, located in front of the Sheraton Maui hotel, at the very north end of Kaanapali Beach. Park your car at the Whalers Village garage, in the center of the Kaanapali complex. It will cost only $3 to $5 to park for the day, but less if you use a *Maui Gold* discount parking coupon. Then enjoy a stroll through the Whalers Village shopping complex as you head toward the beach. Hang a right on the beach and keep walking until you can walk no more. You have arrived at Black Rock, the large outcropping on your left.

It is now time to park your towel and jump in. For clearer water and greater abundance of marine life, swim around the rock, away from most snorkelers. The water is about twenty feet deep and you may see divers below. It is a popular novice dive spot. (Bring your own lunch.) Note: The Sheraton Maui hotel is closed and is being literally rebuilt. But this does not affect the great snorkeling.

Kapalua Beach

Voted Best Beach in the United States—which says an awful lot! This is a pristine, horseshoe-shaped beach with beautiful palm trees lining its edges. It has ample coral and marine life and many beginning divers use it for beach dives. It is two miles north of

Kahana on the lower Honoapiilani Highway, just past the Napili Kai Beach Club at Napili Bay. Look for a tiny blue and white sign that says, "Public Beach Access." You will probably shoot past it the first time out. If you get there before 10:00 A.M., parking is available in the small, twenty-car, free pubic parking lot. Otherwise, park on the road, but check your map for exact location. After parking, walk through the small concrete tunnel to the beach. There is also a concrete walkway that goes around the beach. At the extreme north side of the beach is a small shack that sells only basic snacks, so bring a good picnic lunch, including drinks.

Honolua Bay Marine Preserve

Ready to go off the beaten path? Have someone point it out on your map. Take the main Honoapiilani Highway north until the road narrows, then continue north past Fleming Beach Park (dangerous surf—look but don't swim) and Honolua Bay. Next, around the bend in the road are two bays. The first is Mokule'ia Bay and the other is Honolua Bay. They are hard to find, so look carefully for two dirt driveways on the beach side of the road with cars parked on either side. (Recently, cars were barred from using the bumpy, rock-strewn driveway down to the beach—it seems it borders private property near the water's edge.) It is best to park on the road and walk down to the beach. Do not leave anything valuable in your car, since there are occasional break-ins.

Okay, the beach is not all that aesthetically pleasing, with small rocks and ocean debris dotting the landscape, but there are certainly sufficient patches of sand for your towels, and the bay itself is lovely and horseshoe-shaped. The best part of this beach is its coral and marine life, making it probably the finest snorkeling beach on Maui. You may expect to find many large and colorful parrot fish and turtles. Enter the water and follow the reef to the furthest point on your right, passing over a lot of sand until you reach the coral beds. The bay's coral gardens are a silent testament to the beauty of Maui's undersea world. On the flip side, a storm will cause poor visibility for a few days. When in doubt, stand on the road and look down at the bay, and if you see a brown ribbon of muddy water near shore, this is a sure sign of poor visibility.

Southern Beaches
Makena Beach

This is the largest and best white-sand beach on the island. It is remotely located on the very southern part of west Maui, past Kihei and Wailea, and is a solid winner. Take your lunch and snorkeling equipment, check your map, and then follow the road signs. Head south on Highway 31 until it becomes a small, narrow road. When you finally pass the Maui Prince Hotel on your right, you are one mile from the beach. As you head into the last undeveloped area on west Maui you will see signs for Makena Beach. For the nature enthusiasts, walk to the far northern end of the beach, climb up and over the rock ledge, and then descend into adjoining Little Makena Beach, West Maui's only nude beach. Little Makena also offers some of the Maui's best snorkeling, which includes views of eels and octopus.

Ulua Beach

This fine beach is also south of Kihei. There are two routes you may choose from. If you want to leisurely explore Kihei and its hotels and small shopping centers, take South Kihei Road all the way to Wailea. Or you may take the four-lane expressway (Pi'ilani Highway 31) to Wailea, then go south on South Kihei Road for about one mile. Ulua Beach Park is just past the Stouffer Wailea Beach Resort. Look for a small sign with an arrow for Ulua Beach. The beach has a large free public parking lot and great showers. Follow the walkway past rest rooms and showers and you have arrived. The reef is long and shallow and extends quite a distance. You can even view Molokini from here. Arrive in the early morning, because the winds kick up waves in the afternoon, causing underwater visibility to decrease significantly. Park your towel under the trees at the top of the hill and savor the great view.

Boats, Snorkeling, and Diving

Lahaina Divers: This is Maui's largest diving operation, which offers two- and three-tank trips to Lanai and Molokini. It is located in downtown Lahaina. Prices are about $95 for two tanks and $125 for three. The three-tank dive is cost-effective and more leisurely, since the boat makes only one trip for the day, whereas two-tank boats rush back for a second afternoon run. Call (800) 998-3483 for reservations or a brochure. In Lahaina call 667-7496.

Captain Nemo's: (in Lahaina, on Dickenson Street) The largest dive-accessory shop in the area. Check to see what, if any, boat trips they are running.

Molokini: This is the famous horseshoe volcanic rim jutting out of the water thirty miles or so from Lahaina and fifteen miles from the southwest Maui coast. It is a marine preserve about seventy feet deep and a definite must for snorkelers and divers. But the water may get rough, and boats often abort the trip. Consequently, there is no guarantee you will make it on the first try. The water is usually very clear and harbors prolific marine life. Most boats leave from the main harbor south of Lahaina. You must get up *really* early for this one, but it is worth it.

Another alternative is a long, early morning drive to Ma'alaea Harbor. If you are willing to drive even farther, to the Kihei boat harbor, the boat ride to Molokini is only thirty minutes, compared to the one hour or more to Molokini from Lahaina.

Zodiac Rafting: Hawaiian Rafting Adventures offers a "must-do" adventure. Patty and I had been visiting Maui for many years and thought we had run out of new activities when I spotted a free raft cruise coupon in my Entertainment book. In a flash we were off on a six-person Zodiac raft traveling at high speed from Maui to the nearby island of Lanai. Our raft circumnavigated Lanai, something we had not previously experienced. We stopped to snorkel in pristine lightly-visited coves. We enjoyed the scenery, marine life, and the exhilarating raft trip. If you expect to stay dry *do not* sign on for this trip. This adventure is also expensive, at $120 per ticket, which includes lunch, drinks, and snacks. The current Entertainment edition includes a very valuable two-for-one coupon for a free one-half-day raft adventure with Hawaiian Rafting Adventures. Their price for the half-day trip is $59.

Navitek II: This is Maui's premier snorkel voyage on a fabulous catamaran. It is costly, at $120 per person. For that high tariff you receive a leisurely six-hour cruise to Lanai, with plenty of time to snorkel. The food is tops, and includes a super barbecue. Best of all, the 1996 Hawaii Entertainment Edition has a discount coupon for this one.

Windjammer Cruise: I cannot personally vouch for this one.

However, I am listing it because the Entertainment 1996 Edition offers a two-for-one dinner cruise coupon. Windjammer expects to be offering the same free dinner coupon in Entertainment's 1997 edition. Their dinner cruise off the west Maui coast is regularly priced at $50 for an open bar, prime rib and Alaska salmon buffet. (Did I mention the spectacular views of west Maui, which includes volcanic peaks and meandering pineapple fields from any craft sailing off Maui's west coast?)

Scotch Mist Sailing Charters: This company offers a one-half-day snorkel expedition to the reefs off nearby Lanai, on which you will tour coral gardens and perhaps "mingle" with giant sea turtles. In fact, I have done just that (yes, mingle with turtles) on many occasions. I have a treasured videotape of myself touring coral gardens side-by-side with giant sea turtles at a distance of about eighteen inches—or less. The half-day journey includes juice, fresh pineapple, chips, beer, wine, and sodas. A free two-for-one coupon is available in the Hawaii Entertainment Edition.

Frogman and Seabird: Patty and I took the Frogman half-day snorkel cruise to Lanai. *The Frogman* is a fifty-five-foot catamaran and leaves daily out of Maalaea Harbor. It offers a fun, comfortable sailing adventure, with good food and a happy-go-lucky crew. The daily 7:00 A.M. to 1:00 P.M. trips are priced at $55. Call (808) 661-3333.

➡ **Steve's Tip:** *A fine discount operation runs out of a shop at 834 Front Street in Lahaina. Call (808) 661-8889. Barefoot Cash Back Tours has "wheels" of cards describing almost every available recreational activity on Maui. Customers receive a 10 percent discount for cash or travelers' checks and a 7 percent discount for credit cards purchases. For example, a customer who books Lahaina Divers' three-tank dive for two ($250) receives a $25 discount.*

I first check all available local advertising and my trusty Entertainment book. When all else fails, Barefoot's service and discounts are appreciated, if not overly hefty. Barefoot has been operating for almost ten years and its employees offer helpful and, oftentimes, valuable information on water- and land-based tour options.

Odds and Ends

Lahaina Town: Lahaina's many charms are described throughout this chapter. It retains much of its old world character, with its quaint main street that runs along the ocean. You may enjoy Lahaina anytime. At night, however, it comes to life, with shops and restaurants of every type and description, from Planet Hollywood to the Hard Rock Cafe. The Lahaina Center, behind the Hard Rock Cafe, offers low-cost parking. This is the least congested part of town and a good place to start your walking tour.

The older but still-fun Wharf complex toward the southern end of Lahaina, across from the park with the largest banyon tree on Maui. The Wharf, built vertically on three floors, is full of shops with reasonable prices. At the southern end of Lahaina is another shopping complex (not all that many stores) simply called 505 Front Street. Free underground parking is available. It is worth a quick visit.

➡ **Steve's Tip:** *The Lahaina Center offers a free Polynesian dancing show every Wednesday and Friday at 2:00 P.M. This is probably best if you have children, or perhaps you have enjoyed your first day on the beach and have the smarts to be careful, as in "Let's get off the beach and head into town before we are indistinguishable from bright red, ripe tomatoes."*

So, where is Nordstrom? Sorry, not on Maui! However, those wishing a hint of such a luxurious shopping atmosphere should head for the Kapalua shops complex. It is outdoors and consists of luxury shops, jewelry, art, and more. There is also Whalers Village, the largest outdoor "mall" on Maui. Neither looks or feels like a traditional mall. The new Lahaina Cannery Mall, which looks like a cannery with its corrugated metal roof, is worth checking out. The new Safeway is part of this complex, together with Longs Drugs. Or, you can check out Liberty House when you simply must go for some heavy-duty shopping.

Luaus: Is this your first trip to Hawaii? Or, is this your honeymoon? These are two good reasons to take in a luau. Yes, they are a high-priced, fun way to spend an evening under the stars. The price for a luau is $50 to $55 per person for a full dinner, drinks, and the show. The Maui Hyatt Regency offers one of the best, with fire dancers. Every so often the Entertainment book has a free luau coupon.

Movie Theaters: On the third floor of the Wharf Complex is Lahaina Theater, which shows a variety of the best current films and has three screens. I just learned there is another theater in Lahaina, in the new Lahaina Shopping Center at the north end of town, just behind the Hard Rock Cafe. The 1996 Hawaiian Entertainment edition contains two-for-one Wallace Theater coupons good for both of these movie theaters. These are walk-in coupons and not the mail-in type used in regular mainland editions, so you may easily use them during your stay.

The Hawaiian Experience: A domed theater in Lahaina, the Hawaiian Experience has for several years shown a forty-minute-long spectacular movie entitled *Hawaii Island of the Gods*. The theater may seem small from the street, but it sports a three-story, 180-degree domed screen with theater quality sound. It's ticket booth is in a small store at 821 Front Street, from which you cannot see the theater. It shows a great IMAX-type film on Maui (824 Front Street, 808-661-7111). Good discount coupons are found in *Maui Gold* and, of course, the best is the two-for-one admission coupon in the current Hawaiian Entertainment Edition. This is the kind of diversion that is fun when those tropical rains roll in or after dinner. Shows run continuously until 10:00 P.M.

The Maui Tropical Plantation: A fairly recent attraction created on farmland and found halfway between Lahaina and Maui's major airport at Kahalui, the Maui Tropical Plantation is fun and provides an opportunity to take a tram ride though a living tropical farm. You will see 725 acres of tropical gardens and orchards, including banana groves. The eatery offers incredible fruit delights. This is a pleasant diversion, a good one to consider when you are recovering from that first day's sunburn. Remember, you get another free admission if you have your Entertainment book.

The Trip to Hana: The famous trip to Hana on thirty miles of narrow, winding road is a "must-do adventure" if or when you wish spend a day away from the beach. If you have a four-wheel-drive vehicle or carefully chance it with your rental car, you may circumnavigate the entire island of Maui. The final ten miles, from the Seven Sacred Pools to La Perouse Bay, is the most exciting part of the journey, as you bounce over large rocks and ancient lava flows. If there has been recent rain this route quickly floods.

Most visitors do the fifty-mile, one-way trip from Kahului (near the airport) to Hana. This involves two hours of driving thirty miles of narrow winding roads and crossing forty quaint one-lane bridges. Add forty-five minutes back to Lahaina and your total driving for the day is about five and a half hours. Why go, you ask?

The trip to Hana offers you a unique Maui experience. You may stop and swim in clear pools with refreshing waterfalls. The road passes through an ancient rain forest, finally arriving at the remote town of Hana, which is home to many of the world's "rich and famous." Beyond Hana, several miles down the road, are the famed Seven Sacred Pools. I enjoy climbing to the higher pools, where I sit and watch the rushing water cascading from one pool to another until finally the water empties into the sea. This is nature at its water-wonder best.

➡ **Steve's Tip:** *I noticed a coupon in* This Week *magazine for a Hana tape tour for just $9.95 (regularly $20). If your car has a cassette player, this tape helps to entertain and enlighten during the long hours of driving. If you do not have a player they may provide one. Check this out by calling (808) 661-3333, ext. 5.*

Waimoku Falls: Across the road from the Seven Sacred Pools is a hiking path that leads to four-hundred-foot Waimoku Falls. Join a ranger hike if available by calling (808) 248-7375.

Haleakala Volcano: Haleakala is the world's largest dormant volcano. It is 33 miles long and 24 miles wide. Its crater is 7.5 miles long and 2.5 miles wide. Drive to the cool and windy summit, which is 10,000 feet above sea level, the highest peak in Hawaii. This is another "must-do" adventure on which we have experienced the sensational sunrise. Leave your room at 2:30 A.M. and arrive at the summit at 4:30 A.M. The view from the frosty perch, if clear of clouds, is a moonscape unique to planet earth. Even if it is cloudy, the sunrise is fantastic. Afterwards you can take a short walk or long hike into the crater. Take a sweatshirt, jacket, and hat.

There is shelter at the summit and you can await the sunrise in a glass-walled hut. A trip during daylight, if clear of clouds, is just as rewarding and the walk into the crater is spectacular. Bring lunch and perch yourself on a ledge overlooking the craterscape. The park phone number is (808) 572-7749.

Parasailing: I love parasailing. It offers a wonderful quiet ride and spectacular scenery from a unique vantage point several hundred feet above the ocean. Parasailing off west Maui is the best experience ever. The view of Maui's coast, volcanic peaks, pineapple fields, and nearby islands is superb. These seven-minute rides cost about $40. The current Entertainment edition includes a two-for-one coupon for UFO Parasail in Lahaina. You may find other good discounts but not a free ride in *Maui Gold* or *This Week in Maui*. If you have not tried it, you should! (Note: Regulations prohibit parasailing during the winter whale season months from November to May.)

➡ **Steve's Tip:** *There is one Maui adventure I have yet to enjoy—the thirty-eight-mile downhill bicycle ride from the summit of Haleakala. Presently, many companies offer these rides, using state-of-the-art bicycles with megabrakes. Maui Downhill has run these trips for thirteen years. The better trips include lead and rear guides using radios, and offer breakfast on the sunrise trips. The typical full-day trips run about $100, while Maui Downhill offers an abbreviated twenty-two-mile trip for just $48. Call (808) 871-2155. Also, consider Maui Mountain Cruisers which has ten years' experience. Their price is $99 for the full thirty-eight-mile ride. The operators provide helmets, windbreakers, and gloves. You are picked up at your condo or hotel, bused to the summit, and from there it is all downhill. Remember to check all the magazines for discounts. Also check with Barefoot Tours in Lahaina for their 10 percent discount.*

Maui remains a special place in my heart and mind. For most, a visit to Maui is to fall in love with the island and its people and to look forward to the day when you will be returning. Discover Maui for yourself just as soon as you are able. *Mahalo!*

8

Dirt-Cheap London

London is one of those world-class cities that may justifiably appear on your list of dream vacations. First, I will point the way to air and land packages at true cheapskate prices. With that accomplished, I will provide personal insights, interesting options, and money-saving tips to enhance your London vacation.

In January 1995 Patty and I spent an eight-day vacation in and around London. Our whirlwind London theater experience included *Miss Saigon*, *Sunset Boulevard*, *She Loves Me*, and *The Inspector Calls*. We made three one-day trips to the countryside, visiting Oxford, Stonehenge, Salisbury, Bath, Warwick Castle, Dover Castle, Canterbury, and Leeds Castle. Using Kraft's free travel cash, the net price for the entire vacation package was only $517 per person. This included the airfare from San Francisco, seven nights at Earl's Court Inn, and daily deluxe continental breakfasts. As part of the package American Airlines also gave us a three-day bus and subway pass that we used for intense sightseeing. Did I mention the 11,000 American Airlines program miles I picked up?

Choosing Your Vacation

Off-season travel offers the best rock-bottom prices. Keep in mind that winter travel to England does not necessarily mean horrible weather. In one word, England's weather is unpredictable. Many people use another word to describe it, namely wet. Where exactly does this leave us? I spoke to a friend who traveled to London last summer only to encounter horrid weather every day of his one-week stay. So how does this bode for winter? Believe it or not, in January the rainfall varies only slightly from that in summer months. During our January trip we enjoyed five clear and partly sunny days, with temperatures in the comfortable fifties and sixties. We suffered only a few days of intermittent drizzle. A good way to plan your bargain London getaway is to scan the advertisements in your newspaper's weekend travel section. The best winter rates appear in the late summer, fall, and winter.

In our case, I found American Airlines advertising budget European packages that proclaimed cheapskate prices. Earlier, I suggested travel on American Airlines, assuming most readers are tied in to its superior program as a means of collecting thousands of additional AAdvantage program miles. Our London vacation was one of those golden opportunities. I was totally impressed by America's London on Your Own package, which included six nights, airfare from the West Coast, daily breakfasts, and a three-day London subway and bus pass. The six-night package price was a bargain at only $669 per person. I immediately called American Airlines to learn whether an extra seventh night was available so that I could put my free travel cash to good use. (Most airline packages permit the add-on of extra days.) In this case a seventh night was available at the reasonable cost of $40 per person.

I immediately booked the vacation through Liberty Travel's toll-free number. The $717 price per person was further reduced by $400 with our free Kraft travel dollars for a net price of $517 per person.

In addition to your newspaper's weekend travel section, American Airlines' tour desk is a wealth of information and may be contacted, at (800) 832-8383, for current packages, prices, and brochures. However, keep in mind that some brochures do not reflect all of the airline's latest bargain packages.

United Airlines' 1996 bargain tours include an eight-day land and air package to London for only $692. This package uses the Duke of Leister Hotel and departs from the West Coast. Departures from New York with a higher grade of air service are priced at $625, and from Chicago at $674.

I earned a bonanza of 11,000 AAdvantage program miles by using American Airlines' "London on Your Own" package. In the 1996 program, prices for an eight-day vacation including air, hotel, and breakfast, start at $604 from New York, $653 from Chicago, and $761 from San Francisco or Los Angeles. The math is easy. If you have free dollars to spend, deduct $150 and then get up to 11,000 program miles if traveling from the West Coast. The miles alone equals almost one-half of a free domestic round-trip ticket!

➡ **Steve's Tip:** *When calling American Airlines regarding bargain packages, be sure to request all available information on their selected hotels. Be ready to ask questions about amenities, parking, hotel location, available Underground stops, buses, and so forth.*

Patty and I stayed at the Earl's Court Inn, a twelve-story superior tourist hotel, built in 1971 and renovated in 1992. All of its 505 rooms have a private bath with a shower or tub, hair dryer, radio, color TV, phone, and coffee/tea maker. There is a full restaurant/pub on the second floor. The inn is two miles from Victoria Station and eleven miles from Heathrow Airport. It is only two blocks from the nearest subway, and there is a bus stop directly in front of the hotel.

Our room there was small but very comfortable, and its location proved to be a great asset. By subway it is only three or four stops to Piccadilly Circus, the heart of London. Also on the plus side, because it is on the perimeter of the city we easily drove to the nearby M4 freeway to exit the city for our day trips, which helped us avoid the inner-city weekday rush hour traffic.

The hotel charges $13 per day for car parking. However, I used free overnight street parking and retrieved the car prior to the 9:00 A.M. "free parking" deadline. Each block has a parking ticket box selling day parking tickets that are placed on the car's dashboard.

The inn's daily breakfasts were great! An entire dining room on the second floor serves as the breakfast room, where an international crowd gathered each morning for an assortment of cereals, croissants, jams, jellies, coffee, and tea. Each morning the staff prepared a pot of fresh steaming hot chocolate in response to my special request, and they also produced the skim milk I requested. These filling breakfasts got each day off to a fine start; and they were more than we expected for the bargain price. I have no hesitation in recommending Earls Court Inn as a fine bargain-priced hotel.

Before leaving the states I arranged a car rental for our country day trips through All England Car Rentals at (800) 241-3228. The best part of the rental was their local pickup facility outside central London and only two miles or so from Earls Court Inn. Now we could pick up a car midweek for use during the final three days of our stay. As an extra bonus, we also used the car for our departure run to Heathrow Airport, and incurred no drop-off charge. Rental cost was about $50 per day, which included all taxes.

➡ **Steve's Tip:** *Before we left the United States we purchased an Entertainment publication, the London/U.K. edition. We used the book for everything from pub meals to a free half-day Frames bus tour of Windsor Castle. This coupon saved us $35, more than the cost of the book.*

London Itinerary

To give you an overview, we did four days of sightseeing in London, enjoyed four nights of top-notch theater, and then embarked on three one-day trips to the countryside.

We arrived in London at 7:00 A.M. via a red-eye flight from New York. Our sleeping strategy worked well and I enjoyed my five-seat "bed in the sky." However, four hours of sleep does not quite do it for me. My back-up strategy had us check in to Earls Court Inn and head to Covent Garden. This proved to be an excellent early-morning plan.

Covent Gardens: This is a mostly outdoor experience, with its boutiques, restaurants, street artists, and vendors. The cool fresh air was a wonderful tonic, keeping us wide awake as we took in the sights and sounds. Also, I correctly pegged Covent Garden as a "no brainer." This is not a historic, religious, or political place. Rather, it is a people mecca, a place to enjoy good food, drink, and major people-watching. The outdoor stalls resemble a mini–flea market and offer quality crafted items such as hats, scarves, and gloves. This was a perfect first stop. In the dead center of Covent Garden is a great baked potato restaurant, one of the "in" places these days. It serves huge baked potatoes smothered with every imaginable sauce and topping. (I had an Italian meat sauce. Magnifico!)

I highly recommend any of the half-day city bus tours of London; many conveniently leave from Piccadilly Circus. They are inexpensive and provide an instant view of the city.

London Theater: This activity was high on our list. We booked most of our shows in advance of our trip through one of the most well-respected New York ticket agencies, Edwards and Edwards. Their phone numbers are (800) 223-6108, (800) 366-4845, and (212) 944-0290. I do ask you to appreciate that this is one pleasure that does not come cheap, which was especially true when I insisted on the best close-up orchestra seats available. I am talking third-row center for *Sunset Boulevard* and sixth-row center for *Miss Saigon*. In dollars and cents this luxury set us back $73 per ticket. The prices are similar to those in Los Angeles and New York, though they include a small $6 to $8 charge for Edwards' excellent service.

Madame Tussaud's Wax Museum: Patty and I bit the attraction bullet and entered the world of the famous Madame Tussaud's Wax Museum. I was surprised to find that the museum covers an entire city block. First of all, do not expect to see simple window displays of dull-looking wax figures. This place is an incredible multi-level experience in which visitors become an actual part of most of the major exhibits. No, that does not mean we were doused in wax and placed on display. It does mean you will find yourself walking in and through extended exhibits, among lifelike reproductions of the most loved and feared historic personalities. I marveled at other visitors stopping to take some of the funniest pictures one can imagine. Moments later we joined right in. Patty took an excellent shot of me standing next to Princess Di. The museum is also high-tech, for the visit ends with a Disney-type attraction (similar to "Pirates of the Caribbean" at Disneyland) with a trip through three hundred years of British history. I leave you to imagine the lifelike animated wax figures in this attraction. My rating for this experience is: excellent four-star fun!

Other "must-do" cultural and historic stops included the London Museum, the London Tower, and, of course, Buckingham Palace. Unfortunately the palace tour was not available in January. But I particularly enjoyed our visit to the Cabinet War Rooms built beneath downtown London. This was the heart of the British command center during World War II, and it included Winston Churchill's headquarters. This is my kind of living history. The restored underground complex is at Clive Steps, King Charles St., London. Call (071) 930-6961. I highly recommend it.

Castles and Other Countryside Attractions

Patty and I splurged on a full-day, commercial bus tour using Frames Tours.

Canterbury

Our first stop was the town of Canterbury, which is a two-and-one-half-hour drive east of London. The town is known for one thing and one thing only—it is the seat of the Anglican church and home of Canterbury Cathedral. The cathedral contains medieval tombs of such royals as King Henry IV and Edward the Black Prince. Canterbury Cathedral is most notorious as the site of the murder of Thomas Becket, in 1170. (Yes—1170—long before the United States was a sparkle in anyone's eye.) Four knights of King Henry II murdered the archbishop of Canterbury. I found myself standing on the spot, inside the cathedral, where the evil deed was done. Fortunately, the cathedral survived World War II intact, although its stained-glass windows were temporarily removed. Spend an hour or two studying the cathedral and its history. It is open from November to April between the hours of 8:45 A.M. and 5:00 P.M. From May to October it is open from 8:45 A.M. to 7:00 P.M. Admission is free.

After visiting the cathedral, we then spent an hour or so exploring the lovely town of Canterbury. It has a quaint winding main street with shops of all kinds. We were on our own for lunch and had no problem finding a local pub, where we enjoyed a splendid meal. In short order we were off for Dover, a short drive away on the English coast, about seventy-five miles east of London.

Dover Castle

For more than 2,000 years, Dover Castle was used to protect England's coast from a foreign invasion. More recently, during World War II, the castle housed sophisticated communications. As one of the best-known castles in England, it returns one to medieval times and is a fine artifact of Britain's past: King Henry II built it in the twelfth century. The castle's keep and outer walls are intact and easily toured. The keep is the most elaborate rectangular tower keep in Britain. Best is the view from its top, at a height of about four hundred feet.

Also, below the castle, deep in the Dover cliffs, is Hellfire Corner. This series of underground passages and rooms served as a command post during World War II. The forty-five-minute tour takes visitors to the rooms visited by Winston Churchill during the war. Our full-day tour continued with another short drive to Leeds Castle.

Leeds Castle

Leeds Castle, also known as Maidstone in Kent, is considered the loveliest castle in England. Before our trip I found a photograph of Leeds and decided it was either touched-up or computer-enhanced. No surviving castle could exude the charm and beauty I was viewing—or could it? Known as the Queen's Castle, Leeds was built about nine hundred years ago and was the royal residence for six of England's medieval queens and the country home of King Henry VIII. The castle has been lovingly and meticulously restored and now is the home of a superb collection of medieval furnishings, paintings, tapestries, and other treasures. I am told that tours of the inside of the castle are limited, although our Frames guide got us in.

The castle's setting is beyond even Hollywood's wildest, romantic dreams. It sits on two small islands in the middle of an encircling lake. The lake is itself surrounded by the greenery of park lands covered with thick trees and hills. The five-hundred-acre park also includes lakes and waterfalls. Plan to spend three hours to fully enjoy the castle and its interior. Most curious and fascinating is its unique collection of dog collars. It covers a period of more than four hundred years and is the world's largest! (When I say collars, I mean *collars*, including large metal-studded ones for great danes.) The castle is open from March to October from 10:00 A.M. to 5:00 P.M. and from November to February from 10:00 A.M. to 3:00 P.M. The castle is a one-and-one-half-hour drive east of London. For those with at least one romantic bone in their body, Leeds Castle is an unforgettable "must-see" place. The cost of this fine tour is approximately $55 per person and is worth every penny!

We rented a car for two additional day trips, mimicking commercial tour routes while traveling at our own pace. On our first day trip we drove to Stonehenge, Salisbury, and Bath.

Stonehenge

For me Stonehenge is an ominous, eery, twilight-zone place, like Easter Island. It offers visitors a chance to speculate about the origin of the artifacts and what role UFOs may have played in the history of the stones. Simply stated, it was a "must-see" sight on my list of worldwide oddities. Unfortunately, they did not tell me what I now reveal: Beware the monsoon weather that often soaks visitors from head to toe.

Patty stayed in the car as I headed into fifty-mile-per-hour winds and a rainstorm that would have caused Noah to shudder. In one very "wet" sense it added to the mystique. There I was, walking backward, forging one step at a time, soaked to the bone as wind and water assaulted me from all directions. I counted only four or five other hard-core visitors. Slowly I made my way around the circle only to discover visitors are not permitted to walk the entire 360 degrees. Reluctantly, I had to backtrack from the halfway point. I used my trusty Pentax WR-90, which lived up to its promise of being waterproof. By constantly cleaning the lens, I managed to get about half my shots in sharp focus. By the time I returned to our car I was a human puddle. Later I learned they call this place Salisbury Plain and that this weather, especially high wind, is common.

The circle of monolithic stones is found about ninety miles southwest of London and nine miles north of Salisbury. Britain's most precious stone monuments were "created" about 4,000 to 5,000 years ago. The large boulders used to construct the giant stone pillars weigh two to three tons. To this day, the purpose and meaning of Stonehenge remains unclear. Some believe it was an ancient astronomical observatory used to predict eclipses. In the end one is left to imagine whether this was the site of ancient ceremonies or human sacrifices. Others believe it was the site of a burial ground. Admission is $4. The site is open November to March, from 10:00 A.M. to 4:00 P.M.; June to August, from 10:00 A.M. to 7:00 P.M.; and April, May, and September, from 10:00 A.M. to 6:00 P.M.

Salisbury

Salisbury is home of the famed Salisbury Cathedral, built in the early thirteenth century and one of the best of England's surviving ancient cathedrals. As we entered the town, we were greeted by the cathedral's towering spire. The chapter house contains one of the four surviving copies of the Magna Carta. The town itself offers many shops and pubs. Because of the horrendous weather, our visit to Salisbury was abbreviated, though memorable.

Bath

Bath was the final stop on our first independent day tour, and the best was saved for last. A bit of good fortune permitted the weather to suddenly cooperate.

Bath is a major historical and archeological destination. In 75 A.D. the Romans founded Aquae Sulis, a settlement that later became known as Bath. The Romans applied their advanced engineering techniques to create the Roman baths, and used the area's natural hot springs for recreation and to enjoy their curative "powers." The baths offer some of England's finest examples of surviving Roman structures. The Temple of Sulis Minerva was excavated in the eighteenth century and is open for viewing. The main pump room resembles a large swimming pool in an open courtyard. Today one sees and feels the warm waters feeding the pool from the same hot spring the Romans enjoyed over 1,000 years ago. Inside, we enjoyed viewing the displays of Roman hot tubs, plumbing, and artifacts and excavations in a museum. In the Victorian era the city took on a new life and it was literally rebuilt in the eighteenth century, when celebrities from Queen Anne to Charles Dickens enjoyed visits to Bath. Our visit was fulfilling in every respect.

Bath is also home to Bath Abbey, built in the late sixteenth century. The site has been home to abbeys since the sixth century. The Bath Abbey Heritage Vaults offer an interpretation of the Christian history of the abbey from 75 A.D. to the present. They display findings of recent excavations, including an eight-hundred-year-old skeleton of a woman and some models of Bath comparing the city from about the thirteenth century to the modern day. The Museum of Costumes displays a fine collection of fashions covering the past four hundred years. Sally Lunn's Museum displays the cellars of the oldest house in Bath, Roman and medieval foundations, a nine-hundred-year-old bakery, and stalagmites.

Outdoor activities in Bath include one-hour boat rides on the river Avon and strolling through the Georgian Gardens. The city has recreated the garden to the original (circa 1770) designs of the flower beds, paths, and trellis. In addition, there are many shops, pubs, and restaurants. Bath is another "must-see" destination.

Oxford

The second of our two independent day trips found us driving an hour west of London to Oxford. The weather was finally sunny and dry, which added a highlight to our visit. Of course, the city is best known for eight-hundred-year-old Oxford University. I found myself immersed in a medieval university town. As we left the busy main street, we stepped back hundreds of years in time. Suddenly, stop lights and cars vanished, replaced by numerous ancient college buildings, functioning today as they were five to seven hundred years ago. I could not help but compare the British time line to that of the United States, founded only two hundred years ago.

A fine walking tour leaves hourly from the town's visitor center. Since we missed that tour we set out on our own, trusty Oxford map, available at the visitor center, in hand. The map identified each of the many academic buildings. We followed sign posts to the visitor center at the old school, Gloucester Green. One after another, we viewed the many colleges, marveling at the architecture and durability of these ancient buildings.

Most colleges open their quadrangles and chapels to visitors in the afternoon. Unfortunately, we were touring during the lunch hours. Despite this, we found many open doorways leading to quadrangles. One very interesting quadrangle was built around an old cemetery with horizontal gravestones whose dates stretch back several hundred years. We sat on a nearby bench contemplating the serene scene. In each instance we simply walked in and disregarded the "closed" signs.

Christ Church has the largest of Oxford's quadrangles and the Tom Tower. Bodleian Library is more impressive, with its collection of more than five *million* books, which includes rare books and manuscripts. The Sheldonian Theater was built in 1664 and is still used for concerts today. The Tower of St. Michael at the North Gate is the oldest building in Oxford and has the best view of the city and surrounding countryside from the top of this tower.

Upon leaving the colleges we were thrust back into the twentieth century. The bustling city of Oxford has a charm of its own and more restaurants and shops than one can check out in a single day. We grabbed a couple of sandwiches from one of the student shops and relaxed in an open tree-lined square. This was a splendid, satisfying, and memorable stop. For a moment, just a moment, I felt like heading to the registration office and enrolling. Owing to the fact that our schedule was flexible, we went overtime in Oxford and decided to complete the day with a visit to Warwick Castle.

Warwick Castle

The town of Warwick is ninety-two miles northwest of London and has one of England's best preserved and most popular medieval castles, with fifty-five acres of landscaped grounds and gardens. The original castle was built by the daughter of King Alfred the Great in 914. The original mound and walls survive to the present. The castle was rebuilt in stone in the fourteenth century and became home of the medieval earls of Warwick. To this day it has changed little.

I was surprised to learn that Warwick is now operated by the Tussauds Group, the same Tussaud that owns London's famed wax museum. This translates into one big plus for the castle—a winning Tussaud exhibit, housed within the confines of the castle's private apartments, that is impressive. Tussaud turned this area of the castle into a living museum with thirty wax figures that emulate a "period party." Guests include the duke of Wales, the duchess of Devonshire and the duke and duchess of Warwick. In the drawing room we were amused as we watched and listened to singer Clara Butt performing with a piano accompanist. Perhaps even more fun was the dungeon, with its animated "speaking" wax figures, such as artisans crafting arrows, a blacksmith making iron weapons, and a knight being fitted for battle.

The remaining State Rooms and the Great Hall of the castle offer an impressive array of furnishings, paintings, and art treasures of all kinds and descriptions. The torture chamber offers unique reminders of unkind days. The armory contains a collection of more than 1,000 pieces of armor and weapons, including lifesize horses in full armor.

Warwick lives up to all its promises and is a "must-see" castle. It is intriguing, fun, entertaining, and informative. It is as close as one comes to living history and is certainly an English treasure.

We so enjoyed the visit, the people, and the city of London that we eagerly look forward to revisiting. London is, beyond doubt, one of the great historical capitals of the world.

9

Dirt-Cheap Paris

Paris is like no other city in the world. It sparkles with unbridled beauty and revels in its turbulent history. Barely three months had passed since our return from England where Patty and I were preparing to leave for Paris, the "City of Lights."

Only days earlier I received yet another Entertainment book, this time the Paris edition. Not only was I becoming a collector of international editions, I now had one that was entirely in French. Reading French discount coupons is a real challenge. This trip also marked a milestone of sorts: I was using the last of my Kraft free travel dollars. (More about "dollars and sense" will follow.)

Without doubt, Paris is as exciting a city as it is expensive. This is especially true when traveling in high season. As I expected, our planned April departure met with a substantial jump in air and hotel charges. I was not dissuaded, since "April in Paris" has such a beautiful ring to it. But this time my job was truly cut out for me: I had to come up with a "cheapskate" vacation to Paris in April. Scanning the usual newspapers, I found that the rock-bottom American Airlines package had jumped from $900 for winter season to $1,300 per person for six nights in April. This would simply *not* do!

Enter the Tahiti connection! While reading the weekend travel section, I spotted an intriguing advertisement for a five-night trip to Paris through Los Angeles Airport. The amazing $599 per person package included round-trip airfare, hotel, breakfasts, and all taxes and charges. Now this *was* cheap! The package is run by

France Vacations, using AOM French airlines, through its tour office in Los Angeles. Having traveled to Tahiti several times, we were well acquainted with AOM, the major competitor of Corsair airlines. When landing at Papeete Airport, our 747 jet invariably pulled up to an AOM plane parked at a nearby gate. Both airlines run flights from Paris to Los Angeles and from Los Angeles to Papeete and back.

I called France Vacations and confirmed that, as in the case of our London trip, the extra nights I needed to use the remaining $400 of free travel cash were available—and they were reasonably priced at $45 per night per person. The net cost, after credit for our $400 free Kraft travel cash, was an astounding $565 each. This included nonstop air, an eight-day, seven-night stay at the Hotel Amsterdam in central Paris, daily breakfasts, and all hotel charges. France Vacations rates the Hotel Amsterdam at two stars, which is consistent with the bargain price of the package. Fortunately, AOM provides a brochure called "Le Jardin de Paris," which lists a dozen hotels used in the France Vacations program, and includes descriptions and photographs of the various hotels. We read up on the two- and three-star hotels, their amenities and locations, and choose the Hotel Amsterdam for its price, central location, and small garden. France Vacations may be contacted at (800) 332-5332 for information and a current brochure.

United Airlines' 1996 bargain tour program offers an eight-day, seven-night, air-and-land package to Paris for $656 from Chicago, $770 from New York City, and $745 from the West Coast. Use free travel dollars and the price drops to $506 for an eight-day dream vacation. Call United at (800) 32-TOURS for current package prices.

American Airlines' 1996 "Paris on Your Own" package includes round-trip air, eight-day, seven-night lodging, and breakfasts, and is priced at $789 from New York and $839 from Chicago. The $926 price from San Francisco is too costly. Stick with AOM for the best cheapskate package. Unfortunately, AOM currently flies only between Paris and Los Angeles. (Using an American package offers the extra advantage of adding thousands of air miles to your AAdvantage account. The trip from the West Coast will add about 12,000 miles.)

➡ **Steve's Special East Coast Tip:** *Cheapskate prices and scheduled air travel from Newark or New York (JFK), are available from
Jet Vacations. Their Paris Pas Cher and Riviera Pas Cher packages
offer eight days and seven nights in Paris or Nice, daily continental
breakfasts, and all hotel charges, and are priced at $669 per person.
Since the packages include Air France flights, the price may hit an
all-time New York low of $519 if you use free travel dollars. In Paris
the program includes the Plaisance and Ibis Hotels. Call Jet
Vacations at (800) JET-0999 for brochures. Be ready to use auto
dialer if you have one. Otherwise, be persistent, and you will get
through to one of their friendly operators.*

L'Accordion: Okay, so here is one cheapskate Left Bank restaurant that is not found in any travel guide. Try L'Accordion on Rue
Thoen, near the corner of Rue Monteford. While most low-priced
Paris dinners cost $25 and up, L'Accordion offers a 69-franc dinner
(about $15) that includes an aperitif, appetizer (hot bacon salad or
hot cheese crêpe), four entrées to choose from (we had their half-
chicken coq au vin), and dessert—either flan or chocolate mousse.
This bargain meal includes all service charges. And yes, the
Entertainment book listed this one, so the total bill for the meal
was discounted an *additional* 25 percent! Also, the young crowd
was still spilling into the small restaurant at 9:30 P.M. in the
middle of the week. The bistro sports a cinema motif, with large
posters depicting both American and French films. A great find—
use the Entertainment book!

Rue Monteford Market: There is also a lovely daily street market
on Rue Monteford, a block or so from L'Accordion, where vendors
offer fresh vegetables, meat, flowers, and fruit. Local restaurants
purchase their perishables here in the morning. It's always
bustling with activity, day and night. In the evening, we explored
the area's restaurants, cafes, jazz clubs, sandwich shops, and ice
cream joints, and found a lovely fountain on the corner square.
We thought this area one of Paris's most interesting and quaint
Latin Quarter neighborhoods.

Paris Tips

Hotel Amsterdam: Our room at Hotel Amsterdam was small but "friendly," with everything functioning, including a great heater. Yes, it was cold! We were on the ground floor of the three-story hotel. But this worked out well, since the hotel has a small garden courtyard outside our room. In sunny weather, breakfast is served in the small garden. The hotel has a nicely decorated breakfast room downstairs. The daily breakfast includes coffee or hot chocolate, chocolate croissants, regular croissants, French rolls, and assorted jams and jellies. At Paris prices, this is equivalent to a $10 breakfast.

Better yet, the hotel staff is friendly and attentive. They made a telephone call for me to Les Vedettes de Paris, a company running a Seine boat ride for which we had a free Entertainment coupon. I should add that the boat ride was a highlight of our visit. And on departure day the desk arranged for an engineering student to drive us to Orly airport for a price far less than the cost of a regular taxi.

Coupon Jaune: One way to save money on transportation is to buy a Coupon Jaune and use mass transit. Bring a color passport-size photo (if you forget, most Metro stations have photo machines). Simply ask the clerk at any Metro station for the Coupon Jaune Une Semaine. (A possible glitch, however, is that the card is only valid from Sunday to the following Saturday.) The clerk will issue a laminated card with your photo and protective holder. This card is good for zones one and two, which cover the entire city of Paris, sans suburbs. For sixty-two francs, or $13, it permits unlimited use of all RER trains (which connect Paris to its suburbs), subways, and buses. (A single Paris subway ride is priced at $1.25.) On many days we took eight or more single rides on the transit system with our unlimited pass—a super transit bargain!

Three-Day Museum Pass: This is an incredible buy. A three-day Musée Visite Pass is sold for $27 (127 francs). Purchase a pass at any Metro station or the Paris Visitor's Bureau on the Champs Elysées near the Arch de Triomphe. Feel free to buy the pass at any time, since it is only activated when first used. At that time a date is imprinted on the pass, which is then good for two additional days. The pass offers unlimited entrance to over one hundred museums located both inside and outside Paris. Included are the Louvre, the Musée d'Orsay, the Pompidou Center, and Château Fontainebleau. The single entrance fees usually cost about $7 to $11 per museum or tourist attraction. The pass *is* a supreme bargain!

➡ **Steve's Tip:** *Three of our favorite museums are the Louvre, the Musée d'Orsay, and the Georges Pompidou Center, with its upper-level view of the city. Most museums have free checkrooms for coats and backpacks.*

Fontainebleau

A visit to Château Fontainebleau is one of the three best one-day excursions outside Paris. The other two are Giverny and Versailles. Giverny is the beautiful, county home of painter Clause Monet. For tourists embarking on a "virgin" first trip to Paris, a visit to Versailles is a must. For us the decision was an easy one. Both Patty and I had seen Versailles, but neither of us had visited Fontainebleau. Given our love of history, especially living history, a restored home of French kings and queens was an obvious choice.

Fontainebleau is easy to reach and offers visitors a voyage through some of France's turbulent history. The short journey takes about one hour by train from Gare Lyon to the small town of Fontainebleau. The trains leave at least hourly, and a round-trip ticket costs $15. The admission to the château is $8 but is free for those wise visitors using the highly recommended Musée Visite Pass. Upon arrival at the Fontainebleau train station, take the château bus (a seven-franc fare) for the ten-minute drive to the château.

Fontainebleau was home to French kings, starting in the twelfth century. In 1169 King Louis VII invited the exiled arch-bishop of Canterbury, Thomas Becket, to consecrate his chapel at the château. In 1528 it was torn down by Francois I and rebuilt with the help of Italy's finest artisans. The list of royal residents is long and stretches over centuries. King Henry IV often stayed at the château Fontainebleau and King Louis XIII was born at Fontainebleau. The château was used as the fall residence of kings Louis XV and XVI.

Fontainebleau survived the French revolution unscathed, although its furnishings were sold off and the château was turned into a military school. Emperor Napoleon returned it to its earlier prominence when he made Fontainebleau a state palace. After the palace was refurnished, Pope Pius VII arrived to crown Napoleon emperor of France. Napoleon lived there until his abdication, in April 1814.

We purchased a colorful guidebook and enjoyed a wonderful self-guided tour.

My favorite things inside the château included:

- The emperor's small bed chamber, Napoleon's bedroom from 1804 to 1811
- The Trinity Chapel, which was rebuilt in the sixteenth century, with its ceiling murals reminiscent of the Sistine Chapel
- The gallery of Francois I, with decorated carved panels, frescoes, sculptures, and mostly sixteenth-century Italian furniture
- The ornate ballroom, with frescoes of mythological subjects and a monumental fireplace. (The ballroom was used for grand receptions, feasts, and balls in the seventeenth and eighteenth centuries.)
- The King Francois I drawing room, once the queen's bedchamber and later used by Napoleon as a state dining room
- My overall "unique" favorite was the queen's bedchamber. (Every queen of France since the seventeenth century has slept in the chamber room. Even more impressive is the Marie Antoinette's gilded wooden bed. Though built for the queen, she never slept in the bed since she was beheaded before she could use it, although Empress Josephine did.)
- Napoleon's bed chamber, used from 1804 to 1809

It is easy to spend the entire day exploring this beautifully restored and maintained royal residence. Be sure to leave time to walk through its exterior gardens and grounds. The grounds include the Garden of Diana, dating back to Napoleon and Louis-Philippe; the English Garden, favored by Napoleon; the White Horse Court, which serves as main entrance to the château; the Oval Court, which dates to the sixteenth century; and the Court of the Fountain, which borders the buildings on three sides and a lake on the fourth side. While the grounds are splendid, they do not approach the quality of other Loire Valley châteaus.

We left the château and walked through the town of Fontainebleu, where we stopped at a local delicatessen to purchase fresh French bread, a variety of meats and cheeses, fruit, and sodas. Then, in the pastry shop next door, we spied an array of incredible pastries drissled with chocolate sauce and whipped cream. (Sin! Sin! Sin!) Quaint wooden bus benches provided comfortable seating as we dove into our lunch. We sat back and enjoyed the flavor of a small French town in the afternoon and the perfumed aroma of the fresh flowers surrounding the small fountain in the center island of the street. Then, after a short walk, we were back at the train station. All in all, the day was a fun, memorable, and successful visit to the French countryside.

➡ **Steve's Tip:** *Always carry a few 2-franc coins. Should nature call, a new experience may be at hand. Throughout Paris one will find the true engineering marvels that are its world-renowned public rest rooms. They require a 2-franc coin.*

I could go on and on about Paris, from the museums to the restaurants, to the Metro to the wonderful pastries, to the colorful flowers that grow in tucked-away parks and fountains. Paris should be on everyone's special list of romantic dream vacations. The opportunity to visit Paris is at hand. Take it, and Bon voyage!

10

African Safari: The Ultimate Adventure

Africa! The last frontier! For those of us destined to remain on planet earth, the greatest vacation odyssey awaits right here.

When people think of dream vacations, their minds conjure images of great European capitals and exotic tropical islands. Why is it few people think seriously of the ultimate vacation adventure, an African safari? The obvious answer is the high cost. After all, I have read that African safaris are Johnny Carson's vacation of choice. No wonder people agree that such a world-class vacation is reserved for the rich and famous.

Understandably, most people believe their only access to Africa is through the Discovery Channel. They marvel at video images of herds of elephants marching silently, with snow-capped Mt. Kilimanjaro looming in the background. Other compelling images show prides of lions and their cubs, or herds of tall, lanky giraffes nibbling on treetops. Cable television has truly permitted us to vicariously enjoy the thrill of the African wilderness. Now, more than ever, the very notion of an African safari challenges our collective imaginations.

Given the expense involved, why do record numbers of Americans travel to Kenya each year? In addition to the rich and famous, many retired seniors travel to Africa. Fortunately for them, they have the two ingredients that are essential for a safari—money and time. When your spirit for a safari adventure soars, I can help remove the barriers, both real and artificial, to this vacation of a lifetime.

Although we are neither famous nor wealthy, Patty and I have experienced an African safari adventure not once but twice. I want readers to do the same, to live this incredible experience— and at a price that is no higher than that of a Club Med vacation. I will demystify the exotic journey called an African safari until you are convinced this unique adventure is attainable. Before I point the way, let us cover the basics.

What Is an African Safari?

No, this is not a trick question. I once took an informal poll and found that four out of five people have no clear understanding of the day-to-day reality of an African safari, including its geography.

By far the most popular destination for an African safari is the East African nation of Kenya. To the north Kenya shares borders with Sudan, Ethiopia, and Somalia, to the west with Uganda, including Lake Victoria, and to the south with Tanzania. Its eastern tropical coast abuts the Indian Ocean. Kenya's land mass is 224,961 miles, and its population is approximately fifteen million. Its capital and largest city, Nairobi, has a population of nine million, and its second largest city, Mombasa, on the coast, has a population of less than half a million. Daniel Arap Moi took power as Kenya's one-man ruler and president in 1978. Until recently Kenya had yet to enjoy any trappings of a Western-style democracy. Bowing to global pressures, in 1992 Kenya recognized opposition parties for the very first time. Shortly thereafter, the nation had its first-ever election. As most people anticipated, Moi was victorious and today remains the nation's head of state. The major argument put forth against democratization is the fear of a major outbreak of tribal warfare. Happily, this has not occurred to any large degree, and Kenya continues to be one of Africa's most politically stable nations.

Today Kenya's principal industry continues to be tourism, its second major industry being the export of tea. If one considers the map of Kenya to be roughly square, the equator practically bisects the country. Nairobi is dead center in the southern half of Kenya, just below the equator. A typical Kenyan safari makes a rough circle around Nairobi, exploring the southern half of the nation.

An African safari today means a photo safari, not a hunting safari, as in the past. Let me be clear about this. It is a *capital* crime to hunt Kenya's protected wildlife. The only shooting that occurs on a safari in Kenya is done with cameras and camcorders. In fact, many Kenyans proudly wear buttons that read KILL POACHERS! Photographers find endless photo opportunities every waking moment during their African safari. This is true for still and video photography. With high-quality camcorders, tourists can become Cecil B. De Milles and produce their own cinematic masterpieces.

All Kenyan safaris start from Nairobi. Getting there is both arduous and expensive. The distance to Nairobi from the West Coast of the United States is 15,000 miles, and it takes twenty-one hours by air. U.S. flights reach Kenya via major European gateway cities, including London, Paris, and Frankfurt. Our first trip to Nairobi involved flights from California to New York, New York to Frankfurt, and Frankfurt to Nairobi. Our second visit involved routing from New York to London and London to Nairobi. Although the flights are painstakingly long, there is one positive side to the arduous journey. Flights from New York to Europe are most often "red-eyes," or night flights. In chapter 2, I describe my strategy for sleeping on night flights. While a "red-eye" from the East Coast offers an opportunity to sleep, a good night of sleep often awaits travelers upon their arrival in Nairobi. Most flights arrive in the late evening, about 10:00 P.M., and by midnight a good night's sleep awaits at the hotel.

The best safari packages include a "buffer" day. That means you spend the first day in Nairobi rather than immediately heading out on safari, getting a chance to recover from jet lag. In 1992, we planned to travel on our own during the first week of our Kenya vacation. Realizing the value of the "buffer" day, I planned our train departure for Mombasa, from Nairobi, for 6:00 P.M. rather than the early morning. We were scheduled to arrive at 10:00 P.M. on the previous evening. As they say, the best laid plans... Sadly, our New York flight arrived at London's Heathrow Airport three hours late. In fact, as we were approaching Heathrow, our connecting British Airways flight was already winging its way to Nairobi. It was 10:00 A.M. and we were totally stranded at

Heathrow. We had twelve hours to kill because the next direct flight to Kenya was with an Air Kenya flight leaving Heathrow at 10:00 P.M. American Airlines rescued us and treated us royally, offering us the choice of a $100 shopping spree at the airport's shops or a day room at a five-star hotel. We chose the hotel and enjoyed a $250 room and a great nap.

American Airlines deserves some additional praise. Its staff called Nairobi to inform Unitours of our predicament and advised them of our new arrival time. Since we were traveling with a tour, we had to meet a Unitours representative personally to pick up our train tickets to Mombasa. Our Air Kenya flight arrived in Nairobi at 10:00 A.M. the following day. We picked up our train tickets from the Unitours representative and headed straight for the New Stanley Hotel, where the manager graciously gave us free use of a day room. We napped, freshened up, and took in a local downtown flea market later in the day.

Nairobi, Kenya

Nairobi, one of Africa's most cosmopolitan cities, looks and feels like a major metropolitan city, with its downtown complexes of high-rise buildings, bustling business center, and cars clogging the streets.

During our first visit to Nairobi our package included a half-day tour of the city. Nairobi's major sights include the odd circular International Conference Center, the downtown business area, and the home of Karen Blixen, who wrote the novel *Out of Africa* under her pseudonym Isak Dinesen.

Nairobi has a wonderful indoor craft and flower market that is only a couple of blocks from the town's outdoor flea market. Since we are flea market addicts, we greatly enjoyed Nairobi's market. Open-air stalls line each side of the market's long narrow paths. But remember, the locals are hungry for sales. We were shopping for silk-screen panels and sculpted, wooden animal utensils. At times it got a bit hairy when several vendors simultaneously vied for our business. At one stall we described to the owner the silk-screen scene we were seeking. Immediately, the owner shouted to a young helper, and the young man scurried off and returned in a few minutes with an armful of silk screens. Another young man returned with Coca Colas so we could shop in comfort. Despite the overly persistent sellers, the flea market was great fun.

A word of caution: Nairobi has crime problems similar to those of large American cities. Egos and jewelry should be left at home. Do not wear jewelry when walking Nairobi's streets. I always carry my camera and strap it to my body. Most daytime crime in Nairobi, as one might expect, is mugging or pickpocketing. A "mugging" would be someone grabbing jewelry or a camera. Stick with the crowded main streets at *all* times.

How Many Days in a Safari Week?

I thought I knew the answer to this question until I researched land packages for our first African safari. The following example tells it best. In 1990 I booked the two-week, fourteen-day Explorer Safari with a wonderful tour company called Safariworld. Usually two weeks and fourteen days are synonymous. But it ain't necessarily so on safari.

Let's first reconcile safari mathematics. In calculating your total vacation time from the date of your U.S. departure to the return date, you must think about the "gross number" of vacation days. Then there is the "net time" spent in Nairobi and finally the "net time" actually spent on a safari. How does this work? Tour companies advertise in terms of the "gross number" of vacation days needed for the entire trip. Our fourteen-day explorer safari included two days of flying time traveling to and from Kenya. Our "net time" in Nairobi included our arrival day, one "buffer" day, and one half-day at safari's end. Our fourteen-day package included eight nights at game lodges for a total of eight and a half days of actual safari time.

➡ **Steve's Tip:** *I recommend fourteen days as the minimum for an enjoyable and memorable safari, and the package should include eight nights on an actual safari.*

I imagine that the rich and famous, à la Johnny Carson, enjoy the most opulent safaris. They can afford to use private vans or jeeps and private planes to travel the large distances between most lodges. They use the best deluxe lodges or tented camp-grounds and remain on a safari for as many weeks as necessary to enjoy an in-depth safari adventure. So who needs perfection anyway? The bargain safaris I recommend may be less than perfect but provide a similar unforgettable safari experience. In fact, you will likely stay in the very Treetops Lodge frequented by Queen Elizabeth.

Ultimately, perfection is in the eyes of the beholder. I can only advise. Anyone able to spend more than eight nights on a safari should do so. Because most travelers have time and money constraints, I will talk about minimum requirements. I believe that the perfect length of a safari is fourteen days, with a minimum of eight nights on safari.

The Dollars and Cents of a Safari

This will no doubt give many readers migraine headaches. There is no way around it. Discussing the average cost of an African safari in less than large dollar amounts is impossible. It is an ultimate world-class vacation. The average moderate cost of a fourteen-day safari, including airfare, is about $4,000 per person, or a whopping $8,000 per couple! Presently, the average cost of a high-end safari is about $12,000 per couple. Please do not be intimidated and *do not give up.* I promise the travel picture will brighten significantly.

In the first instance we must break the safari down into its two major components. They include air travel to Nairobi from the United States and the safari land package. Unfortunately, Nairobi is the most expensive air destination in the world. Today, an economy ticket to Nairobi costs $2,500 to $4,000. On the other hand, ticket prices drop to $1,600 if the air travel is part of a tour package.

My strategy is simple and will save you thousands of dollars. I never lose sight of the goal: free airline travel to Kenya and the purchase of the best bargain-priced safari available. Presently, Unitours offers a wonderful seventeen-day Kenya safari (land only) for $1,798 per person. Unitours' special ten-day safari package is offered at the amazing low price of only $998 (land only) per person. The average all-inclusive one-week Club Med vacation, without airfare, will cost about the same. Keep in mind that African safaris are all inclusive, covering all meals, lodging, van, and driver-guide. Also, the most popular safari is a two-week trip that is double the length of the average one-week, all-inclusive vacation.

With free airfare, the equation changes dramatically. The entire safari experience can cost as little as $1,996 for two for a Unitours ten-day safari, and up to $3,596 for two for Unitours' super seventeen-day safari. What about the free air part of the equation? I did say this is a major *goal*. Realizing this goal requires real commitment if this dream adventure is to become a reality.

In chapter 2 I discussed free travel using the American Airlines AAdvantage program, which offers a free round-trip ticket to Nairobi for 75,000 program miles. Members earn two round-trip tickets with 150,000 miles. My winning strategy results in the accumulation of program miles faster than imaginable. I am not overlooking the difficulty in acquiring the necessary 75,000 or 150,000 miles, but Patty and I reached this magic number in less than three years. Having a goal with a workable winning strategy is the key to success. Doubters should consider that offers for free AAdvantage miles abound. As I am writing, MCI is offering new customers 5,000 AAdvantage miles. Simultaneously, Citibank is offering up to 15,000 miles to new depositors. The free Citibank dining program is offering thousands of free miles. By using these free-mileage promotions members can amass 25,000 free miles in less than eight weeks. This is one-third of your first free ticket to Nairobi, obtainable in a matter of weeks at virtually no cost. In this era of competition between airlines and their programs such free-mile promotions are issued almost weekly.

Want more? Presently, a major shirt company is offering five hundred miles for each shirt purchased. I received five hundred miles for my recent stay at a Sheraton hotel. Many car rental companies offer up to 500 miles per rental. By using your Citibank AAdvantage card as I suggested in chapter 2, it is easy to bank program miles at lightning speed. You can obtain most of these miles *without* flying.

Currently, miles obtained today expire on December 31 of the third full year following the year purchased. For example, if 1,000 miles are banked in 1996, the miles must be "spent" by December

31, 1999. This rule permits you more than three years in which to use your miles. Also, there is a mileage cap of 100,000 miles that may be banked each year, which hardly affects you. However, another American program rule can extend the expiration date. This rule provides that whenever members obtains a free-mileage award certificate, they have another full year in which to use it. When miles are cashed in for a travel award the airline gives the member a certificate instead of actual tickets. When the member is ready to travel, the certificate is submitted as payment for a flight. (At this point American issues actual plane tickets.)

Example: By the end of year number three a member has banked 140,000 miles, 10,000 short of the amount needed for two free round-trip tickets to Nairobi. Just before the first 75,000 miles expire, at the end of year three, the member may request a 75,000 certificate. The member now has an extra year in which to exchange the certificate. This time may then be used to bank the 10,000 miles needed for the second ticket, effectively stretching the three-year rule to four years.

Finally, if you lack the necessary miles for a second ticket, consider chapter 4, "When All Else Fails Take a 5 Percent Rebate." You may always combine one free ticket with a second purchased ticket using the 5 percent rebate.

Okay, you have one free Nairobi ticket. However, you have only 40,000 remaining miles, 35,000 short of a second ticket. Use the 40,000 miles for a free trip to London. You may then purchase the round-trip London-to-Nairobi connecting flight on British Airways for just $658! Best of all, this low price is available from any U.S. departure city. Do you have only 80,000 program miles? Then forget the 150,000 needed for Nairobi tickets. Fly free to London and then buy two low-priced London-to-Nairobi tickets for $658 each.

➡ **Steve's Tip:** *Use your free travel dollars! First fly free to London and then book an air-and-safari land package from London to Nairobi. This would include the round-trip British Airways flight to Nairobi ($658) and the Unitours ten-day, seven-night Twiga Safari ($998). The total price from any U.S. city would be $1,506.*

Let's return to the best scenario, two free tickets to Nairobi. This effectively reduces the cost of an African safari by about 50 percent! Safari land packages start at just $998 per person, less 5 percent if using Travelers Advantage.

The Kenya Safari—An Insider's View

Most professional safari videos fail to convey the complete picture of the safari odyssey. They emphasize closeup images of lion "kills" and other tantalizing wildlife scenes. Of course, wildlife plays the pivotal role on a safari. With this introduction out of the way, I will briefly recount our precious few days on the safari trail. Note the safari's pace, the travel time between lodges, and my description of the sights and sounds of our various stops. Consider what the tours accomplished in eight days in the bush. As the safari leaves Nairobi, feel the excitement of a journey to places unchanged over the millennia.

Our safari adventure began at the Safari Park Hotel in the suburbs of Nairobi. Safari Park is a classy hotel built in a countrified setting. Its rooms are in small buildings that dot the landscaped grounds. They have four-posted netted beds and are beautifully decorated in appropriate African motifs. A tall Masai warrior greets guests at the hotel's entrance. The main building and dining room are circular, with immense pointed thatched roofs that speak of Africa. I give the Safari Park Hotel my highest recommendation. If it is not listed in a particular brochure package, it may be available as an upgrade.

➡ **Steve's Tip:** *Safari operators use van-type vehicles configured with a center aisle and double seats next to each window. A four-seat bench stretches across the rear. Since vans may hold up to twelve passengers, be sure to use a tour that provides guaranteed window seating.*

Luck intervened so that we shared our van with only two passengers, one of whom sat up front with the driver. This was as close to a private van as we could hope for. The obvious advantage is an asset for wildlife viewing and photography, both of which require passengers to move from one side of the van to the other. With fewer people to knock into, wildlife viewing is better and taking photos is easier. A freshly washed safari van arrived at our hotel on the morning of our departure—and we were off!

Day One: The safari began! Our van departed Nairobi and headed south to Tsavo West National Park. This is one of the world's largest game reserves, with 1,290 miles of all-weather roads. The van continued through the Atahi Plains and later arrived at Ngalia Safari Lodge. We checked in, enjoyed our first sumptuous safari lunch, and hit the road for our first game drive, ninety minutes, in which we toured the park in search of wildlife. We first stopped for a herd of Cape buffalo and then zebra and flocks of colored birds. The most exciting viewing occurred after dinner. The hotel placed a large piece of raw meat in a nearby tree, easily visible from the edge of the hotel's property. A large lamp provided indirect lighting of the tree branches and hanging meat. Within an hour, "it" crept out of the bush and onto a tree limb. We sat transfixed for twenty minutes as the leopard fed on the meat. This was a major wildlife event! Leopards are primarily nocturnal creatures and are rarely seen on a safari. Already, we were in safari heaven.

Day Two: We completed the tour of Tsavo, stopping at Mzima Springs to view a dozen or so hippos bathing. We then headed to the Masai Amboseli Game Reserve. We stared, our eyes transfixed as we sat in the very shadow of Mt. Kilimanjaro. There it was, the majestic mountain, its peak rising to a height of 19,340 feet and its summit blanketed in white snow.

We enjoyed lunch and an afternoon game drive while viewing many zebra and several wildebeests. A short while later playful Chacama baboons "attacked" our van. Our driver took us to the top of a large hill, where we got out—one of the few times we were permitted to leave the van. The hill, known as Lion Overlook, is a place that was traditionally used by hunters to spot game. As we drove toward the lodge, we viewed a herd of elephants, including several newborn calves. We stopped for photographs at each sighting. The elephants came as close as thirty feet away!

I should briefly discuss vans and their proximity to wildlife. A commonly asked question is, "Just how close does the van take you to the wildlife?" Perhaps the best benefit to photographers is that most wildlife seem to view vans as moving trees; the animals have no fear of the vans. Lions often walked up to and around the van to less than five feet from its windows.

We anticipated new adventures around every bend of the road. As we neared the lodge, we spotted a lone rhino off in the distance. This was a rare sighting and one I will always remember. Suddenly, an ostrich streaked in front of our van. Next came a hyena in hot pursuit. My film of the hyena-ostrich chase is almost comical. (I should mention that the ostrich won! It moved with incredible speed and easily outdistanced the tired hyena.) Velvet monkeys lined many parts of the road. The creatures are enchanting with their black velvet–looking faces.

We stayed at the Amboseli Serena Lodge, with lovely landscaped grounds and a large swimming pool.

Day Three: We left the Amboseli Serena Lodge and enjoyed a final game drive in the park, where I took extraordinary pictures of Mt. Kilimanjaro. One surreal scene shows a string of elephants walking in the shadow of the mountain. We then drove through the heart of Kikuyu country and stopped to enjoy the view of the spectacular Chania waterfall.

We reversed course and headed north toward the Mountain Tree Lodge, one of the spectacular "treetop" hotels built in the forest on the slope of Mt. Kenya. The hotel stands above a nearby watering hole that draws a large number and variety of animals, especially during the night. The hotel uses floodlights to illuminate a pond, with its salt lick, for visitor viewing. There are no regular game drives since wildlife come to the hotel. Amazingly, the hotel staff asked if we wanted to view any particular wildlife in the early morning. We thought for a moment and answered, "Rhino!" Lo and behold, at 3:30 A.M., we awoke to a knock at the door. A voice said simply, "Rheeno, rheeno!" We wiped our eyes and quietly peered out over our balcony to the water hole below, where a Cape buffalo was facing off with a rhino. A battle of giant proportions was about to commence. I grabbed the camera and attempted to capture the moment with several long-exposure shots. The pictures were discernible but definitely of poor quality. The memories, however, will be with us for many years.

A special feature at Mountain Lodge is an underground concrete bunker connected to the hotel by an underground passage. The bunker, with open windows and steel bars, is twenty feet from the edge of the salt-lick pond. I was incredulous as African elephants walked by only several feet from the open window.

Day Four: We continued north and passed a large, colorful sign with block letters that read EQUATOR. Our next scheduled stop was Samburu Game Reserve, one of the richest of Kenya's parks. Our van drove through terrain that became dry and arid as we entered the fringe of Kenya's northern frontier desert. The park is home to the rare Grevy zebra and long-necked gerunuk. The Ewaso Nyiro River meanders through the park, providing a striking contrast to the otherwise arid terrain. Elephants and oryx are often found at river's edge standing under palms, while hippos and crocodiles reside in the river.

Suddenly our van stopped as a small boy led his two camels across the road. We continued to the Samburu Serena Lodge, another picturesque oasis offering comfort and excellent bush cuisine. As our van approached Samburu Reserve, our driver stopped and we drove to a nearby tree. Twenty feet in front of our van were three cheetahs lying in the shade of the large tree. During our stay at Samburu Lodge we viewed crocodiles crawling from a nearby river to the hotel's beach to feed on goat heads placed on the beach by hotel staff. I will let you conjure up appropriate images of this dramatic scene. (Oh yes, we were viewing this from about one hundred feet away, with no barriers between us and the predator crocodiles.) During our game drives we viewed water buck, ostrich, and guinea hens. We also photographed cheetahs, fascinating but ugly wart hogs, and giraffes.

Day Five: The morning started with a farewell game drive. Then, our course reversed. We headed south to the famed Mt. Kenya Safari Club. Actor William Holden originally conceived this plush country club hotel, and to this day it continues to host Hollywood personalities. It is the only lodge in Kenya that has a dress code for dinner. (Yes, I packed a coat and tie for this one dinner.) The hotel's main lobby and sitting rooms sport ornate woodwork fashioned from local hardwoods. This stop is unique since there are no formal game drives. The entertainment at Mt. Kenya Safari Club is truly self-contained. Peacocks lounge on lush extended lawns. Upon our arrival natives were at poolside performing ritual dances to the rhythm of ancient drums. We stood, transfixed, at our room's window staring at the majestic Mt. Kenya, its peak rising 17,058 feet into the heavens. The mountain remains the home of the Kikiyo's divine spirit. The slopes of Mt. Kenya contain a vast array of flora and fauna and the famed and rare Bongo leopards and Serval cats.

The Mt. Kenya Safari Club offers visitors a respite from the usual day of driving to a lodge or morning and afternoon game runs. It offers a giant heated swimming pool and sporting activities, including tennis and horseback riding. The grounds have become a bird sanctuary, with giant Marabou storks flying overhead and standing menacingly along the perimeters of water holes scattered around the lush grounds. These are the largest species of storks and they scavenge for food like their cousin, the vulture. The club is home to hundreds of species of birds that are delightful to observe, especially the large flocks of peacocks and hens.

Day Six: We were back on the road heading in the direction of Lake Naivasha. Our focus changed from big game to Kenya's colorful and varied birds. We stopped for lunch at Lion Hill Lodge near Lake Nakuru, and after lunch marveled at Lake Nakuru. The sight of millions of flamingos turning the lake into a sea of pastel plumage is truly breathtaking. There are three hundred species of birds residing within the park's boundary. Also attracted to the lake's shallow alkaline waters are black-winged stilts, avocets, and ruffs that migrate from Europe to winter there.

Our next stop was Lake Hotel at Lake Naivasha. Upon our arrival, at 4:00 P.M., I had to make a major decision. The manager informed me that a motorized canoe was available for that day's final tour of the lake. However, there were two large "catches:" The tour required a minimum of four persons and I had only twenty minutes to arrange the outing. I spotted the "pizza king"—a fellow tour member and owner of major Cape Cod pizzeria. He and his fourteen-year-old son were game for this aquatic jaunt, and our boat captain did not let us down. The boat immediately headed toward several hippos, moving within a hundred feet of them. We stared, studied, and photographed them before drifting through a bird sanctuary with scores of nesting birds, fish eagles diving for their dinner, and outstanding pink-breasted pelicans. The two-hour boat tour was our un-forgettable highlight of our visit. Did I mention there were *no* mosquitos?

Days Seven and Eight: Our next stop was to be the super finale of our safari. Our van headed for the Masai Mara, the great northern Serengeti Plain in the famed Rift Valley for two days of extraordinary game viewing. This is the place where hundreds of thousands of wildebeest, with their large bisonlike heads, migrate in thundering herds across the grasslands of the Masai Mara. The famed wildebeest migration lasts but a few days, while during the remainder of the year the park holds the greatest number and variety of wildlife of any of Kenya's reserves. Upon our arrival several postmigration wildebeests greeted us.

In short order we checked into wonderful Mara Sopa Lodge, made up of small stone cottages. (In fact, we revisited the lodge during our 1992 Tanzanian safari.) The hotel's small swimming pool overlooks the Serengeti Plain. A young Masai male escorted us to our rooms because a Cape buffalo was roaming nearby. (Note: Cape buffalo are among the biggest and most dangerous of Kenya's wildlife. Each year many Masai women are gored while working in the fields.)

Our daily game drives were superb. Around the bend of the road was a lioness guarding her wildebeest kill. We enjoyed four game drives and viewed lions, elephants, giraffes, foxes, black jackals, wart hogs, wild dogs, and a two-day-old zebra colt.

Later in the day we visited a neighboring Masai village. We expected a "model" village and surprisingly found a fully-func-tioning village no different from those of hundreds of years ago. The village's interior consisted of a large circle of dung huts facing inward, with an interior corral for livestock. During bad weather, the livestock share the huts with villagers. Villagers were friendly and some sold Masai jewelry such as necklaces, bracelets, and rings. The village charges a fee of about $6 that they share with the entire tribe.

Day Nine: This was our final game drive. We found three cheetahs, a lioness on the hunt, griffin vultures lunching on a zebra carcass, and jackals following black-maned lions. Patty and I bid farewell to the Serengeti as our safari came to an unforgettable end. The final drive from the Masai Mara back to Nairobi took four to five hours over horribly potholed roads. At that point we fully appreciated the extra amenity of an A&K safari—its plane flight back to Nairobi.

The knowledge that we were returning to the Safari Park Hotel buoyed our spirits. We returned to the hotel late in the afternoon and had several free hours for dinner. Our plane wasn't departing until midnight. This was the night for our gala farewell dinner at the Carnivore restaurant.

I rented a deluxe van and organized a group outing to the Carnivore, which had been highly recommended. Upon entering the restaurant, we faced a six-foot-wide brick barbecue pit built in the round. It had racks holding several layers of four-foot skewers over the coals. A menu board listed hartebeest, giraffe, crocodile, antelope, and zebra, plus traditional items such as chicken and beef. The waiters wore colorful Carnivore aprons and straw hats. Once seated, waiters approached the table with giant skewers in hand. Every fifteen minutes another waiter and skewer arrived, offering a different barbecued delicacy. This pattern continued throughout the evening. The entire group agreed that our "Carnivore" experience was a most memorable finale to our African odyssey.

Sadly, Patty and I headed to Jomo Kenyatta Airport for our 1:00 A.M. flight to London. Our hearts were heavy as the plane lifted off the runway. Little did we know that fate would see us returning in 1992 for another, different African adventure. I encourage readers to use this itinerary as a guide for your own special journey of discovery. My safari incorporated comfort, economy, and the very best itinerary possible, given our two-week time constraint.

Choosing Your Bargain Safari

Congratulations! You have done it! You have hit the safari jackpot, banking sufficient miles to obtain at least one, and hopefully two, free tickets to Kenya. It is now time to select and purchase a land package in the ever-changing safari marketplace.

The strategy I used for our two safaris worked in spectacular fashion and is equally valid today. Once our free tickets were in hand, I researched all available tour companies and their itineraries, and also obtained and read many books on Kenya. One brochure, from Abercrombe and Kent, was pivotal. It was a wonder to read, although the land packages were too high priced for us.

Unfortunately, Safariworld, the tour operator I selected in 1990, is no longer in business, though it exists in part through a merger with other tour operators. However, Unitours, the tour company I selected in 1992, is still a leader in quality low-priced land packages. I have spoken with a Unitours representative and reviewed the company's current packages. Since our 1990 safari involved most of Kenya's best game reserves, I will focus on that type of land package.

➡️ **Steve's Tip:** *I wanted to see the different lodges as I shopped for our land packages, so I collected every Africa brochure I could find. On average, each one contains at least one photo of a popular safari lodge. Before long I had a collection of most of the safari lodges on my interest list.*

Unitours

Unitours is the company we used in 1992 for our Mombasa-Tanzania adventure. It has been in operation since 1958 and is well known in Europe and Africa. Unitours advertises just about the lowest prices available on safari packages. It also delivers service and quality. When we arrived a day late in Kenya, the Unitours representative was standing at the airport, waiting with our train tickets in hand. When we left Mombasa for our flight back to Nairobi, the Unitours person conversed with local airline and customs people until he got us seats on the overbooked flight. The driver-guide on our Tanzania safari was top-notch.

I recommend Unitours' fourteen-day Kenya Adventure Safari. It consists of ten and a half days of actual safari adventure; it mimics our 1990 Explorer Safari, and travels throughout Kenya. The safari visits the best of Kenya's parks and uses excellent lodges. For comparison I have chosen Abercrombe and Kent's current thirteen-day Adventure Safari, which includes only nine days of actual safari time. At the outset, Unitours' package provides one and a half additional and quite precious days on safari.

Both safaris use the same deluxe lodges, including the Amboseli Serena Lodge, the Samburu Serena Lodge, and the famed Mt. Kenya Safari Club. These account for five nights of the Unitours package. Additionally, the Unitours safari includes a night at either the Ark, Treetops, or Mountain Lodge. (I might remind you that Treetops is the lodge that was visited by Queen Elizabeth some years ago.) All three are the famed "treetop"-type lodges I described and that should be a part of every deluxe safari experience. Patty and I stayed at the newer Mountain Lodge and enjoyed every moment of our stay. The similar A&K safari does not include a "treetop"-type lodge. The Unitours safari also includes a deluxe tented campground, Governors Camp.

However, A&K does offer value for the extra dollars it charges. Its safari package includes two plane flights that shorten driving time. One flight is between points during the safari and the second is a return flight to Nairobi that departs after breakfast on the final day of the safari. On the plus side, Unitours offers more game-viewing hours, with a final morning game drive on the last day of the safari.

The Unitours safari includes Amboseli Park, Lake Nakuru, Mt. Kenya Safari Club, Samburu Park, two and a half days at the incomparable Masai Mara National Reserve, and a dinner at the famed Carnivore Restaurant in Nairobi.

Tour Prices

We paid $1,900 in 1990 for our fourteen-day safari, with eight and a half days of safari time. By doing away with the "buffer" day, Unitours adds extra safari time, for a total of ten and a half days on safari. The price of Unitours' Kenya Adventure Safari, in low season, is a rock-bottom $1,895 for land only. In low season, the A&K Adventure Safari, with one day less of safari time, is priced at $2,600 for land only.

United Touring International (UTI)

UTI has a bargain safari and offers a fascinating low-end safari called its Karibuni Kenya Safari. This is a twelve-day safari that includes two and a half free days in Nairobi and *five* days of actual safari. (It is an abbreviated safari.) So why the recommendation?

Because the price, from the East Coast, is a staggeringly low $1,999 *including airfare to Kenya!* Since this is a seven-night tour, available free travel cash may be used to lower the price by $100 to $200 (see chapter 1). Since airfare alone to Nairobi costs $1,500, this trip becomes the absolute best bargain to be found. There is a hefty add-on of $675 for West Coast departures. This is a great time to use free domestic awards or companion tickets through the AAdvantage program. For information or a brochure, contact UTI at:

United Touring International
One Bala Plaza, Suite 414
Bala Cynwyd, Pennsylvania 19004
(800) 223-6486

Unitours' Bargain Tour

This tour does not include airfare but is an extraordinary package. Unitours' Twiga Safari (tour TWI) is rated as ten days but includes a full six and a half days of actual safari. It offers excellent lodges, such as Samburu Serena Lodge and Lion Hill Lodge. Also, it visits Samburu Reserve, Mt. Kenya, Lake Nakuru, Lake Naivasha, and the Masai Mara. It also provides dinner at my favorite Nairobi restaurant, the Carnivore. In low season the mind-numbing price for this safari land package is only $998! Contact Unitours at:

Unitours
8 South Michigan Avenue
Chicago, Illinois 60603
(800) 621-0557 or (312) 782-1590

For the most part, I have found that tour operators, even wholesale operators, will usually talk to me when I call their toll-free number. It is always worth a try in order to obtain fast information on a tour, or at the very least, a hard-to-obtain brochure.

Flying Doctor Society

All the above safari companies guarantee window seating and participate in the Flying Doctor Society. During our second visit to

Kenya and Tanzania, there were six of us sharing a Unitours van. On the second day of the Tanzanian safari, John, a gentleman in his mid to late sixties had a sudden onset of chest pain. He had a history of heart disease and was on a stringent medication regimen. We were in the Masai Mara, the remote Serengeti, when this happened. Patty and I sat on our veranda and used our binoculars to view a nearby military airstrip. Within three hours of the onset of John's chest pains a Flying Doctor Society plane was landing to transport him to a Nairobi hospital. Handling such emergencies is the major task of the society, and we were more than a little impressed. I later heard that John was back in Texas doing well.

Meals on Safari—Incredible!

Let me begin with a frank admission. I am a lifelong finicky eater, and your basic meat, potatoes, and apple pie kind of guy. When food is gourmet, exotic, or unidentifiable I become concerned. With that said, I happily report that African lodges offer meals enjoyed by all—including me!

In 1990 I was preparing to embark on the greatest adventure of my travel life. The safari brochure promised bountiful and sumptuous meals. I studied a brochure's photo showing a buffet table at an unnamed lodge. Despite my use of high-power magnification, the food items remained a collage of colors. While I am exaggerating, I was curious to know more about dining on a safari. Let's face it, my concern was "survival" in the bush.

In a word, our safari meals in Kenya were very good to superb. In some respects, such as afternoon tea, the Kenyans adhere to British customs established in the days of colonial rule. For the most part, our Kenyan hosts catered to Western palates in fine fashion. At Samburu Serena Lodge we enjoyed an evening buffet barbecue that included beef, chicken, and lamb, and service at all the lodges was always extensive. The number of busboys and waiters attending to us was excessive when measured by American standards.

Generally, breakfasts were ornate and bountiful buffets. Both quantity and quality were always present. Lunch was usually a buffet, while dinners were either elaborate buffets or sit-down meals. I was one with Africa. This was no place to find quiche or Brussels sprouts. It was a gratifying mix of Western foods served with superb rift valley vegetables. Service was excellent to the point of spoiling us rotten. We drank either bottled water or soda during our safari. Why? Because experts recommend this precaution to avoid gastrointestinal illness or other serious diseases. We also avoided uncooked vegetables and unpeeled fruits.

During our 1992 visit we stayed briefly at the New Stanley Hotel in Nairobi. Our room was small, ordinary, and disappointing compared with the room from our earlier stay at the Safari Park Hotel. But on the plus side, the New Stanley has two good restaurants. One is a traditional indoor eatery. The other is found on its roof, next to the refreshing rooftop swimming pool. We tried the rooftop restaurant, which offered a mixed-grill barbecue that was memorable. Besides tasty chicken and steak, we enjoyed ostrich, and I could hardly believe just how flavorful the ostrich steaks were. The taste was closer to beef than to fowl, and I found the meal a marvelous delicacy. This was one meal that did not find me crying "fowl."

Did I mention that the Carnivore restaurant is also a bargain? Carnivore's meals cost about $13 per person for the unique culinary extravaganza.

The Other Safari: Tanzania

Tanzania beckons to all those ready to tread off the beaten Kenyan path. In 1992 we were fortunate to return to Africa for our second safari. The vacation included a one-week visit to Kenya's tropical coast, followed by a safari in neighboring Tanzania. I will give an insider's view of a safari in Tanzania. If finances and time are not factors, then a Kenya safari with a Tanzania extension is, without question, the best of both African safari worlds.

At the time of our visit, Tanzania was an emerging nation. It had, for many years, been under Communist rule. More recently it has come under what locals describe as a benign dictatorship. Politics aside, the practical effect of this political history is that Tanzania has only recently shown interest in promoting tourism. Traditionally, Tanzania's tourist accommodations received a rating inferior to those of neighboring Kenya. However, Tanzania has something very special to offer. Besides its incredible parks and wildlife, it is home to a true wonder of the world, Ngorongoro Crater.

Tanzania is home to a vast array of large animals and birds of prey. The country stretches from the Serengeti Plain in the northwest, to Kenya in the north, Zambia and Mozambique to the southwest and south, respectively, and the Indian Ocean to the east. It also borders Lake Victoria and Lake Tanganyika.

We took Unitours' Tanzania in Depth (TZD) tour. Currently the price is $1,590, which includes six and a half days of actual safari time. Here is a capsule view of Unitours' Tanzania adventure as we experienced it:

Day One: An interesting thing happened on day one of our Tanzania adventure. We never left Kenya. Our van left Nairobi and headed toward the Sand River border crossing, a route that would revisit the wondrous Masai Mara. In fact, the five-hour drive from Nairobi returned us to the Mara Sopa Lodge, one of our favorites. Again I enjoyed a refreshing swim in its small pool overlooking the Serengeti Plain.

Day Two: There was good news and bad news on day two. The bad news was that due to political problems the Sand River border crossing was closed. This meant another five-hour drive back to Nairobi, where we would take an alternate route into Tanzania. What good news could possibly make up for such a wasteful, uncomfortable, and very bumpy ride? The answer is: lion cubs. The fates had decreed an extraordinary wildlife treat for us, one that would live in our memories forever.

Despite the afternoon drive back to Nairobi looming, we had the choice of a hot-air balloon ride over the Serengeti or a final Masai Mara game drive. For us the choice was simple in light of the hefty $325 per person price for the balloon ride, and it turned out to be one of our best safari decisions. Forty-five minutes later we turned a bend in the road and there they were. We had seen them in books, movies, and on the Discovery channel, but there they were—in the flesh. Ahead of us was a pride of lions including adult males, lionesses—and eight to ten cubs!

Patty repeatedly told our driver not to move the van as we continued to shoot stills and video. This was the photo opportunity of a lifetime. The cubs were alert and playful and were having a ball climbing over one another. I suffered goose bumps as one small cub climbed atop a sleeping male lion. At one point a cub came charging out of the bush in a mock attack on an unsuspecting sibling. All of this action took place within twenty to forty feet from our van—a supreme wildlife event that many visitors never experience.

After a restful lunch in Nairobi our van headed toward the nearby Tanzanian border. For the second time fate intervened to provide a near-private van for our safari. In Nairobi, we connected with two couples who had just completed a one-week tour of Kenya. In effect, we were plugging in to the second week of their two-week Kenya and Tanzania safari. In two days John fell ill and he and his wife returned to Nairobi. For the remainder of the safari, Patty and I were accompanied by Jad and Beth, a hip young couple from Ohio. The uncrowded van and excellent company made for a fun and memorable Tanzania safari. Again, four in a van makes for safari heaven.

Our long day's journey continued into night as we crossed the border into Tanzania, arriving in the capital city, Arusha, at 7:00 P.M. Then our van climbed a steep hill, and we finally arrived at our hotel, the Lake Manyara Sopa Lodge. This, the first Tanzanian game lodge, lived "down" to our expectations. It was 10:00 P.M. and we were bedraggled, tired, and hungry. The hotel was gracious and kept its dining room open in anticipation of our late arrival, but on the negative side, the evening entrée was an unidentifiable beef dish consisting of bits of leather-tough meat. The hotel offered sparse accommodations, with bare-bones rooms but a comfortable bed. Our second and final meal was a sparse, no-choice breakfast, basic but adequate, which included milk, orange juice, and cereals. Did I forget the single dish containing five hard-boiled eggs? We did not lose heart, and better days were ahead.

Days Three and Four: Upon checking out of the hotel the van headed down a long hill, and we entered what seemed to be the Garden of Eden, Lake Manyara Park. Not only did we marvel in awe at almost every species of African wildlife, but we soon approached, viewed, and photographed the rarely seen African sleeping tree lion. Lake Manyara is the only place on earth where these creatures are found. Exactly why these lions climb up and sleep on the high branches of trees is unknown. Our driver skillfully took us close to the tree lion, then warned us that vans were not permitted to stop, so we had only seconds to take our still and video shots. We proudly accomplished this task with ease.

The lake itself was a hotbed of wildlife activity, including everything from birds to hippos. In a forested area near the lake, elephants wandered within twenty feet of our van, while giraffes snacked on high bushes. We bid a fond farewell to Lake Manyara and headed west to Serengeti National Park.

Again, we found ourselves visiting the great Serengeti Plain, home to more than 2 million large animals and the site of the great wildebeest migration. This 5,600-square-mile national park is one of the great natural assets of African continent. We stayed at the Serengeti Sopa Lodge for two nights. As with the Manyara Sopa Lodge, the Serengeti Sopa Lodge bore no resemblance to the luxury and comfort found in neighboring Kenyan lodges. However, the architecture of the lodge, which incorporates large natural boulders into its design, is fascinating. I walked through its labyrinth of boulders and winding staircases, finally arriving at the lodge's immense dining room. However, the lack of hot water and the nearly falling ceiling tiles were disappointing. On the plus side, the beds were comfortable and our room had an endless view of the plains. Again, this lodge represented the best and worst of Tanzania's infrastructure. The food was, as we had anticipated substandard. Meals were bare-bones affairs. At breakfast we found a single pitcher of juice and cold cereal.

But the wildlife was incredible. We viewed many prides of lions, wandering wildebeests, cheetah, zebras, giraffes, and much more.

Days Five and Six: We left Serengeti Park and drove for two hours, stopping for lunch at Olduvai Gorge. This is the world-famous archeological site worked by the late Dr. Louis Leakey, who discovered "Lucy," one of the earliest remains of prehistoric humans. Standing above the gorge and viewing the origins of humankind was a cerebral experience, to say the least. After a short stop at the small Olduvai Gorge Museum we moved on for a date with another wonder of the world.

In short order we arrived at the largest intact volcanic crater in the world. Ngorongoro Crater, a collapsed volcano, is approximately ten miles in diameter, with a 2,000-foot rim. Though some large mammals enter and later leave the crater, most species consider it their permanent home. We were standing on the rim, viewing the crater below, when our transfer vehicle, a four-wheel-drive jeep, pulled up. The transfer was necessary because of the rough terrain and steep inclines from the rim to the base of the crater. We grabbed our bags and quickly transferred to the jeep for a two-day adventure. After transferring into a jeep, we descended into the crater, then crossed the crater floor, and then ascended back up to the rim and to our deluxe Tanzanian hotel, the Ngorongoro Sopa Lodge. Our driver compensated for his poor English with his skill at finding wildlife in the crater, including lions, rarely seen leopards, and two scarce rhinos.

I could write volumes about the Ngorongoro Sopa Lodge. The hotel is a virtual palace by any standard. It was the first of six ultra-deluxe hotels built by a German firm, the government contract with the firm intending to boost the nation's sagging tourist industry. The country plans to bring its tourist infrastructure into line with that of neighboring Kenya. We all agreed this first effort was a magnificent success. The opulent hotel had opened for business only ninety days before our arrival. The circular main building and restaurant have twenty-foot ceiling-to-floor windows that look out over the crater. Nearby is the restaurant's lounge and bar, sporting large comfortable sofas facing immense windows.

The guest accommodations consist of a row of large, round cottages split into upper and lower apartments. The bathrooms say it all—with marble floors, bidets, and wall hair dryers. Beyond the oversize king-size bed is a curved sitting area that contains mahogany rocking chairs facing more floor-to-ceiling windows overlooking the crater. The restaurant is a five-star extravaganza, with a five to one ratio of servers to guests. Its four-level dessert cart was beyond culinary belief. For a moment the four of us, Pat, Jad, Beth, and I, concluded that we must be dreaming. Then Beth took photos of the cart to impress her chef friend back home.

Our game drives were spectacular. We viewed and photographed rhinos, buffalos, gazelles, elephants, black-maned lions, hippos, and an array of smaller game and birds. During one drive into the crater, just as we left the lodge, a rare spotted leopard darted across the road just in front of the jeep.

Day Seven: We traveled from Ngorongoro Crater through Arusha while en route to Nairobi. Upon our return, Patty and I "forced" the Carnivore experience on our newfound safari friends, Jad and Beth. Once again, the Carnivore served up a perfect farewell dinner celebration. It was perhaps the best way to mitigate the sadness of our final day in Africa. Several hours later we were winging our way home.

In concluding this section I say, "Think the impossible!" Set your goal and anything is possible, even the ultimate thrill of an African safari!

Photo Memories

The year was 1962. The event was a family outing to Hyde Park, Franklin Delano Roosevelt's county estate on the Hudson River. My hand clutched my most precious possession—my first movie camera, a Yashica 8mm model. Before visiting the president's residence, my family and I visited his nearby grave site. As I stood filming FDR's tombstone, my mother motioned to my right. I ignored her gesture when, to my surprise, I felt her finger poking at my ribs. I turned toward my mother and was perplexed to see her so excited. She pointed over my left shoulder. This time I turned and looked. My eyes opened wide and my adrenaline rushed. Several feet to my right was Eleanor Roosevelt, in the flesh, escorting special guests on a tour of the estate. Within seconds, she began leading them toward the mansion's main entrance, a short distance away. With the speed of a paparazzi, I outpaced Mrs. Roosevelt and waited for her in the mansion's doorway. I firmly stood my ground and filmed the former first lady as she walked past my father, Sam, acknowledged him with a broad smile, and entered the residence. This footage is one of my priceless film possessions.

Over the years my love of photography has expanded to include both still and video underwater photography. My tips and money-saving advice will help you preserve a lifetime of great photo memories.

Point-and-Shoot Cameras

Despite the arrival of home video, 35mm still photography retains its firm grip on the vacationing American public. It is no longer necessary to choose between complicated single lens reflex (SLR) and overly-basic, fixed-lens cameras. Today, there is a new world of sophisticated point-and-shoot and more gimmicky Advanced Picture System (APS) cameras. These cameras use a new-sized drop-in film cartridge so that users never see or touch the negatives. That is a big plus.

Point-and-shoot cameras use 35mm film and offer models in every price range. Most have sophisticated features, are easy to operate, and deliver excellent results. If you decide to purchase a new point-and-shoot camera, I am certain that you have at least two key questions in mind. What is the best camera model and how do you find the lowest possible price?

➡ **Steve's Recommendation:** *I recommend purchasing a point-and-shoot camera with a wide-angle range of either 28mm or 35mm and a telephoto range of 120mm to 140mm. These models are usually priced between $175 and $350.*

Point-and-shoot camera prices range from $100 for a basic model to $450 for an advanced model with features similar to a good SLR.

Camera models are fickle, often changing with the cycles of the moon. When I mention specific models I realize they are periodically replaced by newer and hopefully better ones. Here is my checklist of features you should consider:

Camera weight: Generally the lighter and smaller the camera the better. Currently these cameras weigh between ten and sixteen ounces.

Viewfinders: Compare several models. Look for the largest, brightest and clearest viewfinder image.

Ease of Use: Major controls including the zoom and shutter buttons should permit easy one hand use.

Zoom Lens: I recommend a moderately priced 35mm to 140mm zoom lens.

Auto Focus System: All zoom models use an auto focus system.

Auto Flash With Red-Eye Reduction: Everyone wishes to do away with those devil-eye pictures. The camera you choose must have a red-eye reduction system.

➡ **Steve's Recommendation:** *I like the Pentax IQ quartz date models 140 (35mm to 140mm zoom) and 120 (35mm to 120mm zoom).*

Macro: The macro feature permits you to take extreme close-ups, usually from 18 to 24 inches from the subject. Make sure the model you select has this useful feature.

Waterproof Models: These are ideal for rugged use and for those who enjoy sailing or sunbathing amidst sand and surf. Consider the waterproof Olympus Infinity Zoom 135, with its 35mm to 120mm zoom lens or my favorite, the Pentax WR-90 with its modest 35mm to 90mm zoom lens.

Self Timer: Simply press a button and you have ten to fifteen seconds to run into the picture before the camera shutter automatically goes off. I love this feature.

Backlight Control: Backlight has probably killed as many photos as shaky hands and red eyes put together. The model you select must have a backlight control including an exposure lock button. Read your camera's manual and learn to use this important picture-saving feature.

Panoramic Pictures: Squeeze ten people, left to right, into your viewfinder and take the picture. With or without this feature your print will show the very same ten people. The panoramic feature simply cuts out the top and bottom portions of the scene and stretches the width of the final print from the usual six inches to ten inches. Make sure the camera permits you to change to and from panoramic mode in mid roll. My favored Pentax IQ models have this ability.

Advanced Picture System (APS) cameras have a switch that marks the photo so that it will be printed in any of three available sizes. These include 4" × 6", 4" × 7", and super-panoramic 4" ×

10" photos. At this time I would opt for the tried and true Pentax IQ 120 or 140, or the new Ricoh 130 Super, with panoramic ability rather than the APS models. This still allows users to select two sizes of prints, the regular 4" × 6" or panoramic.

Video Memories

We live in a world of video mania. Today, each of us has the opportunity to create spectacular video films. The subjects, from weddings to safaris, are endless. Some readers may be planning to purchase their first camcorder or an upgraded replacement for that old "dinosaur." I will offer solid tips on how to select the best camcorder, provide basic tips on how to best use existing equipment and save hundreds of dollars on a new purchase.

Why choose a Hi-Band 8mm camcorder? Here are my reasons:

- Overall picture quality, including color, brightness and sharpness, is 30% to 50% better than VHS, VHS-C, and regular 8mm models.
- Unlike VHS tapes 8mm cassettes are smaller and easier to carry.
- 8mm tapes are the only compact video cassettes that permit two full hours of filming.
- 8mm camcorders are the smallest and lightest on the market.
- Unlike VHS tapes 8mm tapes are coated with metal particles so their images will last up to fifty years.

➡ **Steve's Tip:** *How does one create exceptionally bright and crystal clear video images that surpass the performance of 80 to 90 percent of all other camcorders? My firm recommendation is the mail-order purchase of a high-resolution Hi-Band 8mm camcorder.*

Forget VHS-C camcorders that use those small "chunky" videotapes. VHS-C tapes hold only thirty minutes of videotape per cassette at standard speed. A claim that a VHS-C tape can film for ninety minutes is a half truth. Filming at slow, or extended play, does indeed stretch the thirty-minute VHS-C cassettes to ninety minutes, but this type of recording results in the poorest picture and sound quality you can obtain on home video. Is that what you want? VHS-C tapes must be replaced every thirty minutes, or four times during two hours of shooting. Do not miss that all-important "Kodak" moment while fumbling with a tape. In Africa I shot five to six hours of video using just three 8mm cassettes. This would have required *eighteen* VHS-C cassettes. The very thought of thirty-minute video cassettes numbs my photographic senses.

The Hi-Band 8mm camcorder offers the best high-resolution images and hi-fi sounds available. In fact, Hi-Band 8mm images are rated 30 to 50 percent sharper than regular VHS tapes used in most camcorders. The quality of Hi-Band 8mm rivals that of video laser discs. My vote is for the best picture and sound available. End of story!

It is true that the thirty-minute VHS-C cassettes do fit into an adapter that plays on all VCRs. On the other hand, 8mm owners simply run a cord from the camcorder to the VCR. The unmatched virtues of Hi-Band 8mm camcorders warrant a trade-off of the VHS-C adapter.

CAVEAT: Hi-Band 8mm camcorders cost more, but recently prices have dropped. Mail-order savings of $200 to $1,000 reduce prices of Hi-Band 8mm camcorders to well under $1,000.

Recommended Camcorders and Features

My top choices are Sony and Canon brand hi-band 8mm hi-fi camcorders.

I recommend the following camcorder features:

- Tilting color viewfinder with optional spare LCD screen.
- Minimum ten power optical zoom lens.
- Macro focus for great close-ups.
- Built-in titles and special effects.
- Video stabilization system for steadier pictures.

Steve's Special Still and Video Photo Tips

Bean Bag: So, what is the great $10 photo bean bag? Before leaving on our first safari I noticed a small advertisement in

Popular Photography magazine. The advertisement promised that video shots could be steadied simply by using a video bean bag. The more I thought about it the more it made sense. While many video accessories cost $100 or more, this purchase was a solid winner. As others in the van struggled to keep their camcorders steady, I used my amazing bean bag. The reason it works so well is twofold. First, tripods are not practical to set up and use inside a safari van. Second, the van's railing, just below the pop top, is curved so that one cannot place a camera on the rail. Enter the photo bean bag, placed squarely on the curved upper surface of the window railing. My camcorder rested solidly on the bean bag. Any bean bag will do. My associate Nancy kindly made one at home, as a spare, and it worked like a charm.

Bracketing: This is perhaps the most important but least followed of photographic techniques. Here is a fun example: A son attended his parents' fiftieth wedding anniversary. His parents stood behind a huge cake, posing as they prepared to cut the first slice. It was a once-in-a-lifetime "Kodak" moment. The son jumped to his feet and snapped the "perfect" photo. Several days later he stared, horror stricken, at the photo of his parents. His father was standing with his eyes closed as if sleeping in a vertical position. His mother had a grotesque half smile and her tongue hung slightly from her mouth. For a fleeting moment the son questioned whether he is the progeny of alien beings. His confusion was compounded since he had no recollection of any such expression when he took the photo.

Bracketing means that you take more than one picture of an important subject. Is the shot so special that really good results are essential? The truth is that bracketed shots pay for themselves with great results.

Titles: This is a favorite of mine. When I shot my safari video, I carried a white pad and a magic marker. One day, while our van traversed an endless bumpy road, I quickly scratched out the title "The Bumpy Road to Arusha" and stored it in my camcorder's memory. I then chose a quiet scene—blue sky above a herd of zebra —and filmed the title over the sky portion of the scene. My Ricoh camcorder also permits titles to scroll (roll) from the top to the bottom of the screen. I often use this technique on a plane flight as a prearrival shot. Such a title might read "Our Flight to Nairobi."

Leave one or two minutes of tape blank at the beginning of each videotape. You then have the option of adding a different or better title later.

Occasionally a still photo will proclaim the success of a vacation. One good example comes to mind. We have a wonderful picture of Patty and me in Kenya, standing in front of a large sign that reads simply "Equator."

Keep in mind that features are only as good as they are convenient and easy to use. I refuse to "type" titles into my camcorder using tiny buttons. It takes too long and is not worth the effort.

Fades: I love to use fades. My trusty Ricoh has a full fading capability: I can fade into or out of a scene. Just in case this term escapes you, a fade-in is a scene that starts in black or white and then slowly dissolves into the image one is filming. A fade-out is the opposite: The scene being filmed slowly turns to black or white and the sound slowly fades too.

Macro: Let me harp on the word *creativity.* Whether shooting still or video, you should make this feature a part of your photographic arsenal. The possibilities for great close-ups are endless. In Kenya I came upon colorful lizards that transformed into threatening prehistoric monsters when taped at a distance of several inches. (Yes, my Ricoh camcorder can focus to one-half an inch!)

People: I have come to appreciate the uniqueness and diversity of people around the world. Occasionally, local people make the best photographic subjects. In South Dakota, I photographed a dancing Oglala Sioux Indian, and on the Paris Metro I videotaped a musician's uncanny puppet act. Always be aware of surroundings, and do not be afraid to be bold and creative! However, if necessary or appropriate, ask a subject's permission.

➡ **Steve's Rule:** *Always bring a sufficient supply of film on vacation. And keep in mind: the more exotic your destination the higher the cost of film. In Africa a roll of Kodak film costs as much as $10 or more per roll.*

The Wonderful World of Mail-Order Shopping!

Many of you will no doubt find this to be an alien topic. However, prospective camera and camcorder purchasers have one thing in common—they want to pay the lowest possible price. Major chain stores such as Circuit City or the Good Guys generally have good prices. In fact, such stores will usually match any competitor's lower prices for thirty or sixty days after a purchase.

So why bring up the issue of mail order? Why should anyone deal with a seller thousands of miles away? Because mail-order shoppers save hundreds of dollars or more on their favorite purchases. The plain fact is that mail order may appear, on the surface, to be unnecessary and risky. Consequently many shoppers ignore this money-saving option.

Yet I and thousands like me have shopped for cameras and other major electronic items by mail order for decades. I spent thousands of dollars on such purchases and have *never* lost a dime in the process. When, after twenty years, I received my first defective mail-order item, an expensive laser disc player, the dealer immediately sent me a replacement.

First, buy a copy of *Popular Photography* magazine, because it does offer unique safeguards. Flip to the advertisements that take up fully half of the magazine's rear section. Search the beginning of this section for one page called Check Rated Program. The program sets forth the magazine's advertising codes, intended to protect readers making mail-order purchases. The section explains mail-order shopping and tells readers what to ask when placing an order. Those companies who subscribe to the code have, somewhere in their advertisement, a check mark within a small circle that says "Popular Photography Check Rated Store." Then, should anything go amiss with an order, the magazine promises to help resolve the problem. But I have *never* come close to using this service during my twenty years of mail-order shopping.

Your First Mail-Order Purchase

Do Your Homework. First, check *Consumer Reports* magazine, talk to friends, review any available test reports, and window-shop locally. Compare various models of cameras or camcorders using my checklist. Check the "feel" and features of each of the various models. Note the exact model and best local price of the camera you wish to purchase. Make sure to find out whether your selected camera is sold as a kit that includes batteries, a case, and strap.

Check *Popular Photography* magazine advertisements and list the five best prices and dealers.

Read advertisements carefully. If an advertisement simply lists a super-low price but does not state that a U.S. or manufacturer's warranty is included, then it is 99 percent certain the item is grey market. No, a "grey market" is not a place one goes to shop on a horribly overcast day. To sell cameras and camcorders at unorthodox low prices, many advertisers sell "grey-market" products. A grey-market camera is one that was imported into the United States bypassing the licensed U.S. distributor. While grey-market items are perfectly legal, they *do not* have a U.S. warranty. Rather, they are sold with an international warranty that is not honored by the camera's U.S. distributor. The microscopic print on the bottom of the page says that U.S. warranties are available at an extra cost.

Note if the seller lists the street address of its retail store or whether it is strictly a mail-order operation. Note the seller's return policy and the amount of any restocking charge. This is the amount charged for a returned, nondefective item. Keep in mind that mail order sellers make a marginal profit. They expect buyers to know exactly what model they wish to purchase. In the rare instance of a defective product, such as my laser disc player, they will accept the return and quickly replace the item. If a buyer is not pleased with an item, it may be returned. However, dealers are not happy to accept returns of nondefective items. In such an instance the buyer must act quickly, usually within seven to fourteen days, and also pay any applicable restocking fee.

➡ **Steve's Tip:** *I always purchase camera gear that includes the manufacturer's U.S. warranty. Some sellers include the warranty while others charge extra, usually $10 to $25 for it. I do this because I demand the protection of the manufacturer's warranty and also because I am a member of Buyers Advantage (800-553-4948). This wonderful outfit extends U.S. warranties to two full years on all products I purchase. If you explore the small microscopic print on the bottom of the page it will often say that U.S. warranties are available at an extra cost.*

Make certain there is no surcharge for paying with Visa.

Make the Necessary Phone Calls.   Most advertisements mention that their toll-free number is only to be used for placing orders. Despite this, most out-of-state stores will quote their latest price. If they are curt, tell the salesperson you are "considering" paying by cashier's check and need the total price, with shipping and handling. But do this only if you are "considering" that option— right? (Of course, you *may* later decide to use Visa.)

Compare Your Data.   Compare the gathered purchase information. Determine which check rated dealer is offering the best price, with a U.S. warranty and all manufacturer's accessories included. If more than one dealer is in the running, compare return and restocking policies. Also, find out whether the seller charges extra for using a credit card (most do not), and compare shipping and handling charges. Finally, I am prejudiced in favor of a dealer who has a retail outlet in its home city.

Place Your Order!   After deciding on a particular dealer, call and place your order. Follow the suggestions in the *Popular Photography* program. Get the name of the salesperson and purchase order number. Follow up on the order with a fax or mail confirmation. Dealers ship most orders surface UPS so that they arrive in six to eight days. When the order arrives, be sure to check it out immediately. Do *not* complete any warranty papers until the item is thoroughly checked and is functioning properly. In the unlikely event there is a defect in the unit you must return all "virgin" paperwork. If the warranty papers are prematurely completed, you may not return the item but still have the full protection of the manufacturer's warranty.

➡ **Steve's Tip:** *Some cameras, mostly point-and-shoot models, are sold either "à la carte" or as a kit. A kit usually includes expensive lithium batteries worth up to $15, a strap, and case. Yet, a very few mail order operators "invade" camera kits, remove batteries, and try to sell them to gain an extra $15 on the sale. This is a shoddy practice.*

How Much Can You Save?

Here are some amazing examples:

- The Sony Hi-Band 8mm model TRV-70 was selling for $1,580 at local dealers. This state-of-the-art camcorder has image stabilization, digital special effects, a super 24 power digital zoom lens, a swivel four-inch color LCD monitor, and a black-and-white viewfinder. The same camera was available at Abe's of Maine, with a U.S. warranty at the delivered price of $1,099. This is an incredible savings of $481!
- Hi-Band and 8mm for under $1,000? Absolutely! Sony's TR-600 is lighter on price but great on features. It has a 24-power zoom lens, image stabilization, color viewfinder, digital effects and wireless remote. It sold locally for $1,200 (including tax). Beach Camera offered the same camcorder with a U.S. warranty for the delivered price of just $880—another whopping savings of $320.
- Canon's top-of-the-line ES-2000 Hi-Band 8mm camcorder, with 20x optical zoom lens, stabilization, and color viewfinder sold in retail stores for $1,400. Abe's Camera was selling the same camcorder with a U.S. warranty for the delivered price of $940—a savings of $460!
- A solid point-and-shoot choice is the Minolta Freedom Zoom 140EX kit that sold at retail shops for $400 (including tax). Coast to Coast Camera was selling the very same camcorder for $317.
- The Olympus point-and-shoot 3500 zoom model sold at retail shops for $330. It was available from Beach Camera for the delivered price of $250, a savings of $80.
- The Pentax model IQ 120 sold at retail shops for $340. Coast to Coast Camera sold this one for the delivered price of just $247, a saving of $93.

Here is a short list of dealers I have successfully dealt with over the past twenty years:

Adorama: (800) 815-1260 or (212) 741-0052
Abe's Camera: (800) 807-2237 (only check-rated store with toll-free customer service)

Beach Camera: (800) 634-1811; fax (908) 424-1105 (check-rated store)

Camera World of Oregon: (800) 222-1557 or (503) 227-6008; fax (503) 227-7070

Coast to Coast Camera: (800) 788-5555

Focus Camera: (800) 221-0828 or (718) 437-8810 (check-rated store)

Smile Photo and Video: (800) 366-6993 (check-rated store)

Congratulations, you are on your way to years of huge savings on the most current and sophisticated electronic products available. I should emphasize that these dealers sell much more than cameras and camcorders. Many of them sell computers, audio and video components, and telecommunications gear.

11

Moorea, Tahiti: Dream Vacation Extraordinaire

Tahiti most closely resembles paradise on earth. The very name conjures images of primeval tropical beauty. Papeete, the capital city of French Polynesia, is on the island of Tahiti. The island of Moorea, just eleven miles away, is a "Garden of Eden," sans cities, stoplights, and other trappings of modern civilization. It has escaped the ravages of wars, poverty, and the rise and fall of civilizations. Its magnificent bays and volcanic peaks beckoned Cooks ships to land there, and later the *Bounty* laid anchor at Opunohu Bay. Have I mentioned the beautiful French Polynesians, French food, and Moorea's sparkling clear lagoons, rich in marine life?

Moorea is thirty-seven miles in circumference with one encircling road, no stop lights, and no cities. It has small villages that consist of little more than a supermarket and gas station. There are no high-rises. In fact, I have yet to see a single elevator on the entire island. Electricity first arrived on Moorea about twelve years ago. The locals continue to fish and farm as their main livelihood. The best of the hotels are knockouts, with thatched huts on stilts stretching out over clear waters. At night, guests may raise a trap door in their room and view fish in the lighted waters below. These accommodations are expensive and may cost hundreds of dollars per night. We have done one better, staying at a fraction of that cost. Each day, from the balcony of our room or the porch of our bungalow, we have enjoyed the most spectacular view on Moorea—the unmatched beauty of Cooks Bay.

There are good reasons why most people only dream of stretching out on a beach in Moorea. For one thing, travel to exotic and distant tropical islands is by definition high priced. Why, you ask? Because fewer people fly there and hence few airlines service such remote islands. Economically, this translates into very high air fares and hotel prices. This also holds true for Nairobi, Kenya, which is the most expensive air destination the world.

Tahiti is a low-volume exotic tourist destination. Since the dawn of air travel Tahiti has been accessible only to the wealthy. Today the Tahitian Tourist Bureau states that the annual number of visitors to the Tahitian islands equals the weekly number of visitors to Hawaii! This statistic puts Tahiti in perspective. Presently, the cost of a Quantas economy ticket to Papeete from the West Coast is $775 to $875, depending on the season. The cost of a week's lodging can add up to $2,660 (per couple) to the bill for an over-the-water bungalow at the Beachcomber Parkroyal Hotel. Add the cost of meals at upper-end hotels and the price per couple for one week in Moorea is about $5,698. Case closed.

So, how do I translate this into a highly recommended cheapskate dream vacation? Enter bargain tour operators Islands in the Sun, Tahiti Vacations, and Sunmakers Travel Group, which use AOM and Corsair Airlines. These names are not household words, but they are an integral part of my cheapskate travel vocabulary.

In the spring of 1993, I was reading the *San Francisco Chronicle*'s travel section when I came upon a small, one-eighth-page advertisement for a vacation package to Tahiti, placed by Islands in the Sun, a South Pacific specialty tour operator. It announced a one-week trip to Moorea at the incredible low price of $699 per person, which included airfare from the West Coast and *eight days lodging!* Could this possibly be true, I thought? Tahiti for $699? If this checked out, then Patty and I would be packing our bags and winging west over the Pacific. After all, this was not Mexico or even Hawaii, but Tahiti!

Many questions immediately came to mind. How does one follow up on such an ad? Where does one start? What did I really know about Tahiti? What about lodging? At $699 would we be using an outhouse? Overall this deal seemed far too good to be true. But then...the ad said what it said, and wasn't I once told not to look a gift horse in the mouth?

So we did it. Not only did we travel to Moorea in June 1993, we went there again just three months later, in September. We were so smitten with this lush tropical land that we returned to Moorea in September 1994 and again in March 1996. The cost of each of our first two trips was $664 ($699 less the Travelers Advantage 5 percent rebate). Our third trip permitted the use of Kraft's free dollars. We used $400 in free travel cash to reduce the price to just $499 per person. In March 1996 we opted for the Corsair package and again paid only $664 each for an entire eight-day vacation.

➥ **Steve's Tip:** *When I mention Tahiti Vacations' package using AOM or Air New Zealand, free travel dollars, if available, may be used to further reduce package prices. When I mention Corsair Airlines, a charter airline, note that free travel dollars cannot be used. Instead, you can use Travelers Advantage's discount for a 5 percent rebate on the entire package or Pearson Travel's $100 offer. Either way, don't miss the opportunity to use cheapskate bargain deals.*

On each of these visits Patty and I booked Islands in the Sun's basic $699 package, utilizing Cooks Bay Resort for lodging on Moorea. Tahiti Vacations, another South Pacific specialty tour operator, offers a similar eight-day package to Cooks Bay Resort. One important distinction between the two is that Tahiti Vacations uses only regularly scheduled, noncharter airlines, including AOM French Airlines and Air New Zealand, on its bargain Tahiti packages. Sunmakers Travel Group is located in Seattle, Washington, and also offers cheapskate packages to Tahiti, including the same $699 Moorea package offered by Islands in the Sun.

Without further ado, let me assure you that a Tahiti dream vacation is easily within your grasp by using my recommended cheapskate air-and-land packages. Departures are from Los Angeles or Oakland, California. Use my strategies to arrange travel to your West Coast connecting flight. Besides the super low regular fares offered by many major and smaller airlines, use any other available option, such as a free travel program or a free companion ticket. Travel to the West Coast should be either free or cost you no more than $250 to $350 from most U.S. cities. But before delving into specific recommendations, I must mention two related matters.

The Dilemma of the "Wannabe" Vacationer

Let me get this one off my chest and behind us. During our last visit to Cooks Bay Resort I overheard two "mature" women lamenting to their husbands. "This place is terrible!" said one of the women. "I can't believe the small room and those ridiculous open shelves for clothes, not even a dresser," said the other.

I shall refer to these ladies as members in good standing of the "wannabe" clan. First, they and their husbands want to be bargain vacationers and pay incredibly low prices for a hotel on world famous Cooks Bay. To this end they "chose" Cooks Bay Resort. Then a metamorphosis took place and they came face to face with the "wannabe" dilemma. In their heart of hearts they really "wanna be" staying at a $400-per-night over-the-water bungalow for the same bargain price they paid at Cooks. These "wannabes" happily derided their own vacation choice and willingly whined away their week in paradise.

For my part, I pull no punches. Rest assured that my cheapskate Moorea recommendation includes clean, comfortable lodging with private bath and a private lanai (balcony) that offers the best scenic view in the South Pacific. Of course, I discuss the pros and cons of available properties and always offer readers options, such as a bargain-priced upgrade to a private bungalow at Cooks Bay Resort.

The only "wannabe" I am concerned with are the readers who "wanna be" enjoying a world-class dream vacation at an incredible cheapskate price and who make intelligent decisions to achieve this end.

Moorea Recommendations

My cheapskate recommendation goes to Tahiti Vacation's $699 eight-day, seven-night vacation at Cooks Bay Resort. The package uses scheduled AOM French Airlines and departs from Los Angeles weekly on Tuesday evenings. This amazing package includes air from Los Angeles, seven full nights on Moorea, and an interisland flight on Air Tahiti to and from Papeete and Moorea. But remember, weekend departures cost $50 extra. How about my second and third choices? My second choice is Islands in the Sun's $699 eight-day Tahiti Escapes package, which includes six nights' lodging at Cooks Bay Resort.

Of course there are always other options. Are you willing to spend more than $699? Do you require a larger room and more privacy than any hotel room provides? Consider an upgrade to a Cooks Bay Resort garden- or lagoon-view bungalow. Also, just up the road from Cooks Bay Resort is the Club Bali Hai Hotel. Consider this an upscale property that is also located on Cooks Bay. Whichever Cooks Bay hotel you choose, the best possible Moorea experience awaits!

The AOM package provides seven nights and seven full days on Moorea. On the other hand, other packages using Corsair Airlines require that customers leave Moorea one day earlier for an overnight stay in Papeete in order to catch an early morning flight home. We have found Papeete to be lackluster, with congested traffic and run-of-the-mill T-shirt and souvenir shops. Also, by the time one transfers from Moorea to the overnight hotel on Tahiti, there is precious little time left in the day to accomplish any serious sightseeing on Tahiti.

If your package requires the last night to be spent on Tahiti, remember to request the late-afternoon ferry leaving Moorea at 4:00 P.M. This will allow extra time on Moorea before departure.

Booking Your Dream Vacation

Before I launch into a more detailed discussion of Moorea, let's review the options available:

1. Book with ITH and use free travel cash.

2. Join and then book with Travelers Advantage to obtain a 5 percent cash rebate and other valuable freebies, such as a free hotel voucher and/or a $50 voucher offered to new members.

3. To avoid travel agent fees, book directly with either Islands in the Sun or Sunmakers Travel Group. Tahiti Vacations, on the other hand, must be booked through a travel agent, though all the packages I mention may be booked through your local travel agent.

4. Book with Pearson Travel and save up to 7 percent.

Regardless of how these trips are booked, you will enjoy a four-star vacation at a cheapskate price.

When this chapter is finished, turn to the appendix for phone numbers and call the various tour operators to request their brochures. Be sure to ask Islands in the Sun for both its regular brochure and its super-bargain Tahiti Escapes brochure. Ask Sunmakers for its bargain Moorea flyers, in particular the $699 Moorea package. Also request Tahiti Vacations to provide both its regular brochure and its separate bargain flyer describing the $699 Moorea package.

Tahiti Vacations

Tahiti Vacations' Moorea package, using scheduled AOM French Airlines, gets my recommendation. First and foremost, it offers the best one-week Cooks Bay Resort package. I say this is best because the package includes seven full days and nights on Moorea. Want more? When free travel dollars are available they may be used to book this package, since AOM is a scheduled airline. Not using free dollars? The price is still a super cheapskate at just $699 for AOM's Tuesday Los Angeles departures. Since Tahiti Vacations owns Air Tahiti, the package offers another super bonus, interisland flights to and from Papeete and Moorea, ensuring the earliest possible arrival at your hotel. This is more than a $100 bonus when compared to Island in the Sun's ferry transportation to Moorea.

A word about these recommended cheapskate prices. Do not for a moment think the incredible $699 package offered by Tahiti Vacations and other tour operators are limited promotions, here today and gone tomorrow. In 1993 we booked our first Cooks Bay Resort vacation at the $699 price, less a Travelers Advantage discount. These package prices have held steady during the past three years. While the prices are reviewed every six months, Tahiti Vacations and its competitor announced that the $699 package price is again approved through December 31, 1996. If and when the price does increase, it will be nominal, perhaps $50 to $75.

Finally, the risk of flight cancellation, ever present with Island in the Sun's Corsair charter flights, is minimized when using regularly scheduled AOM noncharter flights. The above package, for fifteen days and fourteen nights, is priced at only $954. (Later in this chapter I discuss the three nearby major Moorea hotels, the Club Bali Hai, the Sofitel la Ora, and the Bali Hai Moorea. In each case these hotels are upscale properties that you may wish to consider.)

Also, Tahiti Vacations offers the best bargain price for a Cooks Bay Resort upgrade to a garden bungalow package, priced at $849. See my section on Cooks Bay Resort upgrades for further details.

No free travel dollars? Book through Pearson Travel (no membership fee) or join and use Travelers Advantage.

Call Tahiti Vacations at (800) 553-3477 for updated information on seven- and fourteen-night packages. Tahiti Vacations does not take direct reservations, so book your trip through ITH (if using free dollars), Pearson Travel, or Travelers Advantage.

Islands in the Sun's Tahiti Escapes Program

My second-choice package is Islands in the Sun's Tahiti Escapes Package to Cooks Bay Resort, still priced at $699, or just $664 using the Travelers Advantage 5 percent rebate. This special package uses Corsair Airlines' scheduled weekly charter flights departing form Los Angeles on Sunday evenings and from Oakland, California, on Friday evenings. The vacation includes six nights (not seven) at Cooks Bay Resort on Moorea, one night on the island of Tahiti at the Tahiti Hotel, all transfers, baggage handling, and ferry service from the main island of Tahiti to the island of Moorea, eleven miles away.

Okay, ready for the ultimate cheapskate dream vacation? Have two weeks to spare? The above Tahiti Escapes package to Cooks

Bay Resort is priced at about $869 for *fifteen days and fourteen nights!*
Deduct a 5 percent rebate through Travelers Advantage and the
price is reduced to $825. Yes, two weeks in Moorea, including air
and lodging, for $825 *per person!* And this is *without* using free
travel cash.

➡ **Steve's Tip:** *$699 is a cash price. Islands in the Sun applies a 3
percent surcharge to use a Citibank card or any other charge card.
Beat this one by using Travelers Advantage. Along with the 5
percent rebate, Travelers permits payment by charge card. Travelers
then sends an agency check to Islands in the Sun, saving you
another $21. Also, the above prices have held steady since 1993, and
they are guaranteed for Los Angeles departures through December
1996, when prices may or may not be slightly increased. Also, these
low prices include Friday departures. For reasons I shall soon
discuss, I do not recommend Island's Oakland flights.*

Islands in the Sun employees are ready to help with your
vacation plans. They offer both AOM and Corsair packages. Call
Islands' general number, (800) 828-6877, or their Tahiti Escapes
department, at (800) 642-1881.

A word about gateway cities is in order. This is more or less a
luck-of-the-draw travel situation. As West Coast residents, Patty
and I lost the draw on our Kenya, London, and Club Med
vacations, which departed from Fairbanks, New York's JFK, and
Miami respectively. On the other hand, we are winners when it
comes to Hawaii, Tahiti, and China vacations that depart from
either Los Angeles or San Francisco. East Coast readers are
winners when it comes time to vacation in Europe, the Caribbean,
or Africa.

In all these situations your goal is to get the best available
bargain or free airfare to the American gateway city in question.
Use my super strategies to obtain free American AAdvantage
domestic travel for just 25,000 miles. Or consider bargain carriers
such as Tower Air, which currently charges just $278 round-trip
from the New York area to Los Angeles. Low cost Midwest flights

from Chicago to Los Angeles and San Francisco are available. For example, American Trans Air (ATA) offers a super low round-trip fare of just $218 from Chicago's Midway Airport to San Francisco and $258 from Midway to Los Angeles. Always check your local newspaper's travel section for bargain domestic fares on popular routes to New York, Miami, and the West Coast. Remember. When there is a will there is a bargain travel way!

Scheduled Versus Charter Flights

Confused by "scheduled" air versus "charter" flights? On the plus side, my experience on three Corsair charter flights out of Los Angeles, as well as reports from associates, family, and friends, confirms that all flights departed on schedule or have a one- to four-hour delay. However, our March 1996 Corsair flight from Oakland was canceled. In fact, Corsair canceled all flights for the month of March from Oakland. I discussed this matter with an executive of Corsair's owner, Nouvelles Frontières, and learned that their decision was purely economic. It seems that passenger bookings for March were low, so Corsair canceled all flights except those on the last day or two of the month. Pouring salt on the wound, passengers were given notice of the cancellation as little as three weeks prior to departure. The airline claims its "right" as a charter to protect its interests by such outlandish conduct. Fortunately, such mass cancellations have not occurred with Corsair's Los Angeles flights, although I am told that several single flights, during 1995–96, were canceled because of low bookings. When they canceled the March 1996 flights, Nouvelles Frontières offered three vacation options. Only a small number of passengers were accommodated by option number one: a rebooking on competitor AOM's flight on the very same day but departing out of Los Angeles. The second option was to rebook passengers on Corsair's Sunday evening flight from Los Angeles to Papeete and include a free connecting flight from the Bay Area to Los Angeles. A third option was for passengers to reschedule their vacations at a later date. Of course, a full refund was available to any passengers sufficiently soured to forego their planned vacation. The "rub" with the two-day, delayed Sunday evening departure is the loss of an additional work day due to the midweek (Monday) return, compared to the originally booked Saturday return. One also loses the Sunday "buffer," or rest day, afforded by a Saturday return.

This is another reason Tahiti Vacations' regularly-scheduled AOM vacation is my first and best bargain choice. I have already explained the advantages of this package over the similar Islands in the Sun eight-day package to Cooks Bay Resort. I now emphasize the importance of Tahiti Vacations' use of scheduled air over charter service. This is a good time to mention, again, that Islands in the Sun also offers the eight-day Cooks Bay Resort package using AOM's regularly scheduled flights. Island's package is priced higher, at $799. Remember that all AOM packages permit the use of free travel dollars, if available.

Should you absolutely avoid Corsair's Oakland flights? No, not if you require the convenience of a local departure and accept the risk of cancellation on short notice.

Have I mentioned that getting there is often the worst part of a world-class vacation, as in our missed London flight to Africa? Our philosophy, being seasoned travelers, is to roll with the travel punches whenever possible. We know all too well that long-distance travel on commercial flights, in less than first class, is often one of those necessary evils in travel life. However, the jet age reduces these discomforts to a matter of hours—and then we arrive in paradise!

Ferry Versus Interisland Flights

A word about the choice between a ferry and an interisland flight. It takes twenty minutes to drive from Papeete Airport to the ferry dock in downtown Papeete. The high-speed catamaran *Aremiti II* provides a swift, refreshing, and scenic thirty-minute, eleven-mile ride to Moorea, and we enjoyed this refreshing ferry trip after the long flight to Tahiti. The scenery is spectacular, especially the lush green mountains and volcanic peaks that surround Moorea's dock. Each visit I find myself standing in the open air, at the bow of the ship, taking in the unparalleled surroundings. On the other hand, an interisland flight is faster and may save up to two hours when transferring from Papeete to Moorea.

What to Bring

I maintain packing lists for various categories of travel destinations—"ski" or "tropical." Let me begin with an excerpt from my Tahiti list. The items below are either hard to find on Moorea or are very expensive.

- Canned tuna, turkey, and/or chicken
- Italian or beef salami
- Condiments and utensils
- Lemonade powder, Tang, Crystal Light powders, a funnel
- Large box of cereal
- Six packages of Carnation's Kiss of Cream 1 percent powdered milk (makes six quarts)
- Two, two-quart liquid containers
- Two plastic cereal bowls and two plastic plates with plastic utensils
- Insulated water bottles
- Zippered food bag
- Ziploc bags, both large and small, about four each
- Small steak knife
- Two large mugs
- Noxema, sunscreen, and lip balm

Miscellaneous Items

- A water safe. This is a small, plastic, waterproof container that holds our room key and money while I am happily snorkeling. It costs about $5 and is sold in surfing or diving shops.
- Snorkel fins are essential, since Cooks Bay Resort has only a few available. Other hotels may or may not offer fins.
- Triple antibiotic ointment
- At the minimum, bring one good flashlight (waterproof for night snorkeling)
- A good, small scissors
- A good, small, general multipurpose tool with a screwdriver
- An extra camera battery and the camera's instructions.
- Dual voltage hair dryer for 220 voltage
- Dual voltage curling iron for quick curls, again for 220 voltage

Arriving in Paradise—Papeete

Cheapskate excursions to the Polynesian paradise begin with either of two French airlines, Corsair or AOM. The Los Angeles flights are continuations of flights originating in Paris. Planes arriving at LAX carry a bevy of French tourists en route to their favorite South Pacific destination. Upon boarding Corsair's flights we found the rear section is reserved for U.S. passengers while the forward section is already filled with French tourists.

Once airborne the nonstop flight takes only seven and a half hours from the West Coast to Tahiti's capital city, Papeete. In this regard the nonstop Corsair and AOM flights are deluxe ones.

➡ **Steve's Tip:** *Every airline is subject to delays. My best estimate on Corsair and AOM service to Papeete is that 75 percent of the time these flights leave thirty minutes to two hours late. And 25 percent of the time they leave more than two hours late. On one occasion our Corsair flight left LAX four and a half hours late, causing us to miss our morning catamaran connection to Moorea. Bring a good book, a Walkman, or other delay-survival gear to the airport.*

As our Corsair 747 touched down on the runway at Papeete Airport, Patty and I reveled in the realization that we had made it to Tahiti. Next stop—customs! I always find customs processing, even in a small terminal on an exotic tropical island, to be a drudge that involves check-in lines, the search for luggage, and passport control. So I was not yet one with paradise, but I *was* getting closer!

After we cleared customs, a tour bus took us to the ferry dock in downtown Papeete, a twenty-minute drive from the airport. (Tahiti Escapes and Sunmakers packages include all transfers, from airport to ferry and from ferry to hotel.) The dock area was pleasant enough, with its rest rooms, benches, and a string of food trucks selling drinks and sandwiches. There we eagerly awaited the arrival of our high-speed ride, the catamaran *Aremiti II*, which would travel the final eleven miles to nearby Moorea. On our recent return to Moorea the dock area provided a show of gorgeous sailing vessels. Both the five-masted *Club Med II* and the famed four-masted *Windsong* cruise ships were berthed at the port, one behind the other. What a sight!

Your ferry connection depends on the time of your arrival in Papeete. On one visit we enjoyed the best scenario, arriving at the dock only minutes before the ferry's departure. This ensured the earliest possible arrival at Cooks Bay Resort—by 10:00 A.M. The worst scenario came to pass on one of our trips when our delayed Corsair flight arrived in Papeete about four hours late, which required us to catch an afternoon ferry, at 2:00 P.M.

➡ **Steve's Tip:** *This is important: At the ferry dock, before setting out on a walkabout of downtown Papeete (assuming you have the time) exchange the ferry vouchers in the travel document packet for the actual ferry tickets at the ferry's ticket office.*

Patty and I are true-blue experts at making the best of travel "situations." In this instance we took a leisurely walk through downtown Papeete. Anyone with similar time on their hands should do the same. I enjoyed walking the side streets, where the three- and four-story buildings have wrought-iron balconies reminiscent of New Orleans. But I found Papeete's streets crowded with unsightly traffic. The town's sidewalks are jigsaws of uneven and broken concrete. Parisian-type cafes are scattered throughout the city. Our choices included shopping, doing some necessary banking, or simply relaxing over drinks or lunch while waiting for the ferry.

We did some early "housekeeping," picking up bottled water. By our third visit we skipped the bottled water (more about this topic later) and searched instead for bargain-priced bottles of soda. We picked up a few Parisian-style baguettes at Papeete's best bakery, the Boulangerie Patisseri Eti d'Or, found on Rue de Mal Foch at the corner of Rue Edouard Ahnne, across the street from the Banc de Tahiti. By the time we arrived at Cooks Bay it was very late afternoon.

➡ **Steve's Banking Tip:** *Local banks are closed on Saturdays and Sundays. In this case use the airport's exchange booth, which is always open. On weekdays a better exchange rate is available at the downtown banks. With your back to the ferry dock, cross the main street and turn right and walk about three blocks. Stop at the first bank. All the bank rates are similar, and Polynesian French francs are always available at your hotel. I purchased only $200 in Polynesian francs. (Remember, your goal is to charge everything possible on your Citibank card. A credit card offers the best exchange rate and adds miles to your American AAdvantage account. As of mid-1996 the exchange rate was 85 francs to the U.S. dollar.)*

Arriving on Moorea

There we were, stepping onto Moorea's dock. This was the island of dreams. Civilization was quickly becoming a fuzzy memory. Gone were traffic lights, cities, tall buildings, and crowded, congested streets. Instantly, we knew this was one of the best travel decisions of our lives.

All luggage was off-loaded to the rustic Moorea dock, allowing everyone to "go for it" and find their belongings. We waited and finally heard a van driver calling out the name, "Cooks Bay." Many locals congregated at the dock to sell snacks and fruit, which proved to be an excellent opportunity to buy pineapples, bananas, and mangos. Take your pick!

➡ **Steve's Moorea Rule:** *On Moorea there is a rule: If you see something you want, buy it! Odds are it will not be there later! The dockside pineapples are dirt cheap, about $5 a bunch of six. We later learned that pineapples are not always available at the local "mom-and-pop" markets found near the hotel.*

The van driver gave us the traditional "mini-tour" during the fifteen-minute drive to Cooks Bay Resort, and offered his services for a daily Circle Island Van Tour for $20. (The same tour, purchased from the hotel's tour desk, costs $25.) Once the tour was purchased, we could choose to take it any day of the week. (Tell your tour desk one day in advance. I recommend this bargain-priced tour.) Our van tour lasted four hours and circled Moorea. One stop was Belvedere Lookout, Moorea's most famous scenic overlook. The view is extraordinary. We stood and marveled at Moorea's two principle bays stretched out below, Cooks Bay on the right and Opunohu Bay on the left. (Contrary to popular belief, Captain Cook's ships landed in Opunohu Bay, not in Cooks Bay. This was confirmed years after the event by examining actual drawings made by the crew.) The van then stopped for lunch at a pricy but picturesque floating boat restaurant, the Linareva. We brought a picnic lunch with us and walked down the beach to a quiet spot.

➡ **Steve's Tip:** *If you are staying at Cooks Bay Resort, read this carefully. Take a seat on the van closest to the driver. Designate one person to carry both passports and hotel vouchers. Immediately, upon arrival at the resort, one person should quickly go to register and request one of my recommended room numbers while the other handles the luggage. This way you will beat the large line that will soon form at the registration counter. Rooms are assigned as parties register. Bungalow upgrades are similarly distributed.*

Moorea's Best Cheapskate Hotel

Cooks Bay Resort is my cheapskate recommendation for bargain travel to Moorea. What is so special about Cooks Bay and Cooks Bay Resort? One does not travel to Moorea to sit on a white-sand beach and stare into the ocean. You want to experience the most dramatic location on this lush tropical island. In 1951 author James Michener referred to Cooks Bay as "a monument to the prodigal beauty of nature."

The colonial-style Cooks Bay Resort, built in 1986 amid the unsurpassed beauty of Cooks Bay, has a friendly, small-hotel atmosphere. The colonial building is two stories high. The white lattice trim that adorns the light green façade of the two-story structure is similar to the trim found on colonial buildings in Lahaina, Maui. I have always found Cooks to be quaint and pleasant. The lobby is friendly and airy with an adequate tour desk.

The hotel has lovely tropical landscaping. There are indigenous flowers, palm trees, lawn areas, a refreshing fresh water pool, a poolside cafe, and a small beach.

There is one negative—yes, even in paradise. Roosters! They roam on many properties, including Cooks Bay. In this case they belong to a neighbor and may not, by law, be removed. And they crow early in the morning. If you are a light sleeper, bring earplugs! Also, the hotel is just off the road that encircles the island and there is road noise during the short commute hour from traffic to and from the ferry terminal. By our second trip we were accustomed to it all, and I have heard no complaints from other visitors.

Amenities of the seventy-six rooms include lanais and ocean or bay views. Though the rooms are small, they are bright and airy, with open extended balconies, and they have hot water makers for coffee and tea. Request one from the front desk. There are great showers, refrigerators, ceiling fans with a wall speed switch both a double and a twin bed, a changing area with basic open shelves for clothing, and telephones. The hotel has a lovely fresh water pool, a poolside grill, and a small sandy beach.

Yes, the rooms are small, but they are comfortable. How small? They measure about thirteen feet long by ten feet wide. Additionally, there is a small hallway leading to a mini–dressing area with a sink and a closed bathroom and shower. The room's glass patio doors are the width of the room and allow you awesome views of volcanic peaks while you are reading in bed. The lanai measures a comfortable ten feet by five feet. More than at any other hotel, the balconies here are very real extensions of the rooms and offer sensational four-star views, something money cannot always buy. Guests should immediately take the room's table and chairs and set them on the lanai for the duration of their stay. On each visit we find that our room quickly "merged" into and became a small part of the beauty that is Cooks Bay. During our eight-day visits, we always enjoyed our daily breakfast on the balcony. At other times we simply relaxed on the balcony, staring out over the lagoon. Truly sensational!

Cooks Bay Resort Upgrade

Perhaps you have seen pictures or video of the famed over-the-water bungalows offered by Moorea's best hotels, such as the Bali Hai Moorea or the Beachcomber Parkroyal. These same hotels also offer deluxe private beachfront and garden bungalows. Prices for such top-of-the-line luxury lodging range from $175 to $465 per day. A nonprivate lanai bungalow (two or more units to each bungalow) is priced by the day.

Forget these sky-high prices for a private Moorea waterfront bungalow. We can do infinitely better at cheapskate prices. Fortunately, Cooks Bay Resort recently purchased the adjoining property, formerly known as the Keveka Hotel, which consists of twenty-four bungalows that are both in a garden setting and also at the edge of the bay. On our third visit, we stayed in a garden cottage. While we dearly loved the view from the room's balcony, the garden setting and large private bungalow was a wonderful and somewhat luxurious change.

➡ **Steve's Tip:** *Because most views from the Cooks Bay Resort's regular rooms are superior, I recommend waiting until you arrive at the hotel before deciding to upgrade, then compare your room to available bungalows. If a bungalow is your choice, upgrade and save 42 percent over the cost of a prebooked upgrade.*

Upgrading in Advance

Need to prebook a private bungalow? Then book Tahiti Vacations' TV1510 tour, found in its regular brochure. The upgrade package is identical to its bargain Cooks Bay Resort package but includes a garden bungalow. The price for the upgrade package is $849 for Tuesday departures. The upgrade package with a lagoon-front bungalow costs a whopping $989.

For a garden bungalow the super-low upgrade price upon check-in is $12.50 per person per day and $15 per person per day for a lagoon-front bungalow. With a $699 package, the total price for the week using a check-in upgrade for garden and lagoon bungalows is $786 and $804, respectively.

Most of Cooks' bungalows are recently refurbished and offer an oversize room, a tiled bath area, and stained glass bath area windows. They feature a wood-paneled interior and vaulted ceilings with traditional ceiling fan. Amenities include a queen-size bed, writing table, a large closet with open shelves for clothes, and most also offer a wonderful porch with a table and chairs. The best-located garden bungalows provide exciting partial views of the bay and surrounding peaks. The lagoon-front bungalows are at water's edge and offer incredible unobstructed views of the bay. The three bungalows designated "beachfront" are too close to the restaurant. I recommend against the semiprivate attached bungalows that do not offer a porch, unless you need two adjoining bungalows.

➡ **Steve's Room Tip:** *Room 224 has the best location. Next are rooms 225 and 226. All these rooms are on an inner corner of the second floor so that the building itself insulates against noise. On our second trip we faxed a request to Donny, the manager, and room 224 was waiting for us. These rooms have a terrific view of Cooks' pool, small beach, and the ocean. Other good rooms are 220 to 222, with wonderful views of Cooks Bay and the surrounding mountains. Try to avoid lower or upper rooms directly on the road.*

➡ **Steve's Topless Bathing Tip:** *Historically speaking, the local Catholic churches outlawed topless bathing for all parishioners. Consequently, the bulk of topless sunbathers are tourists. The French at the Sofitel la Ora bathe topless en masse, as one might expect. At Cooks it is more or less an occasional guest thing, a totally available option. Go for it!*

Did I mention the delightful wooden bridge connecting the hotel with a small *motu* (island), where the Le Jardin restaurant is found? Le Jardin is good, not great, but very convenient, which is important in paradise. What's best, a wooden deck encircles the restaurant, including a back patio with wonderful outdoor seating. Special barbecues and feasts are held there.

We often strolled across the bridge, stopping to look down at the lagoon and its prolific marine life. Many people walked by, unaware, as we studied the water and found eels and octopus passing beneath the bridge. Occasionally, we saw one of the famed poisonous scorpion fish swimming throughout the coral. They are beautiful, with five- to six-inch porcupinelike quills sticking out of their bodies. These are the same fish pictured on many T-shirts sold on the island. Behind Le Jardin, near the rear deck, is Philippe Molle's scuba diving shop and dock. To the left of the shop is the recently built pizzeria.

Cooks Bay Resort's Free Activities

The hotel has several outrigger canoes, and I found them generally available and underused. Patty and I found the outriggers a bit tricky on our first voyage, but we persevered and managed to explore the bay. One day we canoed to a buoy, tied up, and had a great picnic lunch while snorkeling over a new reef. Another day we canoed close to the *Windsong*.

Masks and Snorkels: These are available gratis. However, I recommend guests bring their own. Most important, Cooks does supply fins, but they are in terrible shape and there is no place nearby where a guest may rent them. Yes, there is a diving shop, but it chooses not to rent fins, and snorkeling without fins is like swimming with one hand tied behind your back.

Snorkeling: The downside of Sofitel's beautiful white-sand beach is that there is no coral reef. On the other hand, Cooks Bay Resort sits on the edge of a wonderful, active one, where we snorkeled to our hearts' content. This is another reason to bring fins! Enjoying Moorea's prolific marine life is free and one of the best water-based activities on the island.

While I am talking about gear, I may as well suggest light reef gloves. I like to get close to the fish and coral, and the gloves and my Farmer John give me great protection and freedom to explore the reef.

➡ **Steve's Tip:** *Absolutely, guests should bring rubber-soled booties for walking on the coral. Purchase a pair before the trip. The tough soles protect the bottoms of your feet, eliminating the risk of nasty coral cuts that may become infected. Buy good-quality fins, the ones that have adjustable straps and require the use of booties. Also bring a tube of triple antibiotic ointment. Untreated coral cuts can ruin a vacation.*

Farmer Johns: This is an alien term to many. My Farmer John is a thin, one-eighth-inch sleeveless neoprene body suit. While I use it primarily for scuba diving, it is also great for power snorkeling, both day and night, allowing me to stay in the water longer since the suit insulates me from the cold. After hours snorkeling, even seventy-eight-degree tropical water seems cold. Patty wears a lighter suit of lycra "skin."

Back to the snorkeling. A second way to enjoy snorkeling at Cooks is via the convenient ladder located behind Le Jardin restaurant, and off the deck. We have used the ladder for night snorkeling. We climbed down the ladder and—voila—we were in the bay. No coral to walk around and no scorpion fish to step on when snorkeling at night. But at night I also found it difficult to locate the channels leading back to the beach. It was much easier to head back to the ladder. (Did I say snorkeling at *night?* Want to know more?)

Night Snorkeling: I realize that for most people snorkeling is an easygoing daytime activity, an alternative to lounging on the beach; few consider doing it in darkness. I have mentioned that Patty and I are scuba divers. We have gone on many night dives, off beaches and boats. It is always fun and eerie going down with only artificial lights. But night snorkeling is often not convenient, and a good reef is usually not found close to one's hotel. In addition, both entering and exiting the water should be safe and easy. By all these criteria, Cooks Bay Resort proved to be perfect for this first-class marine activity.

Why do it? Because night snorkeling is a fun, unique, and exciting experience. It is an opportunity to experience something completely new—an undersea world hidden from daylight, a world of sleeping—yes sleeping—fish! Often, I hovered above and watched them awaken at my gentle touch. The fish were in a disoriented and groggy state until they got their bearings. A funny scene indeed! On occasion I have held sleeping fish in the palm of my hand. Using my underwater light, I watched the beautiful and poisonous Scorpion fish crawling along the ocean floor. Do not worry, the shy fish are not aggressive and will not attack. Just keep a respectful distance and watch them feeding below. My light also often caught many shiny orange "beads" that appeared surreal. These were the eyes of barber-pole striped shrimp. At times I have also enjoyed "chasing" hermit crabs moving along inside their large shells.

A word about underwater lights. Visit a well-stocked scuba shop and purchase all the necessary gear. A good store will carry reef gloves ($10 to $15), fins ($20 to $30 for low-end ones), Farmer Johns or a short version (an investment of $50 to $75), and a good flashlight. Get as powerful a light as you can afford and one with the widest beam. I bought Patty an Underwater Kinetics (U.K. 1200) that works on D-cell batteries. It is heavy on land but lightweight in water. It is powerful and throws a very wide beam. One set of batteries lasted the week, used two or three times, maximum. The U.K. 1200 costs about $52, on sale; other flashlights cost $20 and up. Also, when snorkeling alone, carry an extra pocket light. Occasionally, a light will malfunction for one reason or another. Bring a spare.

I always use my powerful video light. It throws a strong beam, about fifteen feet wide, that lights up entire coral walls. It is so powerful that I carry a smaller light as well. Then, when I find an eel or other exotic reef fish, I "beam it" with the big one. But video lights cost about $350!

Bargain Activities

Fat Cat: I like this one. The *Fat Cat* is a thatched-roof flat boat used for sunset cruises at Cooks Bay Resort. The leisurely ninety-minute cruise, including one rum punch and music by a local guitarist, is a cheapskate delight at only $10. The boat sails past the famed water huts of the Bali Hai Moorea Hotel. We just kicked back, relaxed, and watched the incredible sunset over the bay. I rate this an easy "must-do." In 1996 Donny was running the *Fat Cat* as needed—depending on guest participation. My own word of mouth caused him to schedule a cruise for our final night. Be sure to book this one early during your stay. If Cooks is not offering the cruise, ask at the tour desk for similar cruises offered by nearby Club Bali Hai or the Bali Hai Moorea Hotel.

Maco and His Friendly Sharks: This new activity is remarkable, and I truly hope this unique adventure continues to be available to future guests. Maco is one of Cooks' long-time valued employees who has created a new version of the traditional motorized outrigger canoe snorkeling trip. He now carries a tuna carcass and has snorkelers join him in the water before he sends out signals that bring the sharks in for lunch. We stopped counting as eighteen four- to seven-foot black-tipped reef sharks swam as close as three feet away. This is a snorkeling adventure above and beyond any other experience. Donny tells me the activity is now nine months old and very popular. It was such fun that we signed up for a second trip during our recent visit. After the sharks feed, the outrigger stops at a second spot for snorkeling. The views of the bay are spectacular, and the price is a bargain at $23 per person.

Cooks' Feasts and Picnic Cruises: These are not exactly bargains, at $43 per person for an evening Tahitian feast and local dance show, or a half-day snorkel cruise to a nearby Motu or another small island with picnic lunch. They are overpriced. In the past Cooks offered the same snorkel cruise without picnic lunch for just $25. Always check with the tour desk and lobby blackboard for current activities.

Other Resorts' Activities

In 1996 the following activities were available through Cooks' tour desk:

Bicycling: In 1996 Cooks gave up on maintaining free bicycles. Nearly new, one-speed bicycles in the lobby are rented by Pacificar at $8 for four hours and $12 for eight hours (per day). I often enjoyed an exhilarating early morning ride along the bay, past the Club Bali Hai Hotel and over the bridge leading to larger market in Pao Pao.

Scuba Diving: One of Moorea's few diver operations, Moorea Underwater Scuba Diving Tahiti (MUST), is located on the Cooks Bay Resort's property. We dove with the long-time owner Philippe Molle and his excellent crew. It offers one-tank morning and afternoon dives. Prices include all gear, and run about $60 with a $30 discount for a five-dive package. Best of all, MUST offers a world-class diving adventure. Philippe also does a daily shark feed! Yes, we dove to fifty feet with at least forty black-tipped reef sharks that were up to seven feet long. Philippe placed us in a circle on the bottom while he held the food—a large tuna head—until the sharks arrived. A fine underwater tour followed, with Philippe's crews feeding one school after another of colorful reef fish. I got fantastic video footage with silhouetted sharks gliding past my camera at a distance of five feet. Philippe offers introductory lessons for about $60.

Dolphin Watching Expedition: This trip is operated by naturalist Dr. Michael Poole, a Ph.D., who has conducted dolphin research on Moorea since 1987. Travel to the dolphins is by the twenty-nine-foot motor boat and includes free hotel pickup. Michael locates schools of spinner dolphins and explains their lives and society at sea. Guests may see humpback whales and touch the dolphins. The price for this half-day trip is $51 for adults, $32 for children six to twelve years old, and $16 for kids under thirteen.

Hiking the Three Coconut Trail: The hike takes participants to the scenic Opunohu Valley Ridge on the flanks of Moua Ra (Bali Hai Mountain). It is an easy beginner-to-intermediate, three-to-four-hour hike that leaves at 7:30 A.M. and costs $32.

Tiahura Ranch Mountain Horseback Riding: The ranch offers two rides daily, except Mondays, from 9:00 to 10:30 A.M. and 4:15 to 5:45 P.M. The route allows panoramic views of the island. The cost is $31 per person.

Deep Sea Fishing: The *Tea Nui*, a thirty-one-foot Bertram twin Volvo 165 h.p. diesel motorboat, offers professional equipment, such as Penn International fishing reels. Captain Chris has fifteen years experience fishing in local waters. Guests fish for blue and black marlin, tuna, wahoo, and mahimahi. The cost is $125 per person.

Dolphin Quest: Want to experience a dolphin "hands-on"? Jay Sweeny is the owner of Moorea's only attraction of this kind. Dolphin Quest is located on the luxurious grounds of the Beachcomber Parkroyal Hotel. The cost is high, at $70 per person. The "experience" is a thirty-minute program where guests, mostly kids and their parents, stand in three-foot-deep water and play with one or both of the dolphins. These are wild animals that spend much of their time in the hotel lagoon but other times head out to sea. As of April 1996 Jay will be offering a scuba option for about $120 per person. Even better, visit the hotel during your island tour, as we did, and watch the free show from the beach only a few feet away.

Motorized Outrigger Tours Around the Island: This is the most adventurous way to see Moorea, and we love it. Albert's Tours and several other tour operators offer this trip. Albert's is just up the road from Cooks, near the Club Bali Hai Hotel. The cost is about $40 per person, and the tour takes most of a day, leaving at 9:30 A.M. and returning at 2:00 P.M. The motorized canoes carry about sixteen passengers and travel inside the coral reef that encircles the entire island. We stopped for snorkeling at two locations. This is a *must-do.*

Photo Safari Tour: We did not go on this tour, but I have heard good things about it. Usually it includes a four-wheel-drive jeep trip that circles Moorea with stops at major points of interest. Unlike the similar and cheaper van tours, it then visits the interior rain forest and waterfalls. The popular half-day tour is priced at about $50.

Day Sailing: In the past we enjoyed fantastic day sailing on Moorea's pristine waters. There are usually one or two boats available for such trips. In 1996 the thirty-eight-foot catamaran *Manu* was offering half-day sails with stops in Cooks and Opunohu Bays. The Lagoon Safari includes sail 'n' snorkel, fishing, shelling, and a dolphin watch. There is one major hitch to this one: You must get transportation to the Beachcomber Parkroyal Hotel, halfway around the island, by the 9:30 A.M. departure time. Since the boat returns at 12:30 P.M. you may wish to add this adventure to your rental car island-circling experience. Call 56-19-19 for reservations.

Miscellaneous Moorea Information

Weekly Car Rentals

The need for a car does not exist once you have entered the Tahiti "time machine" that transports guests back about one hundred years on the Hawaiian time line. Vacations on Moorea are largely self-contained at one's hotel. Free modes of transportation include walking, bicycles, and outrigger canoes. Small markets and local eateries are a short walk from Cooks Bay Resort. In any case, you are saving the cost of a weekly car rental. Chalk up a savings of close to $200. Opt instead for a one-day car or jeep rental.

One-Day Car or Jeep Rental

I recommend you rent a car or jeep for one day so that you may experience your own circle-island adventure. Pack a picnic lunch and head out to explore the sights and sounds of Moorea. You may wish to enjoy Sofitel's white-sand beach or the nearby public beach. Want to explore Club Med? If you tell the gate man you are thinking of transferring to the club for a few days, he will likely allow you on the property. Of course, you should only do this if you are really considering such a move. Then again, at one time or another we all "consider" Club Med, right?

Cooks tour desk will arrange for a car rental or an open jeep. Unfortunately, as of 1996 jeep prices have gone through the ceiling—now at $120. Smaller economy cars are reasonably priced at $60 for a full day. By renting on Tuesday or Friday you can drive to the famous "happy hour" at Club Bali Hai and then enjoy dinner at any nearby restaurant. Many visitors rent a strange-looking French vehicle called the Mega Ranch. It is a two-seater with a T-top. The doors and top are removable, making this a fun vehicle to drive. It comes only with manual transmission. Anyone who rents a Mega Ranch, or any other small car, should check the gas gauge. On Moorea vehicles are often rented with less than a full tank of gas. Do not overfill the gas tank when returning the car. Gas is very costly and you will not use much. (There are only thirty miles of road on the island!) Only replace the gas used.

Public Transportation

On the main island of Tahiti public transportation consists of Le Truck, colorful open-sided trucks that have replaced traditional-looking buses. On Moorea, there is a primitive local bus system. The bus stops in front of Cooks Bay Resort hourly. It costs about $2 and goes in both directions so that you can take the bus all the way to Club Med, on the far side of the island, or to the ferry dock. Always check with Cook's front desk on this one.

Shopping

Forget malls, main streets, and shopping centers. Shopping in paradise is a laid back activity. If one wishes to shop, perhaps for black pearls, the place to go is Papeete.

For light, local shopping, turn left out of Cooks Bay Resort and head down the road a bit. On the right is a boutique and pearl shop. Hang a right from Cooks Bay and walk past Club Bali Hai, where there are several small boutiques. Farther up the road, just over the small bridge, is the town of Pao Pao. Do not get excited, the "town" consists of a market, gas station, and one photo and electronics store. Club Bali Hai has an attractive gift shop that is worth a stop (check for its hours). Cooks recently opened its own boutique that was quite well stocked with local items. I bought a colorful cap for about $12. The store also stocks a nominal supply of sundry items. But shopping at the nearby mom-and-pop market is best.

When bicycling or driving, turn left from Cooks and head down the road. About ten to fifteen minutes by bicycle, on the right, is the famed White House boutique. The White House is striking because it sits back from the road with a wide expanse of green, manicured lawn. Chickens and roosters roam the property.

The largest group of shops is opposite the Club Med resort, with about ten shops selling good quality items. There is also an ice cream–pizzeria that comes in handy for an afternoon snack.

Amazingly, that is *it* for shopping! The paucity of high-priced shops is a built-in money saver. (Another big bonus, in my book! After all, most of us are not going to Moorea to shop!)

➡ **Steve's Resource Tip:** *Call, mail, or write for the best free source book,* The Islands of Tahiti, *published by the Tahiti Tourism Bureau. It usually gives copies only to travel agents, but if you plead your case someone will likely send you a free copy. Call or contact the Tahiti Tourist Promotion Board, 300 North Continental Boulevard, Suite 180, El Segundo, California 90245; (310) 414-8484 or fax (310) 414-8490. My most recent copy is 119 pages and covers all major islands in the chain with sources for all types of activities. This is the book that turned me on to David and his day sail on the catamaran. I wrote to David before our first visit and set up the sail in advance. The book also has lots of information on all aspects of island life. It is well worth the effort to obtain.*

Food and Restaurants in Paradise

We are good travelers and decided to bring some powdered milk (Carnation's Kiss of Cream brand is the best) just in case two factors came into play. First, markets may run out of fresh milk since they stock only a small supply. Buy an extra container or two at the first opportunity. On our recent trip, the markets were out of fresh milk but offered shelf milk. On a prior visit there was a market strike for a couple of days. Powdered milk to the rescue. As long as I am talking about liquids, you may have noticed that my list includes forty-eight-ounce Tupperware containers. We used them to hold lemonade and other powdered drinks, which we mixed with good-old Moorea tap water.

Cooks Bay Resort does state in its guest "rules" that guests may not keep food in the rooms. What about those little refrigerators, you say? I can only say that we followed a rule of reason. We used the refrigerator for liquids and lunch snacks that is about all they can hold.

Many people tell me they have heard about the sky-high prices in Tahiti. Good reason to forego the trip, right? No way! Here is the *real* scoop. First, Patty and I didn't care to waste time on daily restaurant breakfasts. Instead we sat on our balcony eating our homemade repast while we enjoyed a gorgeous view of the bay. We also enjoyed picnic lunches on the beach or on an outrigger canoe in the middle of the bay. Since there is no nightlife on Moorea, dinners were definitely a major entertainment activity in the evening.

The only early evening entertainment to speak of was the famous "happy hour" at Club Bali Hai. Just up the road about a mile, or a twenty-minute walk, is the Club Bali Hai Hotel, which is both a hotel and a time-share. It is the only other hotel on Cooks Bay. We followed Arthur Frommer's suggestion and visited Club Bali's happy hour, confirming that it is a great way to spend a couple of evenings while enjoying the marvelous sunsets. On Tuesdays and Fridays the hotel's open-air bar, with tables at water's edge, has a gathering of expatriates from all corners of the globe. Local musicians play melodious island tunes as the sun sets over the bay. The popcorn is free and exotic drinks are half price, with pina coladas priced at about $3.50. The fun starts when a bell rings at 6:00 p.m. and continues until 7:00 P.M. One night two older ladies, living near Cooks Bay, saw us walking as they were getting into their new, large Mercedes. They were gracious and drove us to the happy hour. Later, when they left, they also dropped us back at the hotel. Do remember to bring a flashlight. The road is very dark, and a light is essential for the walk back to the hotel.

Our restaurant choices were limited since we could not ride bikes at night. The reason for this is the dark, dangerous road and fast night traffic. Choices include walking to nearby restaurants, eating at Cooks, or finding restaurants that offer free pickup and drop-off. Yes, there are taxis, but expect to pay a hefty fare.

Cooks Bay Resort Eateries

Le Jardin: The hotel has a quaint wooden bridge running from the main property to the restaurant, located on a small *motu.* Outdoor dining on the rear wooden deck of the restaurant offers spectacular views of Cooks Bay. Le Jardin is large, bright, and airy. Over the past two years it has changed its menu several times. In 1996 it was once again serving a continental menu. Sample lunch items include a veal sandwich ($5), a BLT sandwich ($4) and a hamburger plate with fries ($10). Dinner items include grilled steak ($13), Pineapple Chicken ($10), and a lamb filet ($14.50). Food reviews are mixed. We rated it good but never great. Le Jardin also serves breakfast daily.

Fisherman's Wharf Restaurant and Cooks Pizzeria: In 1994 a Frenchman opened a pizzeria on the wooden deck, at the rear of Le Jardin. The food was very good. It served many styles of homemade pizza and tasty spaghetti with a choice of sauces. In 1996 the pizzeria was incorporated into the nearby Fisherman's Wharf Restaurant. This is great for families who want to order fish and pizza. The restaurant is not owned by Cooks but does reside on Cooks' property amidst its waterfront bungalows. Its outdoor dining deck offers unmatched sunset views of the bay. Sample dinner entrées include mahimahi ($18), grilled tuna ($16), and grilled chicken ($13). Pizzas are sold in two sizes, priced from $10 to $16. Spaghetti with a choice of sauce is priced at $10. An order of spaghetti and a small or large pizza is plenty for two. Try their special American pizza with cheese, mushrooms, olives, beef, and onions.

➡ **Steve's Tip:** *Think food and related prices in Tahiti are outrageous? If any of these restaurant prices seem a bit on the high side, keep in mind that in Tahiti there are no taxes, and tipping is considered offensive. Yes, offensive! This saves you at least 23 percent on each meal. This must be paradise!*

Rusty's Poolside Snack Bar: The snack bar offers sandwiches and is open from 10:00 A.M. to 3:30 P.M. Foot-long ham-and-cheese or tuna sandwiches are pricey, at about $10. Rusty's also sells half and one-third sandwiches. Want to save big lunch dollars? A daily loaf of French bread at the nearby market costs about forty cents. We make great picnic lunches with homemade tuna and salami sandwiches, cheeses, and sweet fresh pineapple. We made daily quarts of homemade lemonade, Tang, and always had a good supply of soda.

Rusty's Snack Bar Chinese Diner: New at Cooks Bay Resort is Rusty's, now open for dinner and serving a limited Chinese menu. As of mid-1996 the new Chinese cook and owner was serving a basic dinner menu that offered six entrées, including wonderful Chinese beef and onions, chow mein, and beef and vegetables, priced at about $10 per dish. We found two shared dishes quite filling.

Le Pecheur: Hang a left out of Cooks and walk one-fourth of a mile down the road to The Fisherman. Bad new for us came in September 1994, when the restaurant dropped its evening Chinese menu. It now served primarily French seafood. The restaurant's service and food was very good. All in all it is a small and pleasant enough eatery. It is currently open seven days a week, serving lunch from 11:30 A.M. to 2:30 P.M. It serves dinner from 5:30 P.M. to 9:00 P.M. It also offers free pickup and drop-off service, but it is only a fifteen- to twenty-minute walk from Cooks. Sample dinner items include escargot ($8), Mahimahi à la Cardinal with lobster sauce ($21), grilled steak ($16), and roast lamb gigot with fresh ratatouille ($19). How about homemade iced soufflé with Grand Marnier for dessert ($9)? Call 56-36-12 for reservations and a free pickup.

L'Ananas Bleu: For excellent breakfasts and light lunches I recommend this nearby eatery. Turn right when exiting Cooks Bay Resort and walk along the bay. Just fifteen minutes down the road, a few steps past the local Pao Pao Super Market, you will find L'Ananas Bleu (The Blue Pineapple) on the left (mountain) side of the road. This wonderful local eatery serves an incredible array of French crêpes and waffles, with a choice of fourteen toppings. Crêpes and waffles are a bargain at about $3.50 to $4.50. It is open daily from 7:30 A.M. to 3:00 P.M. and is closed on Mondays. They also serve ice cream and delicious milk shakes. Dining is in an open-air setting just across the road from the bay.

Fare Manava: Hang a right out of Cooks and walk twenty minutes down the road. Just past Club Bali Hai are two good eateries. Best is Fare Manava, which is a Chinese restaurant frequented mostly by locals. It is cozy and the food is great.

Typical entrées, such as sweet and sour chicken, run $8 to $9. The pepper steak and onion dish was excellent.

Alfredo's: Directly across the road from the Club Bali Hai is a small Italian-French restaurant, Alfredo's. Owner Syd Pollock divested his ownership in Le Pecheur to devote his efforts to Alfredo's, a place for pizza, pasta, and traditional French-Italian cuisine. We found the food to be excellent, with a full selection of Italian and French entrées priced from $12 to $18 per person. Best of all, it is open every day and provides free round-trip transportation from Cooks Bay Resort. A group of seven of us enjoyed the happy hour at Club Bali Hai, then had a memorable dinner at Alfredos and were driven back to Cooks. For reservations and a free pickup, call 56-17-71.

La Sylesie Patisserie: This small establishment is found about ten minutes down the road from Le Pecheur, in the direction of the Bali Hai Moorea Hotel. You will see a mini-mall of shops on your right, just across the road from the Bank Polynese, which is on the lagoon side of the road. This wonderful eatery is open daily from 7:00 A.M. to 7:00 P.M. It serves breakfasts, lunches, and light dinners, offering salads, pastries, and cakes. Sample items include bananas flambé ($4.50) and chocolate and walnut crêpes ($3).

➡ **Steve's Picnic Lunch Tips:** *Take a right out of Cooks and head for the trusty Super Marché Pao Pao Market, just ten minutes down the road. While making my daily purchase of French bread I noticed the market sells a limited amount of prepared food to go, mostly fried chicken quarters at $2 per item. Better yet, the new owners of L'Ananas Bleu, just five minutes farther down the road, offer a large, whole herb-roasted take-out chicken for $10. Of course, you will be passing the market and can pick up any additional items to complete your picnic lunch.*

Food is a personal thing. You may chuckle, smirk, or follow in our footsteps. As my mini–packing list indicates, we take four to six cans of tuna, canned chicken and turkey, and a large package of salami. We always enjoy our money-saving homemade picnic lunches. Another reason we bring a limited amount of these items with us is that the local markets do not, as a rule, sell identifiable cold cuts such as turkey and roast beef.

Drinking Water on Moorea

In 1994 I read a Department of Tourism flyer that said Moorea's water is chemically treated and safe but recommended that visitors drink bottled water. Get it? Patty, who is my dearest medical expert, declared the tap water fine, and we have enjoyed using it with no problems whatsoever. Want more assurance? The 1995 publication, *The Islands of Tahiti,* distributed by the Tahiti Department of Tourism, declares, "Tap water in the hotels and restaurants is safe to drink." The upscale Bali Hai Moorea tells its guests, "The tap water is safe for drinking." We then have Cooks Bay Resorts handout of weekly activities and hotel rules that states, "The local government officials recommend that you *DO NOT DRINK* the tap water. Bottled water is available at any of our bars." The same flyer declares that "complimentary ice is available at all the bars." Is Cooks telling us that their ice is "sterilized"? I do not think so. I will only emphasize that we have used Moorea's tap water and find it excellent, and the same water is served in carafes, upon request, at every major and minor restaurant. Be sure to explain to a waiter or waitress that you wish a carafe or glass and not a commercial bottle of water.

Other Hotel Considerations

Club Bali Hai Hotel

During each of our four visits to Moorea, Patty and I have enjoyed the famous happy hour each Tuesday and Friday at Club Bali Hai's bayside bar. Cooks Bay Resort and the Club Bali Hai are the only two hotels situated on the most picturesque of Moorea's bays. The hotel is primarily a time-share resort with beachfront and over-the-water bungalows reserved for time-share members. However, there is also a small two-story main building with about twenty hotel-type rooms offered to the public. Room amenities include a double bed, dresser, refrigerator, and air-conditioning.

The grounds, bar, and restaurant are upscale when compared to Cooks Bay Resort. If you want a more "prestigious" property with the same wondrous views found at Cooks Bay Resort, you may wish to consider this option.

Here are the very best prices for this hotel upgrade: A Tahiti Escapes package, which includes six nights at the Club Bali Hai Hotel, is priced at $829. The package provides the seventh night stay at the Hotel Tahiti prior to the departure flight home. On the downside, this package includes a mountain-view room that I do *not* recommend. No, I have nothing against mountains. In fact, Moorea offers knockout mountain views. Rather, Club Bali Hai's mountain rooms do not offer a balcony and they are located in the rear of the main building just off the noisy main road. When considering the Club Bali Hai Moorea, you want their bay-view rooms with balconies that are situated only a few feet away from majestic Cooks Bay. Sunmakers offers the same package with an upgrade to a bay-view room and six full breakfasts, priced at $950. Yes, these rooms have a dresser and air conditioning, and yes, the property is a bit more plush. Is it worth the extra cost of $500 per couple over the Cooks Bay Resort package" I have voted "no" on this one. Want to see for yourself?

Bali Hai Moorea Hotel

The Bali Hai Moorea Hotel is another serious option. It is a classic, one of Moorea's thatched roof, over-the-water bungalow hotels. The Bali Hai Moorea was built by three Americans in the early 1960s and in some respects shows its age. It has a garden, beach, and over-the-water bungalows. Amenities include a swimming pool with a swim-up bar, a tennis court, and free outrigger canoes and snorkeling excursions. It is located between Cooks Bay and Moorea's airport.

Islands in the Sun offers the best price on this hotel upgrade. Its regular brochure package includes scheduled round-trip air on AOM, the interisland ferry to Moorea, six nights at the Bali Hai Moorea with lodging in a lanai room, and the final night at the Hotel Tahiti. The lanai room is a nonprivate bungalow that houses two to four units. The vacation, tour package LD196, is priced at $899. The price is $400 above my recommended Cooks Bay Resort package and includes six and not seven full days on Moorea. Want this same package with a seventh full day on Moorea? Tahiti Vacations offers the same package with two extras: interisland flights on Air Tahiti instead of the ferry and a seventh night on Moorea. The tour (TV1510) is found in Tahiti Vacations' regular brochure and is priced at $959 for Tuesday Los Angeles departures on AOM. Want that private bungalow? Sunmakers offers a similar package with Corsair flights, six nights at the Bali Hai Moorea, one night on Tahiti, six breakfasts, and a private poolside (not ocean) bungalow, priced at a hefty $1,029.

Sample entrées from Bali Hai's restaurant include grilled Pacific swordfish ($22), filet of lamb with garlic butter ($18.50), mahimahi in coconut milk ($17), and sweet and sour chicken ($14). Salads are priced from $6 to $11.

Though Cooks Bay Resort is not as upscale a property as Bali Hai, it has the scenery of Cooks Bay, which is astounding! Cooks Bay also has a wonderful reef that I have discussed at length. One cannot go wrong either way, so long as the pros and cons of each property are considered. If you are on a honeymoon and have extra gift dollars to spend I would not hesitate to recommend one of the upscale hotels or, at the very least, a private garden or lagoon-front bungalow at Cooks Bay Resort.

Sofitel la Ora Hotel

This is my upscale favorite. Unlike other hotels, the Sofitel is somewhat hidden. It is situated off the road and down a long hill ending at the water's edge. It has fourteen tropical acres of flora and the best, longest, and widest white-sand beach on Moorea. As you lie on the beach the ocean is stretched out before you, and in the distance is the island of Tahiti. The hotel is also the most commercial looking, with a rental seaplane parked at water's edge, paddle boats, and every type of water equipment imaginable for rent. It offers eighty garden and beach, wood and bamboo bungalows. It offers complimentary snorkeling gear, tennis courts, and outrigger canoes. Paddle boats are reasonable at $8 per hour. However, since the best snorkeling is a boat ride away, the hotel offers daily ninety-minute snorkel trips, priced at $20. Since the Sofitel is fairly isolated from other hotels or restaurants, you should consider the cost of meals. It offers a daily meal plan, including breakfast and dinner ($60), or three full meals at $86 per person.

➡ **Steve's Video Offer:** *My personal 1996 video offers a unique, in-depth look at Cooks Bay Resort and other nearby hotels. To my knowledge this is the only available video that shows you the interiors of bungalows at the Sofitel la Ora, the Bali Hai Moorea, and Cooks Bay Resort hotels. It also offers tours of the hotels' properties, including a tour of Club Bali Hai grounds. The video offers an in-depth look at Cooks Bay Resort, including the interior of both a garden bungalow and a typical room in Cooks' main building. As an added bonus, my video includes footage from prior visits that include a tour of the island of Moorea, our underwater scuba shark feed, and night snorkeling with the poisonous scorpion fish. The video is high quality, copied from a high-resolution Hi-Band 8mm original. The price of the video, including postage and handling, is $14.95. You may order by writing to:*

Steve's Video
Box 1956
Lafayette, California 94549

The best bargain price for the Sofitel is offered by Island in the Sun's Tahiti Escapes program. This uses Corsair flights and includes six days and nights at a Sofitel garden bungalow, a final night at the Tahiti Sofitel Maeva Beach Hotel, and ferry transportation to Moorea. It is bargain priced at $999. Tahiti Vacations offers its version of a Sofitel package (tour TV 1510) in its regular brochure. For the additional $70 (package price of $1,069), this includes a seventh day and night on Moorea, scheduled flights from Los Angeles on AOM, and Air Tahiti interisland flights.

I personally find the Sofitel a bit too glitzy and commercial. The view of the island of Tahiti is very similar to the view of the island of Molokai from the beaches on Maui. It does not compare to the beauty that is unique to Cooks Bay.

Now that you are a bona fide expert on Moorea and Cooks Bay the choices are all yours. Whether you choose Cooks Bay Resort or another fine hotel, I know you will cherish the memories of your dream Moorea vacation. You owe it to yourself to *go for this one!*

12

The Promised Land: Israel and Beyond

In October 1995 Patty and I enjoyed another great vacation, this time to Israel and its environs. While travel to the Middle East is usually costly, our journey was another cheapskate getaway. This time Patty and I traveled on free round-trip tickets using AAdvantage program miles. The vacation, including side travel to Egypt and Jordan, was one of the most enjoyable travel experiences I have ever had. First, let me expand on the free travel part of the equation.

As I have said, banking the miles necessary for free international travel is easy. In chapter 2, "Better Than Cheap: Free Travel," I describe the ever-present promotions that offer thousands of free program miles. In early 1996 program members could receive 5,000 miles for switching to MCI, 15,000 miles for banking with Citibank, and 5,000 miles for participating in the AAdvantage dining program. By following my super-saver strategies and taking advantage of these free-mile offers you can accumulate 40,000 to 80,000 miles faster than you could possibly imagine. So, what should you do with these miles?

A funny thing happened as I was leafing through my American AAdvantage member's award guide. I came upon the section that lists international sister-airline awards. One group of awards deals with travel to London on American Airlines, with connecting flights to final destinations on British Airways. The final destinations are broken down into five zones. Zone 5 covers

African cities such as Nairobi and Zone 4 covers Middle Eastern cities such as Cairo. Awards for these zones require 75,000 program miles. Zone 3 covers European cities such as Rome, Athens, and Madrid. A Zone 3 award requires 40,000 miles. Why am I telling you this? For reasons unknown to me I discovered that 40,000 Zone 3 miles also allows you to qualify for a free round-trip ticket from any U.S. city to Tel Aviv, Moscow, or St. Petersburg! At that time we had 82,000 miles in our program account. Did we really qualify for two free round-trip tickets to Tel Aviv? The answer was a resounding YES!

I immediately called American Airlines to book a trip to Israel. My travel spirits were immediately dampened by a "good news--bad news" conversation. Yes, our miles qualified for two free round-trip ticks to Israel. But no, it was not possible to book a trip for at least one year! The problem was the final leg of the trip, from London to Tel Aviv on sister airline British Airways. British Airways was booked solid for one full year.

➡ **Steve's Tip:** *Do you know the phrase "clear space?" In our case this was the factor that determined whether or not we would be traveling to Israel. American said they would request British Airways to "clear space" for us on a Tel Aviv flight. Lo and behold, one week later we were told space had cleared. My original call was placed in May 1995 and space had been cleared for an October 1995 departure. Is there a moral here? You bet: Do not give up! Let American do its thing to find you free seats. American came through for us in the same fashion when it was time to book our free trip to Nairobi.*

Bargain Travel Tours

What to do when one is short of the necessary miles for free travel awards? Here are suggestions for bargain air-and-land packages to Israel, Egypt, and Jordan:

Ayelet Tours, Ltd.: This tour company offers cheapskate packages from New York to Israel for only $999. Their best low-season package includes five nights at the Jerusalem Sheraton, a car rental, two lunches or dinners per day, and round-trip air on El Al Airlines. Extra nights are available at $55 per person. Since this particular bargain tour is exclusively offered by Ayelet, it must be booked directly with them so that free dollars may not be used. Ayelet also offers discount tours to Greece, Turkey, and Eastern Europe. Many of their other tours can be booked through travel agents so that free dollars can be used. Contact:

Ayelet Tours
21 Aviation Road
Albany, New York 12205
(800) 293-5389

International Traders: Traveling to Petra and Jerusalem? In early 1996 Royal Jordanian Airlines joined forces with International Traders, a Jordanian-based travel company. Together, they offered an incredible cheapskate package. The eight-day, seven-night package included round-trip air from New York, daily breakfast, guided sightseeing, bus transportation, and all park entrance fees. The tour visited Jordan's capital, Amman, the "Rose City" of Petra, Jerash, the Crusader Castle at Kerak, and the Dead Sea. This entire package was priced at $999 per person or $949 with Travelers' 5 percent rebate. An excellent three-day extension to Jerusalem cost $299. Look for similar programs in late 1996. Call the Royal Jordanian Airlines tour desk at (800) 758-6878 or (212) 949-0060.

Egypt Tours and Travel: Egypt Tours and Travel specializes in Middle East tours, and offers a comprehensive nine-day package to Israel that includes airfare from New York, first-class hotels, all sightseeing transfers, and breakfasts, for the bargain price of only $1,895. If you are using free travel dollars, this price is reduced to just $1,749.

Want to visit Egypt? Egypt Tours and Travel offers bargain packages to Egypt. A comprehensive, sixteen-day tour, priced at $1,649, includes air from New York (add $54 from Chicago). It includes lodging at deluxe hotels, a sleeper train to Luxor, a cruise ship to the temple of Karnak and Luxor with dinner on the ship, and three additional days on a ship, with meals. Sightseeing includes a visit to the tomb of King Tut and the Colossi of

Memnon, a sail to Edfu, a visit to the Temple of Horus, a sail to Aswan, a visit to the Agha Khan mausoleum, air to Abu Simbel, and a visit to the four famous colossal statues dedicated to Amun-Ra, Horakkhti, and Ramses II. Finally, there is a flight back to Aswan, additional cruising, and then a flight back to Cairo. (I hope you could read that in one breath.) If free travel dollars are used, the net cost is reduced to just $1,499. For current tours and a brochure, contact:

Egypt Tours and Travel
4353 North Harding Avenue
Chicago, Illinois 60618
(800) 523-4978, (312) 463-4999; fax (312) 463-4999

The Entertainment Connection

Buy the European Entertainment edition so you may obtain up to 50 percent savings on Israeli hotels. While U.S. editions may contain one or two listings for Israel, the European edition lists between fifteen and twenty Israeli hotels and low-priced kibbutzes in various parts of the country. More about the Entertainment connection follows.

A word or two is in order regarding hotel reservations. Since we arrived in Israel during Succoth, a major Jewish holiday, hotel rooms were scarce and advance reservations were essential. Unfortunately, the hotels would not give us Entertainment's discount rates because it was a holiday week and they were fully booked. Still, you owe it to yourself to try for these discounts, but only Entertainment's international editions contain a comprehensive list of Israeli hotels.

Predeparture Thoughts

If you do not use an Entertainment hotel discount, then book your hotel through Travelers Advantage. Another nondiscount alternative, if you are short on time, is the Jerusalem Travel Center. It is quite helpful and will recommend various accommodations and prices in any Israeli city. You may book directly through:

Jerusalem Travel Center
20 South Van Brunt Street
Englewood, New Jersey 07631
(800) JLM IS US; fax (201) 816-1111

➡ **Steve's Tip:** *Be sure to obtain $50 to $100 in Israeli shekels* before *you leave on your trip. Foreign currency is available through Citibank branches and American Express travel offices that have an international money exchange counter. I ordered $100 in shekels from a local American Express office. Why purchase shekels in advance, you ask? We arrived in Tel Aviv in an exhausted and semiconscious state at 4:30 A.M. With local currency in hand, we grabbed the first available taxi and headed to the bed waiting at our Tel Aviv hotel. As we left the airport, many fellow passengers were still standing on the long line at the airport's currency exchange booth.*

Rental Cars

Rental cars are not necessary in major cities such as Tel Aviv and Jerusalem. We enjoyed walking and took inexpensive taxi cabs whenever it was necessary. Let me repeat that one: *inexpensive* taxi cabs. A twenty-minute cab ride from our hotel in a remote part of Jerusalem to the Jaffa Gate cost only $6. Better yet, tipping taxi drivers is *not* encouraged. (This definitely *was* a foreign country.) If you must rent a car, the daily rate is about $60 to $80 per day. One caveat: Be careful driving. I am told that traffic accidents in Israel are the number-one cause of death of young people.

Traveling to the Promised Land

How should one begin to cover this massive subject? I have reviewed brochures for Jewish, Christian, and Moslem travelers, and for history and archeology buffs. There are brochures for planning bar mitzvahs and others that describe desert exploration safaris. Let us not forget divers, who travel to Eilat, board a dive boat, and enjoy a week or two of intensive first-rate Red Sea scuba diving.

When it comes to visiting Israel and its environs, I am convinced that no two people have identical agendas. But there seems to be at least one common denominator concerning Israel. It is, in one word—Jerusalem—the most fascinating city in the world. No other piece of real estate is such a magnet, drawing masses from every corner of the globe. People arrive daily, by plane, boat, and car. But then again, people have been making this journey for thousands of years. I am not the first to admit that all roads eventually lead to Jerusalem.

From the outset, our approach to this trip was unique. We refused to spend our two weeks doing traditional sightseeing, so we divided the visit into two parts. We spent one week sightseeing in northern Israel and the second week in Eilat, with side trips to Jordan and Egypt. Eilat is Israel's tropical southern resort on the Gulf of Aqaba. Using Eilat as a base, we journeyed to the famed "Rose City" of Petra, in Jordan. Later in the week, on the spur of the moment, we visited Egypt's Sinai desert. The remainder of the week was "water-based," and included a day sailing cruise to Egypt's nearby Coral Island. There we spent hours in the Gulf of Aqaba "playing" with many colorful species of reef fish that are not found in other waters of the world. On other days we relaxed on the beach of Israel's finest marine preserve, only three miles from downtown Eilat.

When recounting our two-week adventure in the Middle East, I emphasize my goal of providing useful, money-saving insights, tips, recommendations, and options.

Tel Aviv

Our British Airways flight from London arrived in Tel Aviv at the ungodly hour of 4:30 A.M. As we exited the airport, I learned there was a thirty-minute wait for a bus to downtown Tel Aviv. Instead, we marched to the nearby taxi stand. In a flash, a fellow passenger accepted my offer to share a taxi into Tel Aviv. Gone was the thirty-minute wait for a bus at 6:00 A.M. The cost was $12, but two bus tickets would have cost $8. We enjoyed the door-to-door service as the taxi dropped us in front of our hotel. Travel from the airport to Jerusalem involves a choice between a bus and a *sherutt*, a shared mini-van that takes eight to ten passengers.

As our taxi neared the hotel my thoughts turned to our master plan. Given the usual hotel check-in time of 2:00 P.M., we would be arriving at the registration desk fully eight hours early. This presented a major problem, namely, what to do until check-in time? My plan went something like this: We would drop our luggage at the front desk, enjoy a long and relaxing breakfast, and then head to the old city of Jaffa for a free walking tour, scheduled to begin precisely at 9:30 A.M. The old city of Jaffa is a major highlight on all visits to Tel Aviv and a refreshing walk would keep us going until our hotel room was ready.

As fortune would have it, the fates intervened at 6:30 A.M. At that moment a prince of a registration clerk told us that our room was ready and waiting for us. In a flash our limp and fatigued bodies fell blissfully asleep.

At 8:45 A.M. we awakened, freshened up, and headed by taxi to the clock tower in Jaffa. Our taxi covered the short distance from our hotel to Old Jaffa in ten minutes, and deposited us at the foot of the clock tower with five minutes to spare. As promised, a tour guide appeared at precisely at 9:30 A.M. and we set off with a group of about twenty visitors. We looked at one another and then knew—really knew—that we had arrived in the Promised Land!

➡ **Steve's Tip:** *Write to the Israeli Government Tourist Office and request their wonderful booklet, "Israeli Events." It contains listings of holidays, country-wide events, and events in major cities. It saved us big dollars in Jaffa by listing the free walking tour. An expert volunteer guide meets visitors at the town's clock tower. Contact:*

Israeli Government Tourist Office
21 Hill Road
Waltham, Massachussetts 02154
Or call the Israel Ministry of Tourism at (800) 596-1199.

Jaffa

For the past four thousand years Jaffa has been a significant port on one of the major trade routes of the Middle East. The Bible states that cedars arrived at the port for use in building King Solomon's Temple. It talks of Jonah fleeing from God via Jaffa, and the New Testament mentions apostle Peter performing a miracle there. Over the ages the city was conquered time and again by such as Roman legions, Richard the Lion Hearted, Napoleon, and Turkish sultans. After World War II the city became part of the British mandate until the war of independence in 1948. Today Jaffa is touted as one of Tel Aviv's main tourist attractions. Our walking tour visited one of the world's oldest flea markets and then took us past ancient buildings, many still functioning as shops, bakeries, and artist studios. The sights and sounds were marvelous. Perhaps best was the view of the Mediterranean Sea and the beach-lined coast of Tel Aviv. Other highlights of Jaffa include the following:

- Church of St. Peter (circa 1888)
- Andromeda's Rock
- Jaffa lighthouse (1936)
- The Citadel clock tower (1901)
- House of Simon the Tanner
- The Antiquities Museum of Tel Aviv
- Jaffa synagogue (1740)
- Al Mahmoudiyeh mosque (1812)
- Ancient but ongoing flea market
- Diaspora Museum

We spent the afternoon visiting Tel Aviv's famous Diaspora Museum. It offers marvelous Judaica collections and exhibits that dramatically recreate the history of Jewish communities from all corners of the globe. Then we were ready for another nap and headed back to our hotel.

My choice of the Center Hotel, a member of the Atlas hotel chain, was a good one. The hotel has fifty-six small, recently refurbished rooms and is on a quiet pedestrian walkway just one hundred feet or so from Tel Aviv's famous Dizengoff Square fountain. Unfortunately, prices in-season and during religious holidays are high. The price of the room was $75 per day, which included a fine daily breakfast, but the best thing going for the Center Hotel is its great downtown location, just off Dizengoff Square. You may contact the hotel directly for rates and reservations at:

Center Hotel
2 Zamenhoff Street
Tel Aviv, Israel 64373
Tel: 03-6296181 or fax: 03-6296751

➡ **Steve's Tip:** *Did I mention phone cards? In Israel the phones take a prepaid local phone card instead of coins. They are sold at post offices, cigarette shops, markets, and bus depot newsstands. Ask for a ten- or twenty-call card.*

Later, we walked in and around Dizengoff Square. It is only several blocks from the Mediterranean and is a main attraction in the city. Architecturally it is a most unusual accomplishment. The public square is elevated above the traffic, with about six busy intersecting streets below, and it has descending walkways that connect with each of the adjoining streets. A famous multicolored circular fountain sits atop the square. Each evening it comes alive with a light, sound, and water show. As the water cascades and pulsates in time with music, the fountain rotates. Locals either love or hate the fountain. We found it charming and enjoyed the many street artists who routinely perform in its shadow. The bustling nearby streets offer a plethora of shops, cafes, and restaurants. Dizengoff is truly a "happening" place, and is one of the best night spots in Tel Aviv.

My plan for our second day was to leave Tel Aviv. Of course, we wanted to see everything, but that was impossible. I decided to do the unthinkable and take two intensive day tours by bus. Tours are the fastest and easiest way to see the country in the shortest possible time. I opted for one northern tour to the Golan Heights and a second tour to Massada and the Dead Sea.

Two major tour companies in Israel are United Tours and Egged

Tours. Both have excellent color brochures listing available itineraries. While the companies assign identical numbers to most of its respective tours, some tours are available only through one company or the other. For brochures, write to:

United Tours
113 Ha'Yarkon Street
Tel Aviv, Israel
Tel: 03-6933410/11;
fax: 03-6933408

Egged Tours
11 Sunrise Plaza, Suite 302
Valley Stream, New York 11580
Tel: (800) 825-9399;
fax: (800) 825-0980

Here is my list of United's best tours departing out of Tel Aviv. In parentheses is the number of the identical Egged tour:

- Tour no. 200 (same): Day city tour of Tel Aviv. It visits Old Jaffa, the Jaffa flea market, Jaffa port, St. Peters Church, and the Diaspora Museum. The cost is $23.
- Tour no. 231 (230): A full-day tour to Massada and the Dead Sea. The cost is $61.
- Tour no. 258: One-day tour to Caesarea, Acre, and Rosh Hanikra. The tour goes north up the coastal highway to Caesarea, where visitors tour Roman and Crusader ruins. The tour continues north through Haifa to Rosh Hanikra and the Lebanese border. It also explores an underground crusader crypt. The price is $55.
- Tour no. 280: Full-day desert safari. This tour of the Judean desert visits Mt. Montar, which is 524 meters or 1572 high. From atop Mt. Montar the tour stops to view Jerusalem and the Moab Mountains. From the cliffs above Kidron Canyon one views the Marsaba Monastery, the largest monastery in the Judean desert. Next is a one-hour hike to St. Georges, a fifth-century monastery, and Eliyahu's Cave. The price is $59.
- Tour no. 243 (243 and 244): Golan Heights, Hammat Gader Hot Springs full-day tour. We took this one. First it bisects Israel, traveling from the Mediterranean coast to the Golan Heights. We traveled on the coastal highway to Hadera, then east inland to Afula and Tiberias. We drove along the shore of the Sea of Galilee and across the Arik Bridge to the Golan Heights. After viewing the Syrian border we visited the Israeli city of Katzrin, recently built in the heights. The tour

moved south to the famed Hammat Gader Hot Springs and ancient second-century Roman baths. Both the baths and the springs are spectacular.

➡ **Steve's Tip:** *The hot spring's restaurant used to be self-service. It now has waiter and waitress service that is slow. Rather than kill a precious hour for lunch, bring your lunch and enjoy a picnic on the beautiful lawns and gardens near the pools. Be sure to leave at least thirty minutes for touring the Roman baths.*

Jerusalem

Without question, Jerusalem is the most unique city in the world. It is the cradle of three of the world's great religions and draws visitors of every faith from every corner of the globe. We wisely decided to devote four days to Jerusalem. Patty and I spent three glorious days exploring and savoring the city. On the fourth day, which happened to be the Sabbath, we took a full-day tour to Massada and the Dead Sea. I will not attempt to make an itinerary for your visit to Jerusalem. What you see and do depends, in large part, on your personal agenda, whether religious or historical.

For most visitors the Old City *is* Jerusalem. For the two of us, the miracle and joy of this unique place began when we passed through the Jaffa Gate. As I entered the Old City, I felt transported back to another era of human civilization. On that first day we walked for four hours with our trusty map in hand, and visited the Christian, Moslem, Jewish, and Armenian quarters of the city.

David Street: David Street is a long, narrow, winding street that is home to the world's most ancient bazaar. Imagine a bustling, crowded street fair in continuous operation for thousands of years. We marveled in disbelief as the street meandered downhill, toward the Gate of Chains, which leads to the Dome of the Rock. We stopped every ten or fifteen feet to check out the shops or open stalls of every type, kind, and description. David Street also divides the various quarters. To the left is first the Christian, and then the Moslem, quarter. To the right is first the Armenian, and then the Jewish, quarter. Most of old Jerusalem's shops are on David Street and in the nearby Christian and Moslem sections. Merchandise is set out in front of the open stalls or shops. There are clothing shops, food stalls, and countless souvenir shops selling ceramic, silver, bronze, gold, and jewelry items. There are leather shops, tea shops, religious shops, and eateries. In short, if you enjoy good flea markets, bazaars, and street fairs, then David Street is, pardon the expression, "heaven sent."

Yes, there is more to Jerusalem than shopping. During our three days of touring Jerusalem we saw as many highlights as possible. In the Old City we visited the Church of the Holy Sepulcher, the Way of the Cross, King David's Tower (the Citadel) and the Western (Wailing) Wall.

➡ **Steve's Tip:** *There is one money-saving reason to contact the Israeli office of tourism before you depart for Israel: maps, maps, and more free maps. You may ask the Israeli Tourist Office for several free maps. The touring map of Israel is a great 14" × 20" color map of the entire country. It also includes a city map of Eilat and three other local regions. Be sure to also request the excellent Jerusalem and Tel Aviv city maps. At local travel shops these sell for $10 to $20 each.*

Dome of the Rock: Our several attempts to see the Dome of the Rock were in vain. The hours when the Dome was supposed to be open to tourist seemed to vary. Each time we appeared at the "right" time an unfriendly Jerusalem policeman informed us it was the "wrong" time. We were stopped cold at the Gate of Chains at the Moslem end of Hashaifshelet Street, which is the continuation of David Street. Finally, we tried the Lions Gate in the Moslem quarter and that too failed. Good luck on this one!

Jaffa Gate: Our favorite Old City section was inside Jaffa Gate, near King David's Tower. It is a great place to people-watch while enjoying lunch. There are two cafes, but neither one impressed me. At the entrance to David Street there is a shop selling fresh hot apple cakes and chocolate buns that are cheap and delectable.

Back toward the Jaffa Gate there is a stand where you can buy shwarmas, the Middle Eastern equivalent of Greek gyros. The sandwiches are great and cost only $3. We enjoyed our brown-bag lunch and watched people scurry by, a supreme pastime in Jerusalem. There is also one resident camel available for photos and rides.

Schindler's Grave: It is Jewish tradition to place a small pebble on a tombstone in memory of your visit. We visited a Christian cemetery just south of the Zion Gate, outside the city wall. One gravestone stood out among the hundreds of tombstones. It was covered with literally hundreds of small stones piled on top of the horizontal gravestone. Inscribed in the gravestone is the name Oscar Schindler. If you wish to view the grave of this real war hero, then head for the Zion Gate. With the gate at your back, cross the busy street and turn right. Continue to walk and a double wrought-iron gate will be on your left. The second large gate leads to the Christian cemetery, with crosses over the gravestones. If the gate is open, walk in. A caretaker will approach and instantly lead you to the Schindler grave. You will descend a small staircase to the lower part of the cemetery. At this point look for the horizontal tombstone covered with pebbles. Remember to give the caretaker a small tip.

Ben Yehuda Mall: The best local night-time entertainment is the Ben Yehuda Mall. It is a six-square-block section of street open to pedestrian traffic only. King Solomon Street intersects one end and is open only to foot traffic. Both streets are downtown and an easy one-mile walk from Jaffa Gate. This "mall" is a hotbed of fun and activity, with hundreds of locals and tourists enjoying its many shops, boutiques, cafes, fast-food eateries, and restaurants. Both young and old enjoy strolling through the mall at night, meeting and visiting with friends, stopping for a "nosh," and taking in the local street artists.

Other Sights: The new city of Jerusalem, that part of the city that lies outside the old walled city, offers additional endless sightseeing options. We visited the Knesset, or parliament building, the Supreme Court building, the holocaust museum Yad Vashem, the famous model city of Jerusalem at the Holyland Hotel, and the Great Synagogue.

Special Jerusalem Tips

Walking Tours: One day we walked from the Knesset to down-town Jerusalem, stopping at the Great Synagogue and then moving onto the Jaffa Gate. This is a great cross-city trek that traverses many different neighborhoods and gives one a real "feel" of the city and its people. The walk takes about three hours with the various stops. Do not miss the Supreme Court building and Rose Park and Hanasi Garden, found a hundred yards or so from the Knesset building. Also check out the Great Menorah, presented to Israel by Great Britain, which stands about twenty feet tall. It is found across the street from the entrance to the Knesset building.

Hotel Location: Our hotel was too far from the center of town, especially since we did not want to rent a car. Stay at a hotel near the downtown area.

Sabbath: During holidays and Sabbath the city of Jerusalem shuts down. Public transportation, museums, Jewish and kosher restaurants, and shops close at 3:00 P.M. on the Friday afternoon before the Sabbath. For those who are not Orthodox Jews, Satur-day is the best time to schedule a full-day tour out of Jerusalem. The Sabbath is also a fine time for my recommended walking tour. On Jewish holidays there are often religious street processions. After our Succoth walk to the Great Synagogue we joined a religious procession of several thousand Jewish observers heading to the Wailing Wall in the Old City via Jaffa Gate. There was singing and dancing in the streets, truly a moving experience that neither one of us will forget.

Machine-Gun-Toting Civilians: Before our trip I read nothing about machine-gun-toting, twenty-year-old "civilians" casually walking the streets of Israel's major cities. Usually, they are found near tourist areas, including beaches. Not to fear—they are off-duty or reservist soldiers or licensed ex-army civilians. The government encourages them to carry their weapons, especially in tourist places, including crowded streets, the downtown mall, and the beaches in Eilat. A visible armed force discourages terrorist attacks against tourists. Actually, we found ourselves feeling quite safe whenever we noticed these armed individuals in the area—a necessary precaution in Israel, but quite a shock to Americans.

Terrorism: For years my mother thought of Israel as a great but dangerous place to visit. I met an Orthodox Jewish New Yorker on a Jerusalem tour bus. Evidently, an Orthodox-looking friend was stabbed in broad daylight in the Moslem section of the Old City by the Damascus Gate. This type of violence is rare in Jerusalem. The reality of Israel, including Jerusalem, is that tourists are *not* and have never been targets of crazed terrorists. Yes, when you ride a local bus, your risk increases. If you want complete safety, take a taxi. My conclusion is that 99.9 percent of the time tourists visiting Israel are totally safe. Does this mean you should visit the Moslem quarter of the Old City late at night? No!

Sightseeing Bargain: Egged Tours provides tour no. 99, the Circle Line Bus Tour. For a nominal fee of about $2, this tour travels around Jerusalem visiting major tourist attractions and areas. The bus ticket allows tourists to disembark and then reboard at any of its thirty-six stops, which include the Rockefeller Museum, the Knesset, Yad Vashem (the holocaust museum), the Holyland Hotel (home of the famous model of old Jerusalem), Gethsemane, the Lion's Gate, the Church of the Resurrection, and the Mount of Olives. The bus finally loops back to the Old City past the Lions Gate and ends at Jaffa Gate. The tour runs Sunday through Thursday from 10:00 A.M. to 4:00 P.M. and Fridays and holidays until noon. It departs from King David Street at the large intersection north of Jaffa Gate. As you stand facing the Jaffa Gate, the bus stop, not well marked, is a couple of hundred feet to the left, just past the large intersection. If you see the bus coming, just wave at the driver, who generally will stop to pick you up even if you are not at the stop.

Model of Jerusalem: I have mentioned the model of the city, which is found at the Holyland Hotel. This is a justifiably popular attraction that was five years in the making. The model is a large replica of Jerusalem that shows the city as it existed at about the Second Temple period, before complete and total destruction by the Romans. The model was painstakingly built using the same materials as was used in the original buildings. It was incredible! As we walked around the large sprawling outdoor model, we could visualize the social, political, and military aspects of biblical life in Jerusalem in 60 B.C. The model also shows fortifications and various levels of housing. For the technically minded, the model is built to a 1:50 scale. The Holyland replica is often used in biblical films and documentaries. This is a "must-do" sightseeing stop.

United Tours Departing From Jerusalem

Following are my recommended United Tours departing out of Tel Aviv. Again, the parentheses contain the tour numbers of the identical Egged tours.

- Diamond Center: This tour is free and given daily, except Saturday, and includes a half-day tour of Jerusalem. It visits the nearby Ramat Rachel Kibbutz, takes in a view of Jerusalem, and then tours the National Diamond Center. Simply have the hotel call United to arrange a morning pickup.
- Tour no. 101: This is a one-half day tour of the Old City of Jerusalem. The price is $21.
- Tour no. 204 (102): This one-half day tour includes a mountaintop view of Jerusalem, a visit to Yad Vashem (the holocaust museum), and Bethlehem. The cost is $20.
- Tour no. 131 (130): This is the big one! We took this full-day tour to Masada and the Dead Sea. It also heads east into the Judean desert. We passed bedouin camps, a kibbutz, and then turned south along the west shore of the Dead Sea. The tour then headed for Masada. At the base of the desert plateau we took a cable car up to the top to King Herod's ancient fortress. The view of Syria, Jordan, and southern Judea was as unobstructed today as it was in ancient times. Then we visited the popular Ein Gedi Spa on the Dead Sea. The price of this tour is $58, and I highly recommend it.
- Egged tour no. 158: This is an endurance test. If this your only chance to explore Israel's Mediterranean coast north of Tel Aviv, then take it. The tour leaves Jerusalem and travels west to Tel Aviv and north to Caesarea (mimicking United's tour no. 258 from Tel Aviv). It leaves at 6:30 A.M. and costs $58.

Masada

Masada is a "must-see" place. It was the mountaintop fortress of King Herod and the last stronghold of the Jewish zealots. Another piece of history is in order for those who do not watch *Ancient Mysteries of the Bible*. Masada is the dramatic story of hope, pride, and defiance of almost a thousand men, women, and children facing destruction by the Romans.

The story of the mountaintop city began in ancient times, when it first was a military lookout. In 150 B.C., when Jews sought a haven from hostile Greeks and Syrians, they built a military fortress on the plateau on the top of the mountain. Later, in 40 B.C., King Herod fled to Masada when rivals threatened his life. His fortress was approximately 2,000 by 750 feet. King Herod's palace was literally a castle in the sky. It was a bastion of luxurious living, with mosaic tiled floors, beautifully decorated walls, real Roman baths, and a large, outdoor swimming pool. The fortress was impregnable on all four sides.

In 66 A.D. the Jews once again revolted against Roman rule, and the Romans defeated the rebels in northern Judea. However, a small group known as Sacarii remained entrenched at Masada. They numbered around nine hundred men, women, and children. They had sufficient stores of water, food, and other supplies to last for years. At least two defensive walls protected their mountaintop enclave. The Roman commander, with 7,000 to 10,000 soldiers, laid siege to Masada for more than three years. The Romans had multiple encampments that encircled the mountain but made no headway. Finally, the Roman soldiers constructed an ingenious stone and gravel ramp for the troops to march directly up to the fortress. When the Sacarii saw the completion of the ramp and coming assault, they knew that they would all die come the light of day. That night the rebels met and decided that suicide was more appealing than death at the hands of the Romans. Only two women and five children survived to recount this story to the Roman historian Flavius Josephus.

The tour of Masada includes a cable ride up the mountain. From the cable stop at the top there are an additional seventy steps up to the plateau. The view of the Dead Sea and endless desert is thrilling. Those who are not on a tour may take a one-hour hike up the mountain if they are in good physical shape. The ruins at Masada include remnants of houses and walls, the oldest synagogue in Israel, ritual bathhouses, enormous food storage houses, and remnants of Herod's Temple, with its rose mosaic tiles. (Seventy water cisterns scattered throughout the area held enough water to last eight years.) The remnants of the Roman encampments are visible from the plateau.

If you can get there at night, there is a sound and light show every Tuesday and Wednesday. Do *not* miss Masada!

Eilat, Jordan, and Egypt

The next day we headed to the central bus depot and bid a fond farewell to Jerusalem. Finding your way at the bus depot is tricky. Despite our best efforts we almost boarded the wrong bus. Do your best to get in the right line and then double-check with the driver. We finally boarded the correct bus and took off on the five-hour journey to the southern resort of Eilat. The fare was a reasonable 46 shekels, or $15 each.

➡ **Steve's Tip:** *When traveling by intra-city bus to or from Eilat, buy your tickets three days in advance. All bus seats are reserved; no seats are guaranteed for last-minute ticket purchasers. I have great video of seatless young people sprawled on the floor in the aisle looking very uncomfortable.*

Eilat is the most southern city in Israel and its only port with access to shipping routes through the Red Sea. The resort is on the Gulf of Aqaba, only a couple of miles from the Egyptian border to the west and the Jordanian border to the east. An article I had read said that Eilat is overrated as a tropical paradise. It referred to the city as a commercial shipping port that lacks the look and feel of a lush tropical resort town such as those in Hawaii. Yes, it is true that Eilat is on the edge of a desert and is surrounded by barren mountains, so there are no lush, green tropical gardens. However, we loved Eilat. We found that the physical port facilities were a couple of miles outside the city and not an eyesore. There were no lines of ugly super-tankers ruining our view of the gulf. Eilat is a vibrant resort bustling with young Israeli tourists visibly enjoying a respite from their tense and stressful lives. But activities in Eilat are limited. Of course, one can vegetate on Royal Beach, but who travels halfway around the world to sack out on a lounge chair? I anticipated that six days in Eilat might be too long, so before we left home I booked a two-day adventure to Jordan and the Rose City, Petra. We also signed up for a one-day trip to Egypt's Sinai Desert and the seventh-century Greek Orthodox monastery of Santa Katerina.

Evenings in Eilat are fun affairs, with thousands of people enjoying the promenades along the beach. There are many cafes and restaurants from which to choose. Street and craft artists line the promenades, offering additional diversions. Shopping, dining, and people-watching are favorite night-time activities.

Lodging in Eilat

October is both high season and a holiday month. In the end we opted for comfort and convenience, staying at the Riviera Apartment Hotel, built in 1989. The hotel is part of the large Isrotel hotel group, which incudes the King Solomon Hotel. This association allows guests to visit the nearby Royal Beach Hotel's wide beach and use its lounge chairs. The Riviera offers studio, one- and two-bedroom units. We had a super studio with a large veranda overlooking the pool. The grounds include pools for both adults and kids, and every unit comes with a kitchen. The Riviera also has one of the only mini-markets in the area. We paid a whopping $106 per night, definitely a high-season or holiday rate. As you will soon learn, the hotel fully cooperated with our departure for Petra and our return two days later. You may book directly.

Riviera Apartment Hotel
North Beach, Eilat 88000
Tel.: 07-334141; fax: 07-333939

➡ **Steve's Tip:** *Planning to visit Petra? Then arrange to check out of your Eilat hotel for the night you will spend in a hotel in Jordan— don't pay for two hotels for the same night. Most Eilat hotels will cooperate, since a visit to Petra is the most popular tour outside Eilat.*

Coral Beach Marine Preserve: A resort town is a resort town is a resort town. Anyone want a lounge chair on Royal Beach overlooking the Gulf of Aqaba? Patty and I are not pool people, and any old beach will *not* do! Instead we opted to relax on a gorgeous beach that had local marine life and we spent the better part of two days enjoying the local marine preserve called Coral Beach. The preserve is a couple of miles west of Eilat on the road to Egypt. The number 15 bus reaches the preserve in just fifteen minutes. (The fare is only ninety cents!) We had our own snorkels and masks but rented fins. On the negative side, the main road and traffic abuts the beach. Otherwise, it is a great place for sun, snorkeling, and fish. In fact, to preserve the coral, the beach sports a walkway that takes visitors past the coral and then provides steps into the water. (It does not get any easier than this.) We spotted eels and gigantic orange parrot fish not found in the Caribbean or the Pacific. The entrance fee is $4, and (optional) comfortable lounge chairs go for another $2.

Coral Beach Snuba: The Coral Beach Nature Preserve has a SNUBA program. This allows one to go underwater to a shallow depth of about fifteen feet. Participants breathe on an air line that they connect to a floating surface compressor. The floating compressor moves with the swimmer and is quite an ingenious system. The sessions last about thirty minutes and cost a hefty $50.

Kings Wharf Promenade: This promenade is on the canal behind the King Solomon Hotel and across the street from the Riviera Apartment Hotel. This classy promenade becomes lively after dark. The quarter-mile walkway sports a variety of eateries, from the Yacht Pub and an Indian Restaurant to Pizza Hut and Ben and Jerry's Ice Cream. The Red Sea Sports Club arranges all types of water-based activities, from live aboard dive boats to deluxe snorkel cruises.

Royal Beach Promenade: Continue on to the Royal Beach Hotel boardwalk, with its fine upscale shops and restaurants.

Downtown Promenade: Walking the downtown promenade is a great evening activity. Upon crossing the marina's pedestrian bridge one enjoys about a half-mile of restaurants, shops, street artists, and craft people selling their wares.

Dolphin Reef: Dolphin Reef is a highly-touted local attraction that includes a private beach and their own trained dolphins. It offers visitors a unique opportunity to go swimming or even scuba diving "with dolphins." The basic price of admission ($8) allows one to view the training of the dolphins. The swimming and diving-with-dolphins experience has an additional price tag of $20 to $30. Entrance to the private beach is free after 5 P.M.

Jules Verne Observatory: The Jules Verne is a high-tech mobile underwater observatory. It appears to be right out of a sci-fi story and is a fun activity.

Coral Island Snorkel Cruise: We booked a great snorkeling trip on the sailing schooner *Oriona* through the Red Sea Sport Club. It cost us $45 each for the five-hour excursion. The masted schooner *Oriona* sailed into Egyptian waters to Coral Island, just beyond the Taba–Egyptian border. The sail was superb and the two hours of snorkeling was great fun. As expected, the crew and passengers created a party atmosphere, serving up a delicious roast chicken lunch. Those wanting to go ashore have a fine time exploring the restored Crusader Castle, which covers the entire island.

Other options include desert jeep tours, camel tours, and Bedouin belly dancing dinner shows under the desert stars. Here is my list of United Tours best tours departing out of Eilat:

- Tour no. 515: Tour to the Pillars of Solomon and the Timna Copper Mine. This half-day tour travels twenty-five kilometers north of Eilat, visiting Solomon's Pillars (fifty meters high) and the Mushroom, a natural rock formation formed by the effects of wind and water on the sandstone. Timna (6,000 years old) is the oldest producing copper mine in the world. The tour stops at the Egyptian temple to the goddess Hathar, with its ancient rock paintings, and then stops at the Yolvata Kibbutz. The price is $38.
- Tour no. 530 (Egged): Tour to Masada and the Dead Sea. I recommend this for the few, if any, people who missed Masada when they were up north and much closer to it. The tour from Eilat backtracks two-thirds of the way back to Jerusalem and therefore includes much too much time on the road. The cost is $68.
- Tour no. 580, Santa Katerina Monastery: Okay, we took this one impulsively. After all, what is a day in the Middle East if

one is not crossing a new border? This full-day tour took us into Egypt and the Sinai Desert. We crossed the border at Taba and drove along the Gulf of Aqaba past the Coral Island Marine Preserve with its fully-restored, twelfth-century Crusader Castle. We passed an Oasis and stopped at an overlook to view the endless desert. The sight was inspiringly and serenely beautiful.

We continued on to the sixth-century, Greek Orthodox Santa Katerina monastery. The interior is filled with ancient artifacts, just outside is the "burning bush," and off in the distance is a path to a bluff that offers a view of Mt. Sinai. I was particularly impressed with one room in the monastery that had floor-to-ceiling wire cages. One cage contained hundreds of skulls and the other contained hundreds of other bones, including hands and feet. We were told these belonged to former residents of the monastery. (Was this an extreme effort to avoid the high cost of burial?) The tour concluded with a tented bedouin lunch. Total cost is $55.

Petra: The Rose City

Where is Petra and why visit it? Do you recall the film *Indiana Jones and the Last Crusade?* It not only stars Harrison Ford and Sean Connery, but also the breathtaking ancient city of Petra. Do you recall the awesome rose-colored temple, hand-carved into the façade of a large mountain? The final scene depicts Indiana Jones and his father escaping on horseback through a winding, narrow gorge only three meters wide and two hundred meters high. The romantic adventure film was shot on location in the "Rose City" of Petra. Petra was a wealthy city on the trade routes from the Far East to the Mediterranean cities. Its abandoned buildings and temples have survived the ravages of time. Today, Petra is an inspiring reminder of the ancient and vanished civilization of Nabatea.

Our timing was perfect. Only one year before we arrived, Israel and Jordan signed an historic peace treaty allowing Israeli tourists to visit Jordan and Petra for the first time in recent history. So you can appreciate the city, I will quickly recap its 2,600 years of history.

Petra is northeast of Eilat, in Jordan. Travel time by bus or car is five hours, through miles of desert and mountains resembling

America's southwestern states. Today Petra is Jordan's number-one tourist site. In fact, eighteen new hotels were under construction during our visit in October 1995.

From 1200 A.D. until 1812, Petra was truly a lost city. Only local bedouin tribes knew of its existence, and they told no one. The city is an architectural marvel, with temples and tombs carved into the sandstone faces of the surrounding mountains. Your introduction into the ancient world of Petra starts when you walk between the narrow, shaded, winding canyon cliffs leading to the entrance. Suddenly, around the final bend, the light becomes brighter until a vision of a monumental, pink palace magically appears before you. The first sight of Petra is of the famed treasury building, by far the most famous and photographed structure in the city.

The ancient Nabateans ruled this area, protected the trade route through the region, and built the city of Petra between the third and sixth century B.C. Each temple and building was painstakingly hand-carved out of the colorful sandstone mountains. Most tourists visit for several hours, but the city is so large it would take three full days to cover it all. The houses, tombs, and palaces display early Greek, Roman, and Egyptian influences.

Amazingly, in 63 B.C. the Nabateans successfully defended Petra from the Roman legions of Pompeii. Petra was thought to be impenetrable. The king of the Nabateans wisely negotiated with the Romans to let them be until after his death. Then, in 106 A.D., Petra came under Roman rule and development. Roman influence is everywhere, from the columnated main street to the ornate carved capitals and building decorations.

Archaeologists believe that 20,000 to 35,000 people inhabited the city at its zenith. Petra's success resulted from the protection it offered the caravans traveling the trade routes from Mesopotamia to Arabia. Everyone stopped in Petra for safety and respite from the harsh desert.

In the fourth century a major earthquake caused the trade routes to shift north to Syria and the city began to decline. Petra was subsequently conquered by the Byzantines, then the Arabs, and finally the crusaders, who promptly built their own fort, which still stands as witness to the city's changing fortunes.

Until August 12, 1812, the city was unknown to Western

civilization. That year a Swiss explorer, Jonathan Burkhardt, vowed to find the legendary city. Disguised as a Moslem pilgrim, he had his bedouin guide lead him to Petra's entrance, where he stood in awe. After a quick look at the carved temples, he knew what he had found. Burkhardt returned to Europe and announced his discovery to a fascinated world.

In more recent times, due to greater interest and the influx of tourists, the Jordanian government moved the resident bedouins to nearby, newly-constructed housing. Many bedouins still visit Petra daily to sell souvenirs. I purchased necklaces and camel bone boxes from men, women, and an adorable seven-year-old boy.

The famous Treasury building, found near the entrance to Petra, is about 85 meters wide and 125 meters tall. Its shades of red seem ever changing, as sunlight first bathes the edifice and later retreats. The sandstone interior, believed to have served as a tomb, offers a wonder of cascading colors and designs. Just down the road is another major sight. A Roman amphitheater, built in the second century, seats 2,500 to 3,000 people. Nearby are the Royal Tombs, the Corinthian Tomb, and the Palace Tomb, which sticks out of the mountain. Up the road is another major site: the remains of the Roman highway, built about 2,000 years ago and lined with giant columns. As I rode my camel on this ancient highway, I could easily imagine a Roman legion marching in formation behind me. We climbed a large staircase to reach the museum, which displays many interesting artifacts from various explorations of the city.

➡ **Steve's Tip:** *Take the camel ride starting at the Roman amphitheater and ending at the museum. Three or four young boys patiently awaited customers for their deluxe camel excursion to the museum. They dress the camels with ornate layers of colorful rugs. After a little bargaining they take any form of currency. I paid $4 for the ride, and Patty took great photos. Later, Patty and I took a camel ride for two down the mountain and back to the amphitheater. We were tired from hours of walking, and the ride down the mountain was relaxing, scenic, fun, and romantic. The trip back only cost $8 for two.*

The Petra Vacation Package

This was an expensive package. I had my local travel agent book United's Jordan-Petra Tour no. 582 before our departure for Israel. Since United Tours does not have a U.S. office, the travel agent faxed our reservation, and we paid with our Visa card. Although the brochure price is $159, it does not cover meals or the entry fee to Petra. We paid $229 each for a tour that included overnight lodging in Petra, the $30 per person entrance fee, two lunches, and one dinner. As with London theater tickets, not all world-class experiences come cheap. On the plus side, the $458 package became an incredible two-day vacation experience in Jordan. It included the following:

Day One: We departed Eilat and crossed the border into Jordan. The border crossing is friendly enough but wastes two to three hours of the morning (through passport checking, payment of border fees, and buying Jordanian dinars). Our next stop was Jordan's Red Sea port city of Aqaba. Upon arrival we stopped to visit a medieval monastery. Patty and I took off for a short walk to the city's newly built park at the water's edge, where the Gulf of Aqaba was outstretched before us. Off to the right, only several miles away, was the city of Eilat, with its skyline of resort hotels. The tour included a wonderful lunch at the Ali Baba Restaurant, and then we had an hour to walk around downtown Aqaba. We strolled through this ancient Jordanian town, exploring many colorful shops. Our tour continued through the Jordanian desert to Wadi Rum, an ancient dry river bed that stretches all the way to Saudi Arabia. Finally, at about 7:00 P.M., we arrived in Petra. United's hotel selection was a fine one, the three-star Edom Hotel, built only one year before. The room was large and comfortable, with a mock mini-bar that contained only two bottles of soda. The long day ended when we met our fellow passengers in the hotel's restaurant for a lovely dinner.

Day Two: Our two-day trip geared us up for a great finale. The day started early, at 7:30 A.M. The early morning strategy is crucial. Hordes of tourists from all parts of Jordan arrive at the park between 10:00 A.M. and 2:00 P.M. Also, the weather is cooler in the early hours, before the heat of the midday sun. Did I mention that our hotel was only several hundred feet from the entrance to the park? We toured Petra for approximately five hours, including the leisurely thirty-minute hike into the park. Options included a horseback ride through the famous winding canyon that is the entrance into Petra. Seniors may opt to ride a horse-drawn cart into the Rose City. At the conclusion of the tour we returned to our nearby hotel. Lunch was scheduled for 1:00 P.M., after which we loaded luggage onto the bus and headed back to the border. At this point we were exhausted but also totally satisfied with the unparalleled Petra adventure.

➡ **Steve's Tip:** *Don't be shy about asking for what you want. We were dusty and tired from five marvelous hours of hiking, camel riding, and generally dealing with the dusty mountain terrain. I approached the Edam Hotel's manager and requested a day room. He was friendly but said no. I eventually convinced him otherwise, and we agreed on a $5 fee for the room. Then Patty and I enjoyed showers as never before. On the return bus ride, fellow passengers moaned with the anticipation of a shower in Eilat. We just sat and smiled.*

Visiting Petra was a thrilling and unforgettable experience, an ultimate adventure into the past. In every respect, it was worth the price. I give it my highest beyond-cheapskate recommendation.

13

China on a Shoestring

China! Today merely mentioning "Mainland China" invokes fleeting images of the mysterious Orient. Imagine! While our fledgling nation enjoys its period of infancy, a mere two hundred years of democracy, China records its history of imperial dynasties, stretching more than four thousand years! With the emergence of the Pacific Rim countries as a global force in today's world, China and its 1.3 billion citizens may hold the key to international peace and cooperation. China will be a formidable force in the oncoming century. Although a journey to this ancient land, found halfway around the world, hardly seems a proper candidate for a cheapskate's adventure, rest assured that it is!

What is a cheapskate China tour? How did we travel? Where did we go? How were we treated by the locals and did we really eat Chinese food three times a day? I will conclude this cheapskaters guide with thoughts and tips on our recent world class adventure.

Tour operator China Focus Travel describes this seven hundred-mile China odyssey, as an introduction to the "old and new China." The Historic China Tour started in Shanghai, circled northeast and ended in Beijing. We traveled through the country by bus, day train, an overnight train, and by plane.

In June 1996 Patty and I packed our bags and again headed to the farthest gate at San Francisco International airport. There we boarded our Air China Boeing 747 jet and headed west, very far west. Our tour commenced in cosmopolitan Shanghai. Then we traveled to the ancient cities of Qufu, home of Confucius, and Tai'an, home of Mt. Tai and one of China's five ancient sacred mountains. The six-city tour also included one day in Suzhou, the Venice of the Orient visited by Marco Polo. One day was spent in Jinan, the regional capital of north China in centuries past. The tour concluded in China's capital, Beijing. We spent three days touring the city and climbing the Great Wall.

Incredibly, this all inclusive and fully escorted tour was priced at just $999 for low season January and February 1996 departures. We traveled in June, high season, and enjoyed fabulous weather. The cheapskate price for our high season trip was just $1,399. Not only that, we used $300 of FREE Nabisco travel cash to reduce the total price to $1,249 each!

At least half our U.S. tour group of thirty-seven traveled from East Coast and Midwestern cities. Incredibly, China Focus included free air travel from Los Angeles to San Francisco for the group's L.A. residents. All agreed this was by far the lowest priced China Tour available anywhere.

On the downside, while waiting to depart the airport, I noticed that they outfitted about one third of the China Air 747 Jet passenger section to carry cargo. Consequently, we felt like sardines on the thirteen-hour outbound flight. (On the return flight, however, Patty and I sat in business class with more than ample space.) The on-plane service was excellent with a continuous supply of food and drinks, plus three free full-length movies. In thirteen "short" hours we were at last setting foot on Chinese soil in the mysterious land of Kubla Khan and Marco Polo. We arrived in the famous port city of Shanghai.

Shanghai

How does the sightseeing work? We were met at Shanghai airport by a Chinese guide who spoke excellent English and who traveled with us from day one until we waved him a fond farewell at Beijing Airport on day twelve. He was a key ingredient in making this tour a delightful experience. A local guide from each city accompanied us on the bus and directed our sightseeing. The quality of the local guides ranged from good to excellent. On occasion our main guide came to our rescue when the local guides did not understand a question or concern of the group.

Upon arrival in Shanghai, airport officials immediately passed us through customs, and our guide whisked us onto a comfortable tour bus, which delivered us to the Qianhe Hotel, a beautiful new high-rise sporting a marble-tiled lobby, wood-paneled elevators, and clean comfortable rooms. After a great night's sleep, we opened our drapes and marveled at the expansive nineteenth-floor view of a haze-covered Shanghai. We were more than satisfied with this first omen of fine, if not elegant, Western-style four-star-quality lodging. All rooms on the tour have twin beds and include a refrigerator/mini bar stocked with sodas, juices, and liquor. Also, room service supplied and refilled a large Chinese-style thermos of boiled, hot water upon request.

Electricity is 220 volts and hotel outlets require two different two-prong adapters, as recommended by the Magellan catalogue. The hotels were weakest in the "electric department" because often wall outlets did not function. However, the maintenance personnel were quick to do the repairs.

Shanghai is a city of 13 million residents. It is the most Westernized and industrialized of China's cities and is the country's major port. Its access to the sea is by way of the Huangpu River. Shanghai is by far the most prosperous city in China. On day one of our tour, we visited a "village," or local neighborhood, celebrating its forty-fifth anniversary. Individual costumed groups of local seniors performed tai chi exercises with swords or fans in hand as they paraded down the street. A score of young children lined both sides of one narrow street and displayed their watercolor paintings of their neighborhood. Schoolchildren were dressed in their spanking new red-and-white school uniforms. Then a drum band of fifty or more young men dressed in ancient warrior costumes of red and gold pounded ancient military tunes. On a makeshift stage three old women in full costume and makeup acted a "Chinese opera."

Next, we visited an actual, one and one-half room apartment of a typical retired couple. Our final stop was at a rundown, neighborhood medical clinic.

On the second day of our tour we visited Shanghai's bustling, cosmopolitan waterfront. The extensive street running the length of the water front was named the Bund by the Europeans in the nineteenth century because they built their commercial banks and financial centers on this street. Main attractions are the Bank of China, Citibank, the Peace Hotel, the customs building, and other shops and businesses both large and small. Then we walked through Huangpu Park alongside the river next to the Bund.

Next we visited the Yu Yuan Bazaar and marveled at the number of shops and street vendors selling all kinds of goods. Masses of bicycles and people were visible in every direction. Because of our fast-paced schedule, we had little time to shop. The tour guide whisked us to the nearby incredible Yu Yuan Gardens first built in 1559 by a retired official of the Ming Dynasty. Walls separated the three sections of the park, which contained circuitous walkways, secret gardens and lotus-filled pools. A large stylized dragon laid upon the top of the wall, and its body extended the wall's entire length.

Our final stop was the first of many Buddhist temples, the famed Jade Buddha Temple with its impressive eight-foot-high bejeweled statue of Buddha brought by monks from Burma.

Suzhou: The Silk Capital

Late that same afternoon after leaving the Jade Buddha Temple, we boarded a local train to the nearby city of Suzhou, fifty miles west of Shanghai. The ninety-minute trip took us through a countryside covered with rice paddies and then to the Nan Lin Hotel.

The picturesque city of Suzhou, founded in the fifth century, is famous for its picturesque lakes, ponds, and miles of winding canals. In the thirteenth century, Marco Polo enjoyed his visit to this unique city that was once referred to as the "Venice of the Orient" and the "Silk Capital of China." On the third day of our trip, we visited a government silk factory and viewed a production line of silk thread being spun from real cocoons. Of course, a visit to the silk shop followed.

We also toured the city of Suzhou, visited local pagodas and famous gardens and cruised one of Suzhou's canals. At 6:30 P.M. we boarded our overnight train to Qufu, the hometown of

Confucius, three hundred miles northeast of Suzhou and halfway to Beijing.

➡ **Steve's Tip:** *When may tour members properly revolt? Read on.*

Patty and I and fellow tour member Helen volunteered to take a sleeping compartment in a train car far removed from the remainder of the group. We found our sleeping compartment and settled down for a smooth, quiet overnight journey. Our deluxe private overnight train car was clean and comfortable. Toilet facilities were sadly lacking and typically Chinese as in sans toilet seat. One of those "grin and bear it" local customs!

Several train officials came by and insisted that we share our compartment with a stranger who had purchased the empty fourth bunk in our compartment. We refused! Why you ask? Because the three of us were travel companions and this was our bedroom for the night. All accommodations on our tour were to be private. All our belongings and money were in the compartment. Helen, a single woman traveling alone, strongly objected to sharing her compartment with a stranger. I stood gallantly behind Helen, as she blocked the door, preventing both the man and the officials entry into our compartment. At the next train stop, the officials summoned our guide from his compartment at the far end of the train. Our guide reluctantly agreed to purchase the vacant bunk for $30 thus assuring our privacy. We all three slept comfortably as our train sped through the night. The next day we found ourselves "heros" of sorts, as we recounted the episode to fellow group members.

Qufu: Home of Confucius

Confucius was one of China's greatest philosophers, a thinker and scholar who founded Confucianism. His spiritual and moral influence on China has continued since the sixth century. He became a teacher in mid-life and received official recognition at age fifty. After his death, followers built the Confucius Temple with its forest of birds and simple gardens and the family Kong Mansion in Qufu. Over the centuries, imperial rulers have sojourned to Qufu to pay homage to the man and his heritage. They bestowed titles of honor on his descendants who lived in the mansion. Confucianism developed into a state religion and survived for two thousand years until the early twentieth century.

Our visit to Qufu included stops at Confucius Temple and Kong Mansion. The temple grounds include a forest with its thirteen pavilions, carved columns, wall engravings, and the Great Hall of Achievements, the main structure in the complex. Later that afternoon, we visited the tomb of Confucius and the tombs of descendants in the Kong family graveyard.

The Queli Hotel in Qufu was by far the weakest link in our hotel chain. Our room required maintenance work to get a lamp and refrigerator to function. Next, the hotel ran out of hot water for the night. In the morning, a steady stream of hot water provided welcome showers. Despite its ornate lobby and costumed lady greeters, the hotel, perhaps due to its remote location, fell far below our Western standard. It was the only such hotel on our tour.

Tai'an: Home of Sacred Mt. Tai

We traveled for several hours from Qufu to Tai'an, home of Mt. Tai, or Taishan, one of China's five sacred mountains. Although the mountain is only 4,998 feet high, it is considered the most important because the rising sun strikes this part of China first every morning. Consequently, according to historical records during the past centuries, seventy-two emperors of various dynasties offered prayer and sacrifices on Mt. Tai.

Our morning was spent visiting the city's major attraction, the Dai Temple, which is dedicated to the gods of Mt. Tai. The complex is considered the grandest of China's ancient temples. Its main pavilion, the Heavenly Blessing Hall, was built in the year 1009 and is one of China's three largest palaces.

The next choice was an easy one. We could walk seven miles and climb seven thousand steps to the summit of Mt. Tai. Or we could take the eight-minute cable car ride to the upper plateau and then walk the remainder of the way to the true summit. Take a guess! We chose the cable car ride from the Zhongtian Gate, which traveled 6,200 feet with a rise of 1,821 feet. Okay, despite the cable car ride, real exercise lay ahead. The remaining long walk and stair climbing were steep. This effort took about forty minutes, with short stops to check out vendors, shops, and perhaps catch our collective breath. Peering into several storefronts, I noticed sets of cots used as accommodations for visitors wishing to catch a sunrise view or continue their journey the following day. We savored stunning views in all directions as we ascended to the peak. One could not help but feel humbled by the mist-shrouded view of the surrounding lush green countryside. We truly enjoyed the heavenly view of kings atop the most majestic of China's sacred places.

Our fondest memory of Tai'an is an evening stroll Patty and I took down a main street. The fast pace of our group tour rarely afforded time to explore on our own, so we took full advantage of this wonderful opportunity. Our hotel's location placed us near blocks of stores, crowded streets, and colorful street vendors. Given the rarity of Western visitors, we found children reacting to us as if we were extraterrestrials. At my first utterance of English words, vendors would smile and attempt to negotiate by scribbling Arabic numbers on the palms of their hand.

At 6:00 P.M. the street transformed dramatically. Entrepreneurs set up cooking tables, platforms, Karaoke equipment and barbecues. In no time, outdoor cafes were serving live eels, fish, crayfish, crabs, meats and all types of salads and vegetables. Table after table displayed, artfully prepared tempting sample dishes. These were content, happy, well-fed, hardworking people. CNN is not available to the public. Consequently, people in these smaller cities have little information about life outside China. They do not measure their lives by our Western standards and appeared quite content. People everywhere offered friendly gestures. However, the language barrier gave us little opportunity for communication other than to bargain, using international gestures with paper and pen. This was a down to earth one-on-one experience with Tai'an's hardworking residents. In Tai'an we again enjoyed excellent lodging, this time at the Laio Dong Mansion.

Jinan: In Jinan we visited the Yellow River that in the summer was a mere trickle. We visited the city's famed source of a thousand springs, the Lake Da Ming Hu. We spent the afternoon boating on the Lake and viewing the Lotus plants and pavilions that surround it.

Beijing and the Great Wall

On this trip the best was saved for last. From Jinan we took a one-hour flight to China's capital city of Beijing. The remaining three days of our visit were spent savoring the wonders of this legendary city and its equally renowned historical surroundings.

We wasted no time during our final days of touring. Our arrival at Beijing Airport was uneventful. I was astonished at the number of international aircraft from nearly every Western nation parked at various terminals. This is truly a cosmopolitan, International airport. Quickly, we were heading toward Beijing by bus via a two-year-old ultramodern freeway. We were heading for our first stop, Beijing's famed or "infamous" Tiananmen square!

We spent half an hour meandering around Tiananmen Square. We studied monuments and nearby buildings and then visited the mausoleum where Chairman Mao's embalmed remains were on display. Mao rallied a million Chinese followers in the 1950s on this square. And here the same number queued up in 1976 to pay their last respects.

Before leaving home I jokingly told friends and family that I would ask guards at the square to point me to the former location of Miss Liberty, the replica of our own Statue of Liberty built by protesters in 1989. While Miss Liberty is sadly long gone, ironically, the square is only a short distance away from shops selling Western goods, everything from designer sun glasses and Seiko watches to hamburgers from the world's largest McDonald's. Western influence is obvious. We even visited the Beijing branch of the Hard Rock Cafe. Yes, a 100 percent genuine and classy branch of the famous restaurant is located on the ground floor of the Landmark Hotel, our Beijing residence.

After lunch we spent hours exploring the largest royal palace in the world, Beijing's "Forbidden City," also known as the Palace Museum or the Imperial Palace. Movie buffs know this palace as the location of Bernardo Bertolucci's film *The Last Emperor*. For five hundred years this extensive cluster of imperial structures was off-limits to ordinary Chinese people. The outer courtyard of the palace complex included the emperor's reception buildings, royal working quarters, triple marble terraces for pomp and circumstance, and libraries. The inner courtyard contains the royal living quarters and several thousand bungalows for concubines and eunuchs, with hidden gardens and walkways and decorated pavilions. Artistic beauty was everywhere, especially in the details of the ornate statuary, marble carvings, and rooftop ornaments. Our group agreed that our visit was rushed and far too short, a price we often paid for this comprehensive ten-day tour.

Next morning we headed north toward the rural, forested area that is home to the Ming Tombs, the underground resting place of thirteen of the past sixteen Ming emperors. We descended underground and visited one Ming tomb. The lack of decoration, artifacts, or wall designs, usually so visibly displayed in other culture's imperial tombs, was disappointing. However, the tombs and surrounding park were preludes to the big event just up the road.

We spent the remainder of the day at the Great Wall, one of the seven wonders of the world. We arrived at the busy Badaling section of the Wall in early afternoon. The first sections of the wall were built around 700 B.C. In 221 B.C. the first emperor of China united all the sections. The Great Wall was last rebuilt in the Ming Dynasty nearly 600 years ago. This section's full length is nearly five miles. Badaling was considered a strategic section of the Great Wall since it protected Beijing from northern attacks through the mountain passes. The wall is 24 feet high and 15 feet wide, built of rectangular slabs of stone with watchtowers placed at strategic overlooks.

Every dignitary to China hikes the Great Wall. So did we. Patty and I huffed and puffed as we climbed one staircase after another leading to a watchtower on the high point on the ridge. Views from either side are awesome. Curved sections of the Great Wall seemed to "dance" across distant ridges, through the surrounding mountains and countryside, finally disappearing in the misty horizon. The very notion that this structure was built before

Columbus set sail for America boggles the mind. Although Columbus had no opportunity to purchase "I sailed the Atlantic Ocean!" tee-shirts, we could purchase a score of sweatshirts and tee-shirts claiming "I climbed the Great Wall" for ourselves, friends, and family. Visiting the Great Wall was an experience of a life time!

On our last day in Beijing we visited the imperial Summer Palace, considered one of the world's top historical sights. The Ming emperors expanded the resort in the seventeenth century. Royals would leave the confines and official duties of the "Forbidden City" and escape to the Summer Palace. Here the emperors would enjoy nine to ten months of rest and relaxation while still performing government duties. The famed Long Corridor impressed me. This outdoor-covered walkway is 2,100 feet in length, and its pavilions and roof are decorated with 8,000 colorfully painted historical scenes. The walkway offers a stunning view of Lake Kunming on one side and various landscaped hills and gardens on the other side. At the end of the walkway is the surreal Marble Boat built by Empress Dowager Cixi in 1888. This famous, immobile, solid marble boat sits at dockside. We wasted no time in exploring the ship from its marble floors to its filigree ceilings. This was a "believe it or not" kind of sight. The main Summer Palace building, with its museums and exhibits, was extraordinary. This last historical stop was a world-class crowd pleaser.

Later that afternoon, Beijing was finally ours! By popular demand, and some negotiation with our tour guide, we arranged for shopping on one of Beijing's best and busiest shopping streets, Wangfijing Street. Patty and I exercised our tourist's right to "shop till you drop"! The stores ranged from common clothing stores to major city department stores. Street vendors hawked beautiful leather jackets and coats, silk ties, and shirts in their cubbyhole shops. For instance, a Seiko watch store was next to a common shop.

A nearby government luggage shop had shelves filled with well-made local luggage. We bought a large bag for a mere $9 that was essential for packing our many purchases.

One side of this busy street was currently under construction. A joint venture project financed by a Hong Kong investor was building Beijing's newest and largest office and shopping complex, one city block long. The new economic game in China is joint venture investments. These capitalistic partnerships with the government bring billions of overseas dollars into the Chinese economy. Today, Panasonic, Hyundai, and Sony advertising have replaced the political billboards of the past. All of this bodes well for a new era of cordial relations between China and Western nations.

I happily pondered these serious but upbeat thoughts as our departure time drew near. In the hustle and bustle of the Beijing Airport, we gave a sad farewell to our guide, to Beijing, and to China and her people.

Miscellaneous Tidbits

By the time of our arrival in Beijing, for the better part of seven days, we had eaten Chinese food three times a day. On our last day, while walking in downtown Beijing, we looked up and gazed with delight at the "big M." We bolted across the street to the world's largest MacDonalds and downed Big Macs, Cokes and fries!

Okay, let me explain this. Our meals were good to very good but not excellent compared with Chinese-American dishes at home. Most lunches and dinners were served in nonhotel restaurants. They served meals family-style with nine to twelve dishes placed in the middle of the table on a lazy susan. Only 10 percent of the dishes were spicy. Entrees included vegetable, fish, chicken, and pork dishes, plus an occasional beef dish. Beer, soda, and water were always served.

Is the food similar to American Chinese food? The answer is yes and no. They served us versions of fried rice, sweet and sour chicken and pork, Chinese roast duck (once only), and a pepper-steak-and-onion dish. One day we lunched at a deluxe Mongolian barbecue restaurant. Breakfasts contained strange and sometimes unidentifiable items. The promised "American breakfasts" failed to appear until our final three days in Beijing. I suffered seven days sans milk, cereal, and juices, eating instead toast, fruit, egg rolls, and occasionally some form of pork, ham, or sausage. Being a milk drinker, my strategy of bringing Swiss Miss Hot Chocolate drink packets was a winner. Since hot water was always available,

I always had a hot milk drink.

When dinner meals became boring, I ordered items from the restaurant's regular menu. Dishes were bargains and priced at $3 per dish for beef or chicken entrees. Bottled water was sold everywhere. Speaking of drinks, Patty and I used our Tahiti strategy. We mixed Crystal Light fruit drink powder with bottled water. Then we froze a half-filled container in the refrigerator. The following morning we topped off the bottle and then enjoyed hours of ice cold lemonade for the rest of the tour. I should emphasize that cold drinks are a rarity. My overall assessment of both food and service is definitely positive.

Despite my strong travel disposition and my total adherence to bottled water, I and others suffered some type of minor digestive distress. I had the mild queasy stomach that reacted well to Patty's preferred medication, Lomotil.

➡ **Steve's Tip on Tips:** *Arnold requested forty dollars per person to cover tips for all bus drivers and guides. This was a most reasonable amount considering the ten days of intensive sightseeing that covered some seven hundred miles.*

Overall Patty and I agree this trip was extraordinary and one of our finest world-class global jaunts. It was a unique travel adventure, our first to an Asian nation, and one filled with new cultural, historical, political, and human experiences every hour of every day. It is an understatement to say this was an exceptional cheapskate vacation! I give this China vacation my highest cheapskate recommendation.

14

World-Class Bargain Vacations

By now you appreciate the reality of exotic bargain vacations. Perhaps you have planned a trip to Tahiti or Paris. If not, there are still endless opportunities for new and different travel adventures. Keep a constant vigil to spot the best of the vacation bargains that abound in the present travel marketplace, and be prepared to move when you find the right package. Use all the assets at your disposal, whether free travel dollars, American AAdvantage miles, or a combination of both. In rare cases, such as Tahiti ($699) and China ($999) packages, the advertised offers qualify for my highest cheapskate rating whether or not additional discounts are used.

The goal of this chapter is to enrich and enlighten your travel spirit with ideas and resources. Following are examples of tour packages that were available in 1996. They reveal many current low-cost tour operators and airlines. The packages depart out of various U.S. gateway cities, such as New York, Miami, Dallas, and Chicago. Often free travel dollars can be used to reduce these bargain prices further. For example, a seven-night package from New York to Cancun, including air and hotel, is net priced at only $259.

Use this chapter as a gateway to the world, from the Swiss Alps to Bangkok and beyond. I have done my best to ensure that all packages use scheduled air so you may use free travel dollars. I provide names and addresses of most tour operators so you may obtain current information on tours of interest. Of course, tour prices and features often change. Additionally, tour operators may substitute charter air for scheduled service. Use this chapter as a guide to tour operators who specialize in great bargain vacation packages.

Before I discuss global travel packages, I wish to emphasize the importance of using available resources. Talk to fellow travelers, obtain brochures from local travel agencies, and study weekend newspaper travel sections. The *New York Times* and the *Los Angeles Times* are unparalleled in their coverage of travel in general and of the East Coast and West Coast in particular. Contact airlines that have their own tour departments, such as American, United, and Delta, to name just a few.

➡ **Steve's Tip:** *Let me emphasize that world-class cheapskate vacations are often found at our doorstep. We always try to travel on American Airlines and earn program miles. Check American's Fly AAway Vacations packages to Hawaii, the Caribbean, Florida, Las Vegas, ski trips, Europe, and Costa Rica. Call (800) 321-2121, or for European trips call (800) 832-8383.*

Consider subscribing to an excellent and inexpensive monthly magazine called *International Travel News (ITN)*. *ITN* has 50,000 subscribers and is the only publication entirely devoted to overseas travel. Its format includes 170 pages chock full of news features, travel articles, and bargain travel advertisements for trips to every corner of the globe. *ITN* is a valuable resource for travelers to foreign destinations outside North America and the Caribbean. Also, as an independent publication, it has no affiliation with any firm in the travel industry. The magazine sells at travel shops for $2 per issue; a subscription costs $16 per year. *ITN*'s editor assures me that *Cheapskate's Guide* readers will receive a free current copy for the asking. To order a subscription or to request a free copy, write to:

International Travel News
2120 28th Street
Sacramento, California 95818
(800) 366-9192

A Word About Domestic Vacations

I could write an entire book that lists the best domestic air-and-land packages available from major U.S. cities. However, the reality of the travel marketplace is that such packages change daily, weekly, and monthly. Many factors affect current deals. The state of the economy, the cost of running airlines, and even the change of seasons affect the pricing of vacation packages. Both major airlines and smaller local ones regularly advertise their bargain package vacations in local newspapers. Together they offer a smorgasbord of diverse, exciting, bargain-priced, air-and-land packages.

While the focus of this guide is on international travel, I will offer a good example of bargain packages available from one major independent airline, American Trans Air.

American Trans Air

ATA provides both scheduled and charter services from San Francisco to Chicago. In chapter 7 I discuss the incredible cheapskate packages available to Oahu and Maui. Pleasant Hawaiian Holidays uses ATA's scheduled, noncharter flights from the West Coast. In July 1996 they priced an eight-day package to Maui at just $519 (only $369 using free travel dollars). It included round-trip airfare, a condo for seven nights, and a rental car for the week.

Contact ATA and request their current Amber brochure. ATA's expanded service area includes departures from Indianapolis and Chicago. They offer rock-bottom prices on packages to Florida, Las Vegas, Phoenix, Mexico, Nassau, and Grand Cayman. Most important, the Amber brochure lists ATA's scheduled flights. Call American Trans Air at (800) 225-2995 and ask for their vacation desk.

Following are two sample packages available from ATA. In each case the packages include round-trip airfare on scheduled ATA flights, hotel for seven nights, and all taxes and transfers. The brackets represent departure cities:

Las Vegas: Lodging at Days Inn or Town Hall Hotel costs $417 from Chicago or $360 from Indianapolis; at the MGM Grand Hotel it costs $560 (from Chicago only).

Orlando: Lodging at the Best Western Plaza or the International Hotels: $374 from Chicago or $396 from Indianapolis.

World-Wide Destinations

Australia

Quantas Airline recently announced a fantastic Aussie vacation package that included round-trip air to Sydney, five nights at a five-star Sydney hotel, transfers, and a three-day transit pass, and all this for an incredible $1,048. But that was just the beginning. After all, how much of Australia can one see in five days? I contacted Quantas and had them add nine nights in Cairns on the Great Barrier Reef. Now, by using $500 in free travel dollars, the fifteen-day, fourteen-night Australian odyssey hit a low of $1,113 per person. Do not expect to see anything like this price in high season, but for those ready to pounce on a golden "Down Under opportunity," keep an eye out for this package or a similar one. Be sure to contact the airline's tour desk for information on money-saving, fourteen-night packages. A word on seasons. Low-season bargain vacations are from April through the end of August. Shoulder season is the months of March and September to November. High season is December through February.

More recently, in early 1996, I have seen air-only deals for as low as $698 round-trip to Sydney. Always call the airline and see if they offer an add-on land package of seven or fourteen nights so free travel cash can be used. Call Quantas at (800) 227-4500.

The Canary Islands

Enjoy the year-round subtropical climate of the world-famous Canary Islands, off the coast of North Africa. A great choice is the five-star Hotel Melia Tamarindos on Grand Canary Island, an island of scenic beauty and sandy beaches. The five-star hotel is situated on San Augustine Beach on the southern part of the island. Enjoy the hotel's spacious grounds and gardens. Amenities include twenty-four-hour room service, elaborate pools, and a game room. An eight-day stay is priced at $1,034 (or $884 using free travel dollars). A two-week stay, using free travel cash, is priced at only $1,225, including air from New York or Boston. Add only $44 for air from Miami and only $138 for air from Los Angeles. See the Spain and Portugal section for details on Skyline Travel contacts.

This ten-day package, from New York, is priced at $1,399, including air and hotels. Contact:

Adventure Travel
915 Highway 35
Middletown, New Jersey 07748
(908) 671-9000

The Caribbean and Costa Rica

Dolphin Cruises: The Dolphin cruise line offers seven-night sailings from Miami to the eastern or western Caribbean. Its ships visit ports such as Playa del Carmen, Cozumel, Montego Bay, and Grand Cayman Island. The cruise price by itself is $445, whereas the cruise including air from Miami is $545. Take a further discount using free travel cash to reduce these prices to $295 out of Miami, or $545, which includes air from Miami.

Carnival Cruise Line: Their Mexican Riviera seven-night cruise departs from Los Angeles and costs just $549 per person. Caribbean seven-night cruises are priced at $534.

Holland Cruise Line: Its eight-day, seven-night cruise to the Caribbean is priced at $599. Or use your free travel dollars and enjoy the cruise for only $449.

Jamaica: Here it is—eight-day, all-inclusive Jamaican packages at cheapskate prices. Jamaica Air's tours offer all-inclusive Jack Tar Village at only $822, or just $672 using free travel cash. This package includes air from Miami or Ft. Lauderdale, all meals, unlimited cocktails, land and water sports, nightly entertainment, and all tips. The same package, substituting the famous Sandels all-inclusive resort, is priced at $1,091 or just $941 using free travel dollars. Call Sandels Resort at (800) 523-9770.

Aruba: This package from New York includes eight days at the Hotel and Casino five-star resort, air, a deluxe ocean-view room, tips, taxes, and daily buffet breakfast. The price per person is just $799. Also, the package from Newark, including air (on Air Aruba), Americana Hotel (ocean view), taxes, and daily breakfast buffet costs $799. Contact Players Choice Tours at (800) 79-Aruba.

Costa Rica: This eight-day, seven-night package to Costa Rica includes four nights in San Jose and three nights in Jaco Beach. The vacation also includes four dinners and round-trip transportation on American Airlines from the West Coast. Package rates start at $699. For details and brochures contact:

GAT Holidays
Pier 27, The Embarcadero
San Francisco, California 94111
(800) 258-8880

➡ **Steve's Note:** *Generally, cruise brochures are readily available at all local travel agencies. If you wish to use free travel dollars or obtain a 5 percent rebate, you must book directly with ITH or Travelers Advantage. Also, cruise lines routinely advertise their latest bargain fares in weekend newspaper travel sections.*

Greece

Tourlite International is a New York–based tour operator specializing in Greek tours at super bargain prices. Their eight-day, six-night Athenian tour is priced at $779. Their deluxe nine-day, seven-night land-and-cruise combination tour is priced at $1,059. These packages include round trip air from New York, transfers, most meals, and all sightseeing. Available free travel dollars may be used on the seven-night package. Call Tourlite at (800) 272-7600 or (212) 599-2727 and request their brochure for current details.

Italy

Perillo Tours: Perillo Tours offers a great cheapskate getaway to Rome. Their off-season, eight-day Roman Holiday package costs only $999. It includes scheduled round-trip air from New York, Boston, Chicago, Miami, Houston, Detroit, or Cleveland via Al Italia Airlines. West Coast departures add $199. The tour also provides six nights' lodging at first-class hotels, daily buffet breakfast, limited sightseeing, transfers, and hotel taxes. Free travel dollars do not apply to the six-night package.

The Roman Holiday itinerary provides for a late-evening departure from the United States and an early morning arrival in Rome on day two and sightseeing on day three. Days four through seven are free days. The tour provides five and a half days in Rome. The return flight leaves Rome on the morning of day eight, a Saturday departure. (Many other tours charge extra for premium weekend travel.) This is super bargain price for such a deluxe eight-day tour. You may contact:

Perillo Tours
577 Chestnut Ridge Road
Woodcliff Lake, New Jersey 07675
(800) 431-1515 or (201) 307-1234

Jet Vacation Tours: Jet also offers a bargain package from New York to Rome. The seven-night package includes round-trip air on Air France, seven nights lodging at the superior Delle Muse Hotel, daily breakfast, and hotel fees. The total price is $871, or $721 using free dollars. Jet offers another interesting vacation, its Diamanti di Italia, three-city package to Rome, Florence, and Venice. This includes air from New York on Air France, ten days and nine nights in Italy, transfers, sightseeing, and daily breakfasts. It is priced at $1,334, or $1,184 using free dollars. Contact:

Jet Vacations Tours
1775 Broadway
New York, New York 10019
(800) JET-BROCHURE

Mallorca

This largest of the Balaeric Islands provides scenery, small coves, beaches, and a colorful history dating to the Bronze Age. Stay at the four-star Hotel Cal Vinas in the Paguera resort area on the border of a cove beach. Enjoy windsurfing, sailing, and canoeing. An eight-day vacation, including air from New York, hotel, transfers, and daily breakfasts is priced at $862, or $712 using free dollars. Want to stay on for another week? Pay only $885 for a total of fifteen days. This is another fine Skyline Travel package.

Mediterranean Cruises Departing From Florida

Regency Cruise Lines' transatlantic cruises are offered as twelve- or fifteen-day voyages from Ft. Lauderdale to the western Mediterranean. The cruises leave Ft. Lauderdale and then sail to Bermuda, Madeira, Lisbon, Cadiz, and Barcelona. The twelve-day cruise is a bargain, priced at $1,194. The net price with travel cash is $1,044. The best cheapskate deal is a fifteen-day cruise priced at $1,694, or use free travel cash to reduce this to only $1,444. For an extra $99 Regency will add a two-day extension that includes two nights lodging in Lisbon plus a half-day city tour.

Mexico

American Trans Air (ATA) offers great Mexican vacation packages that include scheduled round-trip air, seven nights' lodging, and all transfers and taxes. The flights depart from Indianapolis, ATA's gateway city. Here is a small sampling:

- Cancun: Hotel Margarita $442
- Cancun: Two-bedroom suite (for four people) at the Costa Real $584
- Cozumel: Hotel Presidente $742

Cancun: This package, from New York, includes air on Aero Mexico, seven nights' lodging at Holiday Inn Centro, transfers, and taxes for $409. The eight-day Cancun/Chichen Itza/Merida Mayan Explorer Tour is just $649. Contact Liberty Travel at (212) 363-2320 or (212) 349-5610.

Mexican Riviera: Carnival has hit a new low on this one. They reduced 1996 cruise prices to only $549, or $399 using your free travel dollars. We are talking about a full seven-night cruise from Los Angeles.

Morocco

Central Holidays offers one of the best exotic packages I have seen. It includes eight days and seven nights at Club Valtur in Agadir, Morocco. I am told that Club Med is part owner of this renowned property. The amenities of the Club Valtur package include:

- Round-trip air on Royal Air Morocco
- All transfers
- Superior class lodging
- Twenty-one meals, including wine
- A free half-hour message
- $20 of club money (beads) per person
- All sports, including golf and tennis
- Free entertainment

The incredible price is $979. Air Morocco is a scheduled airline, so free travel dollars reduce this price to $829 for New York departures. Contact:

Central Holidays
206 Central Avenue
Jersey City, New Jersey 07307
(800) 935-5000

Panama Canal Cruise

Regency Cruise Lines offers a seventeen-day canal cruise from San Francisco, with free air, which includes port stops at Puerto Vallarta, Zihuantanejo, Acapulco, Costa Rica, Cartagena, Grand Cayman, and Tampa. The total price, including free airfare, is $1,499. Since this cruise is more than fourteen nights you can use of $500 of free travel cash, reducing the net price to $1,249 per person. The same cruise is also available from Los Angeles with free return airfare for just $1,599 for sixteen days, or a net price of only $1,349 using free travel cash. Call (800) 753-1234 for brochure AT50.

Panama Cruise From Los Angeles: This sixteen-day Regency cruise includes stops at Puerto Vallarta and Zihuantanejo and a transcanal passage to Ft. Lauderdale, for only $1,199, or use free travel cash to get a super-bargain price of only $949.

Russia (USSR)

GT Corporation offers an incredible fifteen-day Moscow to St. Petersburg cruise that includes nine ports of call, four days in St. Petersburg and four days in Moscow. Bargain prices for cruise only (no air) start at $799 for a four-person stateroom. This includes all meals, wine, caviar, land excursions, entertainment, lectures, and transfers. Free travel dollars apply.

GT Corp. World Trade and Travel
2610 East 16th Street
Brooklyn, New York 11235
(800) 828-7970, or (718) 934-4100; fax (718) 934-9419

Spain and Portugal

Portugal: Tour operator Skyline Travel offers the best of Portugal at bargain prices. Tours use Iberia and Air Portugal. This bargain vacation to Lisbon includes air from New York or Newark, seven nights' lodging at the Hotel Rex, taxes, and daily breakfast. The package is priced at $845, or $695 using free dollars. Better yet, if you can stretch this one to fifteen days the price is only $1,076, or $826 if free dollars are used. Contact Skyline and ask for its Portugal and Spain, Freestyle Vacations brochure. Contact Skyline at:

Skyline Travel
376 New York Avenue
Huntington, New York 11743
(800) 645-6198 or (516) 423-9090; fax (516) 423-9094

Estoril/Cascais: Want sun, fun, and Lisbon rolled into one glorious package? Try Estoril and Cascais, which are a thirty-minute train ride from Lisbon. Estoril is quite close to Sinatra's wonderful palaces, the Mafra baroque monastery and Queluz, with its famous pink palace and extraordinary gardens. Relax at the Baja Hotel, a three-star hotel that faces the beach. The recently renovated hotel features beautiful views of the bay and a covered rooftop swimming pool. A one-week package is priced at $867, or a net price of just $717 if you are using free travel dollars. Want to stay for a comfortable two-week getaway? Use $500 of free travel dollars and pay $820, which includes air from New York or Newark, hotel, taxes, and daily breakfast. This is also a Skyline Travel tour. See above for Skyline contact information.

Madrid/Seville/Barcelona: Madrid is truly one of Europe's great cities. Visitors enjoy its outdoor cafes, limitless shopping, and cultural treasures such as the Prado museum. Seville is one of

Spain's ancient and most romantic cities. Visit its Gothic cathedral, Moorish Alcazar Palace, and Maria Luiza Park. Then there is Barcelona, home of Picasso, Miro, and Dali. Enjoy its striking architecture and savor its famed Catalonian cuisine. Net prices for an eight-day vacation, including air from New York, taxes, and daily breakfast, are:

- Madrid: lodging at Tryp Capital Hotel, priced at $972, or $822 using free dollars.
- Seville: lodging at Macarena Hotel, priced at $1,036, or $886 using free dollars.
- Barcelona: lodging at Majestic Hotel, priced at $1,094, or $944 using free dollars.
- Want to stretch your vacation to two super-bargain weeks? Use $500 in free travel cash and pay $859, $909, and $1,093, respectively. Skyline Travel offers these packages.

Costa Del Sol: Are you are tired, burned out, and ready for *one month* of beachfront vacation in Torremolinaos Spain? This one is almost too low to believe. The one-month package includes air from New York on Iberia Airlines and four weeks lodging at a beachfront studio apartment-hotel. The fantastic low price is only $999. Use free travel dollars and pay an astounding $749 per person. Contact:

Sun Holidays
7280 West Palmetto Park Road
Boca Raton, Florida 33433
(800) 422-8000
Fax (407) 393-3870

Benidorm: GAT travel offers fourteen-night packages to Benidorm, Spain. They include round-trip air on either United Airlines or Iberia (from the East Coast), fourteen nights' lodging at the Poseidon Palace, and three meals daily. The total price is $1,099. Since the packages uses scheduled airlines, a whopping $500 in free travel dollars may be used, reducing the net price to $849. Ask either ITH, Traveler's Advantage, or your travel agent to contact GAT travel.

Switzerland

Anyone for a ski vacation to Interlaken? For $1,049, this Zurich package includes air from New York on Swiss Air, transfers, seven nights at the four-star National Hotel, daily breakfasts and dinners, and all taxes. Contact Adventure Travel at (908) 671-9000.

Turkey

Pacha Tours specializes in Turkish package tours. Currently they offer an all-inclusive, seventeen-day Turkish Delight tour. The package includes round-trip air from New York at the bargain price of $1,395 per person. For details and a brochure, contact Pacha Tours at (800) 722-4288.

Epilogue

We are all tempted to enjoy easy bargain travel to nearby destinations. Those on the East Coast flock to the Caribbean while we on the West Coast head to Mexico. I believe you deserve more, much more. Every day we read of the rich and famous who are enjoying world-class vacations. Patty and I have lived these very dream vacations to some of the world's most exotic destinations. And we have done it on a shoestring budget.

In my introduction I asked that you ignore artificial barriers. Hopefully, you now appreciate just how easily you can rise above the ordinary vacation crowd, how you can reach out and experience your dream vacations, whether it is an African safari or the delights of French Polynesia. You are equipped to be the most savvy of international travelers, rivaling those in the jet set. Unlike all those infomercials, there is no real estate for you to buy and no $200 packet of tapes to listen to. Instead, you may sit back and wait for free travel cash to roll in. Or you may find yourself receiving free travel awards and companion tickets for making normal day-to-day purchases. Those of us "in the know" appreciate that something for nothing does indeed exist in our user-friendly travel universe. Be bold and daring. Only the timid should spend their hard-earned dollars to visit overcrowded Caribbean and Mexican resorts while the rest of us are savoring the beauty of unspoiled Moorea in Tahiti.

Above all, let your imagination be your guide. When you opened this book you likely believed that world-class travel, to Africa, the Middle East and Tahiti, was beyond your grasp—and your pocketbook. All of that has now changed in a big way. Never let go of your dreams! Savor them and live them, one by one. Enjoy world-class vacations and relish memories that will last a lifetime.

Appendix:
Essential Cheapskate Contacts

Africa

United Touring International
One Bala Plaza, Suite 414
Bala Cynwyd, Pennsylvania
19004
(800) 223-6486

Unitours Africa
8 South Michigan Avenue
Chicago, Illinois 60603
(800) 621-0557, (312) 782-1590

Aruba

Players Choice Tours
(800) 79-ARUBA

Caribbean Islands

Sunshine Tours
(800) 879-5371

Costa Rica

GAT Holidays
Pier 27, The Embarcadero
San Francisco, California 94111
(800) 258-8880

China

China Focus Travel
870 Market Street, Suite 603
San Francisco, California 94102
(415) 788-8660
Fax: (415) 788-8665

Cruise Lines

American Hawaii Cruises
(800) 765-7000

Celebrity Cruises
(800) CELEBRITY

Crystal Cruises
(213) 340-4121

Cunard Cruise Lines
(800) 7-CUNARD

Delta Queen Steamboat
Cruises
(800) 240-9752

Norwegian Cruise Lines
(800) 262-4NCL

Princess Cruise Lines
(800) LOVE-BOAT, ext. 55

Radisson Seven Seas Cruises
(800) 424-3964

Seaborn Cruise Line
(415) 391-7444

Hawaii

Pleasant Hawaiian Holidays
Vacation Packages
(800) 2-HAWAII; (800) 242-9244

Royal Kahana Reservations/
Brochure
P.O. Box 1956
Lafayette, California 94549

Israel/Middle East

Ayelet Tours
21 Aviation Road
Albany, New York 12205
(800) 293-5389

Center Hotel
2 Zamenhof Street
Tel Aviv, Israel 64373
03-6296181 (Fax) 03-6296751

Egged Tours
11 Sunrise Plaza, Suite 302
Valley Stream, New York 11580
(800) 825-9399 and, (516)
825-0966
Fax: (800) 825-0980

Egypt Tours and Travel
4353 North Harding Avenue

Chicago, Illinois 60618
(800) 523-4978, and (312)
463-4999
Fax: (312) 463-4999

Israeli Government Tourist
Office
21 Hill Road
Waltham, Massachusetts 02154

Jerusalem Travel Center
20 South Van Brunt Street
Englewood, New Jersey 07631
(800) JLM IS US
Fax: (201) 816-1111

Riviera Apartment Hotel
North Beach, Eilat 88000
Tel.: 07-334141; Fax: 07-333939

Royal Jordanian Airlines
(800) 758-6878; (212) 949-0060

United Tours
113 Ha'Yarkon Street
Tel Aviv, Israel
Tel.: 03-6933410/11
Fax: 03-6933408

Italy

Jet Vacations Tours
1775 Broadway
New York, New York 10019
(800) JET-BROCHURE

Perillo Tours Italy
577 Chestnut Ridge Road
Woodcliff Lake, New Jersey
07675
(800) 431-1515; (201) 307-1234

Jamaica

Sandels Resort
(800) 523-9770

Magazine, Catalogue

International Travel News
2120 28th Street
Sacramento, California 95818
(800) 366-9192

Magellan's Travel Catalogue
P.O. Box 5485
Santa Barbara, California 93150
(800) 962-4943

Mexico

Liberty Travel
(212) 363-2320; (212) 349-5610

MexSeaSun Tours
Mexicana Airlines
(800) 531-9321

Morocco

Central Holidays
206 Central Avenue
Jersey City, New Jersey 07307
(800) 935-5000

Paris

AOM French Airlines
(800) 892-9136; (310) 338-9613
Fax: (310) 670-7784
Los Angeles information:
(310) 416-9068
Paris information: 49-79-12-34

France Vacation
Airport Boulevard, Suite 1120
Los Angeles, California 90004
(800) 332-5332; (310) 645-3070
Fax: (310) 645-1947

Phone Cards

American Travel Network
10211 North 32nd Street, Suite A5
Phoenix, Arizona 85028
(800) 477-9692

World Link
3399 Peachtree Road N.E.
Lenox Building, Suite 400
Atlanta, Georgia 30326
(800) 432-6169

Spain/Portugal/Mallorca

Skyline Travel
376 New York Avenue
Huntington, New York 11743
(800) 645-6198; (516) 423-9090
Fax: (516) 423-9094

Sun Holidays
7280 West Palmetto Park Road
Boca Taton, Florida 33433
(800) 422-8000
Fax: (407) 393-3870

Switzerland/Canary Ialands

Adventure Travel
915 Highway 35
Middletown, New Jersey 07748
(908) 671-9000

Tahiti—Moorea

Alberts Car and Jeep Rental
Circle Island Tour
(689) 56-13-53; 56-19-28

AOM French Airlines
(800) 892-9136; (310) 338-9613
Fax: (310) 670-7784
Los Angeles: (310) 416-9068
Papeete: (689) 43-25-25

Aremeti II Catamaran Ferry
(689) 56-31-10

Cooks Bay Resort
Box 30
Pao Pao, Moorea
French Polynesia
(689) 56-10-50

Horseback Riding Stables
(near Club Med)
(689) 56-17-93

Islands in the Sun
760 West 16th Street, Suite L
Costa Mesa, California 92627
(800) 642-1881
Fax: (714) 548-1654

Lagoon Seafari Moorea (sailing)
(near Park Royal Hotel)
(689) 56-19-19

Steve's Video
Box 1956
Lafayette, California 94549

Pacificar Tahiti (rental car)
56 Rue des Remparts

(Ponts de l'Est)
B.P. 1121
Papeete, Tahiti
French Polynesia
(689) 56-11-03 (Moorea)
(689) 41-93-93 (Papeete)

M.U.S.T. Philippe Molle (scuba
diving) (at Cooks Bay Resort)
Box 336
Moorea, French Polynesia
(689) 56-17-32; 56-15-83
Fax: (689) 56-29-18

Sunmakers Travel Group
100 West Harrison Street
Seattle, Washington 98109
(800) 255-7380
(206) 216-2905

Tahiti Vacations (AOM)
9841 Airport Boulevard, Suite 1124
Los Angeles, California 90045
(800) 553-3477; (310) 337-1040
Fax: (310) 337-1126

Upa Polynesian Parasail
(near Park Royal Hotel)
(689) 56-19-19

Travel Cash Giveaways

International Travel House
24 Columbia Road, Suite 210
Somerville, New Jersey 08876
Fax: (908) 429-1022

Nabisco Consumer Information
Services
100 DeForest Avenue
Box 1911

East Hanover, New Jersey
07936-1911

Nabisco Special Offers
P.O. Box 7147
Easton, Maryland 21606-7147

Travel Discounts

Entertainment Publications
P.O. Box 1068
Trumball, Connecticut 06611
Orders: (800) 374-4464

PriceCostco Travel
(800) 800-8505

Travelers Advantage
Box C32123
Richmond, Virginia 23261
(800) 843-7777

Travelers' Travel Pak Insurance

Downtown Travel
1609 Locust Street
Walnut Creek, California 94596
(510) 945-9004
Fax: (510) 945-8081
(Mailed requests for applications
will be honored.)

Travel Insured International
National Distributor for TravelPak
(800) 243-3174

Turkey
Pacha Tours
(800) 722-4288

Russia

GT Corp. World Trade and Travel
2610 East 16th Street
Brooklyn, New York 11235
(800) 828-7970; (718) 934-4100
Fax: (718) 934-9419

Index